STUDIES IN ASIAN AMERICANS
RECONCEPTUALIZING CULTURE, HISTORY, AND POLITICS

T0316022

Edited by
Franklin Ng
California State University, Fresno

A ROUTLEDGE SERIES

STUDIES IN ASIAN AMERICANS: RECONCEPTUALIZING CULTURE, HISTORY, AND POLITICS

FRANKLIN NG, *General Editor*

TAIWANESE AMERICAN TRANSNATIONAL FAMILIES
WOMEN AND KIN WORK

Maria W. L. Chee

Routledge
Taylor & Francis Group
New York   London

Published in 2005 by
Routledge
Taylor & Francis Group
711 Third Avenue
New York, NY 10017

Published in Great Britain by
Routledge
Taylor & Francis Group
2 Park Square, Milton Park
Abingdon, Oxon OX14 4RN

First issued in paperback 2013

Routledge is an imprint of the Taylor & Francis Group, an informa business

International Standard Book Number-10: 0-415-97330-9 (Hardcover)
International Standard Book Number-13: 978-0-415-97330-4 (Hardcover)
International Standard Book Number-13: 978-0-415-65432-6 (paperback)

Library of Congress Card Number 2004026256

Library of Congress Cataloging-In-Publication Data

Chee, Maria W. L.
    Taiwanese American transnational families : women and kin work / Maria W.L. Chee.-- 1st ed.
        p. cm. -- (Studies in Asian Americans)
    Includes bibliographical references and index.
    ISBN: 0-415-97330-9
    1. Taiwanese Americans--Social conditions.   2. Women--United States--Social conditions.
    3. Immigrants--United States--Social conditions.   4. Labor--Social aspects--United States.
    5. Women--Taiwan--Social conditions.   6. Transnationalism.   7. United States--
    Emigration and immigration.   8. Taiwan--Emigration and immigration.   9. Family--
    United States.   10. Family--Taiwan.   I. Title.   II. Series: Asian Americans.

E184.T35C47 2005
305.895'1073--dc22   2004026256

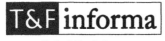

Taylor & Francis Group
is the Academic Division of T&F Informa plc.

Visit the Taylor & Francis Web site at
http://www.taylorandfrancis.com

and the Routledge Web site at
http://www.routledge-ny.com

Dedicated to the memory of my late first uncle
who loved me as his own daughter

Contents

Acknowledgments

Fruition is a process, and many people have lifted me along the way. I am indebted to the women and men who kindly shared their experiences and thoughts without which this book would not have materialized. This book is largely based on my doctoral dissertation. I thank the Fulbright Foundation, the Social Science Research Council, the Pacific Cultural Foundation of Taiwan, the Pacific Rim Research Program of the Office of the President, University of California and the Graduate Division of the University of California, Riverside (UCR). They had funded in part various stages of my project from initial dissertation workshop to the completion of fieldwork. Further, I appreciate the following institutions that had financed my dissertation-writing: a Dissertation-Year Fellowship from the Office of the President, University of California and a Graduate Student Resident Fellowship from the Center for Ideas and Society, UCR. The Chiang Ching Kuo International Scholarly Exchange Foundation generously awarded me a doctoral dissertation fellowship. I regretfully declined that fellowship due to award overlaps.

During my preliminary visit and subsequent fieldwork in Taiwan, I received much assistance and hospitality, including many sumptuous meals, from several local scholars including Professors Nora Chiang, Chang Chueh, and Tseng Yen-fen of the National Taiwan University; Professor Chen Hsiang-shui of the Tsing Hua University; Drs. Chang Mau-kuei, Chang Ying-hua, Allen Chun, H. H. Michael Hsiao, Hsu Cheng-kuang, Lu Yu-hsia, Wu Chi-yin, Yeh Chun-rong, and Yi Ching-chun of the Academia Sinica, Taiwan. The Director-General Chang Ying-chang of the Academia was instrumental in bringing me to its Institute of Ethnology as a visiting associate during my year in the field. The staff and researchers at the Institute as well as the Institute of Sociology never failed to be friendly and helpful. Commissioner and Professor Chang Li-ching of Tung Hai University and Professor Inge Chen Ying-chin of Chung Yuan Christian University have showered me with warmth and personal friendship unto this day. Many others also made my year in Taiwan memorable.

Dr. Nicola Piper at the Australian National University, and Professor Mina Roces with the University of New South Wales in Australia commented on some of my writings. Professor Vivian-Lee Nyitray at the Department of Religious Studies, UCR first pointed me to the Center for Women Studies at the National Taiwan University. Jay Lin, J.D. of Taiwan, Professor Gary A. Dymski of UCR, Professor John M. Liu of the University of California, Irvine, Pastor John Lee, Yi-ping Hsieh and Eva Han provided assistance in various ways. I am thankful to all of the above.

I am grateful to the Department of Ethnic Studies at UCR. It practically financed my entire doctoral education by repeatedly granting me teaching assistantship and lecturer assignments. The Department provided exceptional professional training and development opportunities; whereas Professor and Chair Alfredo Mirandé has given me intellectual inspiration as well as support. The faculty residents, especially Professors Karen Pyke, Ruth Chao, and Masako Ishii-Kuntz, assisted me during my residency at the Center for Ideas and Society, Winter Quarter 2002, UCR. The reference librarians and circulation desk personnel of the Rivera Library facilitated my research at all times. Janet Moores and Maria Mendoza at the Interlibrary Service jovially greeted my constant bombardments and urgent requests. I hope my appearance had not caused any anxiety attack.

I thank my dissertation committee members. Professor Christine Ward Gailey guided me in women's studies along with irresistible gastronomic delights such as Beijing duck and bread pudding. She thoroughly critiqued the chapters on women. Professor Eugene Anderson commented with efficiency and diligence on my draft chapters as they became available. His interest kept up my momentum and morale. Professor Paul Gelles deserves special recognition. He had strongly supported my admission to the Department and has since counseled me on my career continuously. He was responsible for the improved structure and organization of this book. Professor Michael Kearney introduced me to transnational studies. I owe my intellectual tutelage to the Department of Anthropology and unaccountable assistance to its office staff, especially Joye Sage and Valerie Smith. All the faculty members in my Department have spoiled me with friendliness and high regards.

I am particularly thankful to series editor Professor Franklin Ng who recommended this book for publication and who provided much needed suggestions, to associate editor Kimberly Guinta who has been helpful in making this book a reality, to Professor Min Zhou who took interest in my research and in me as a junior member in Chinese American as well as immigration studies. Professors Ling-chi Wang and Him Mark Lai also assisted in the process. Their friendship and support had warmed me in the solitary hours necessary for writing. A note of thank goes to UCR Interim Vice Chancellor Robert Nava, J.D. He generously provided coaching, guidance, advice, encouragement, and work load flexibility while I served as his special assistant during the preparation of this book. I cherish his friendship.

Finally, my gratitude goes to my extended family. My mother and sister have always believed in me. Uncle James and Aunt Patty have offered continuous moral support as well as financial assistance if ever needed. Cousins Kathy, Francis, their children and grandchildren, Cousins Sandy and Brad and their children all have given me a family in southern California. My darling son Aldous blesses me with the pride and joy of being a mother. I am immensely grateful to Professor Lawrence Davidson for his superb fathering work. In my moments of weakness, long-time close friends Connie, Masano, and Ellen readily supply empathy, words of wisdom, and solidarity to walk me through crises.

I live with the confidence of support from my colleagues, friends, and relatives. How do I thank thee? I cannot even begin to count the ways.

Maria W. L. Chee
Riverside, California

Introduction

This book focuses on transnational families divided between the United States and Taiwan. By transnational families I refer to split household arrangement where one spouse lives with the child(ren) in one country while the other spouse lives in another.[1] What happens to non-working class women and their husbands when the wife and children migrate to the country of destination,[2] while the husband remains to work in the country of origin and send "remittances" to support them? At both macro and micro levels, this project studies the above contemporary phenomenon that is widespread in several Pacific Rim countries including Australia, Canada, New Zealand, United States, Hong Kong, and Taiwan.[3]

My interest in this subject arose from my membership in a transnational extended family that transcends Hawaii, the Mainland United States, Australia, and Canada; as well as my keen awareness of the powerful impact on everyone's life by politics, economics, and larger forces in society. If one questions whether current transnational practices will continue in the next generation, the Chinese experience provides a ready answer. Chinese have been leading transnational lives since at least the seventeenth century when a large number of them migrated to Southeast Asia.[4] Such living continues unto this date. Like anthropologist Kroeber posits in his theory of supraorganic, the individual participant passes away, but the phenomenon of transnational families persists across generations, often due to personal aspiration as well as socioeconomic and/or political dynamics of the nation-states involved.

My personal background stands as one living proof. In direct contrast to the claim that Asian transmigration to the west is recent (see, for example, Bun, et al. 1995), my family's transnational tradition has continued for five generations between East and West. For almost three decades I have been living in the United States whereas my mother, sister, sister-in-law and my nephew reside in Toronto, Canada. My brother is a computer engineer. In

1

1996 he left Canada for East Asia to assume a job that paid twice as much as his former one in Toronto. He would base himself in Hong Kong and the economic zone called Shengzhen of southern China. My brother and his wife were a young couple with a son who barely turned eight at the time. Husband, wife, and child would reunite during school vacation and holiday seasons. That was the plan.

I was talking to my sister-in-law on a long distance telephone call one Sunday morning in 1996, shortly after my brother had left home. "How are you feeling? Are you doing okay?" I asked her. She responded to my concern as follows:

> Oh yes, I'm just fine. Don't you worry. I have my parents and brothers here. Your mom and sister are here. Your ancestors did the same thing, don't you remember? They all left home and went away to work. The only difference is that in the old days they went away from China to the Hawaii and the Gold Mountain, now we just let your brother dig gold in China. As long as he sends home the money! And he promises to guard his body.

My sister-in-law reassured me and invoked our family history to support her claim.

The above conversation epitomized the geographical reversal in migration patterns between other countries and China in the past, and between the United States and Taiwan in the present. In recent decades, men (and occasionally women) have been working in China, Hong Kong, or Taiwan as business owners or professionals, and send money to support their families in Australia, Canada, New Zealand, or the United States. In times past, men left their wives and families in China to perform stoop labor in the Americas, Australia, the Caribbean, Hawaii, Southeast Asia and elsewhere in the world (for the dispersal of Chinese in the diaspora, see Pan 1990, 1999). They were expected to send remittances back to China to support their families.

Beginning with my great-great-grandfather in the late 1800s, at least one man in each succeeding generation went to Hawaii to make a living, leaving his wife behind to care for children and parents-in-law in China. I remember early childhood days in Hong Kong with aunts and great aunts who lived alone or with their children. I also heard stories from some of these women about their lives. One summer afternoon in California in the 1990s I went to visit a cousin's mother-in-law afflicted with cancer. She was in her 70s. We were alone in her quiet hospital room. I sat on the edge of her bed. The sterile white linen enhanced her pale shrunken cheeks. She started to murmur, as if talking to herself,

He came back from Honolulu and took me into his house. Then he went away. I had a child. Then he returned some years later and then left and I had another child. I had four children and that means I spent time with him four times in my life. Don't marry someone that way.

While the husband lived in Hawaii all those years, this woman resided with his first wife and her children under one roof in China. In my cousin's home in California, I saw a black and white picture of the two mothers with their own children in a family portrait. The husband was missing.

Why did these men and women of the past lead separate lives in split family arrangement across national political borders? What kind of lives did they live? Such families were forged at the intersection of "race" and class within historical contexts, with consequences that affected women in various ways due to their gender.[5] Further, these families were at once transnational and yet grounded by the power of the state. The nation-state maintained territorial demarcations for historical Chinese American transnational families. Their experiences demonstrate the intense power of macroscopic forces beyond individual's control, and the micro responses of individuals who reacted to such forces.

Hune (2000) urges researches on contemporary transnational families to elucidate gender dynamics in Asian America, and I undertook this project on Taiwanese American transnational families. Silence is easily interpreted as absence. I want to give them a voice, to show how women and men act and react to the sociopolitical and economic forces of their time and space only to emerge triumphant, compromised, or otherwise. I want to give these Taiwanese Americans a presence in contemporary American consciousness, to augment our understanding of these people and their transnational split-households experiences.

THE STUDY

In 1997 when I first caught wind of the transnational families split in Taiwan and United States, I immediately sensed that there might be more than met the eyes. Were there not lots of stories from my relatives? It was because of my familiarity with such past that I became sensitized to this issue in the present. My claim to knowledge about these women arose from my birth into a family of successive emigration from the ancestral country of origin, a tradition of sojourners from China to the West that resulted in transnational families split in multiple nations-states. Therefore, this book started with situated knowledge (Haraway 1988). As suggested by Dorothy Smith, social research must be reorganized by placing the researcher "where she is actually situated . . . making her direct experience of the everyday world the primary ground of her knowledge" (1987: 91). My belonging to a transnational family tradition had sensitized me to certain issues; it had also motivated me to embark on this project.

Bourdieu (1984) posits that within the French national context, members of different class backgrounds actively acquire cultural practices and tastes that distinguish them as members of their class. My work extends this aspect of class reproduction to consider transnational contexts, in the acquisition of skills and symbolic capital that contribute to class reproduction in a rapidly changing development context, that is, Taiwan. Bourdieu neglects to consider the gendered nature of class reproduction, as do early migration studies scholars. The inclusion of women in migration studies began in the 1970s and 1980s, while research on gender and migration emerged in the late 1980s and early 1990s. Studies in this phase look at gender and migration with a meso-level perspective at such social institutions as family, community, and social networks as if the larger society and world order do not matter. The current stage of feminist immigration scholarship emphasize gender as a key constitutive factor, and begin to consider a much wider context that includes globalization (Hondagneu-Sotelo 2003). Mahler (1999: 82) highlights "gender, class, age/generation, mobility and regionality" as "key characteristics to investigate" in transnational studies. In particular, she points out the following areas needing development in the literature: the beneficiaries of transnational activities, and their relationship with power and privilege.

This book examines the intersection of gender, class, race/ethnicity, generation, and international migration in a global political economy, with attention to its impact on non-working class women as workers, mothers, and wives in transnational families split between Taiwan and the United States. I examine the causes and changing nature of immigration from Taiwan to the United States, as well as its impact on local communities in southern California. I study families split between Taiwan and the United States, and argue that the formation of transnational families is primarily a strategy to maximize return on productive and reproductive labor, facilitated by participants' non-working class position in a global political economy, to maneuver disadvantages encountered at the local level that involves race/ethnicity and generation. Despite the many observations on the harmful effects of globalization on local populations (Lewellen 2002), these families benefit from a global political economy due to their privileged socioeconomic position in society, albeit at the expense of women's career advancement and personal gratification. Hence, the effect of globalization on the local is also class specific. Further, it is primarily women who absorb most of the cost in their transnational family strategy. Thus, this strategy and migration is gendered. The impact of international migration and transnational practices on these women are not uniform. The experiences of the women as related in this research demonstrate a variety of circumstances and conditions that affect them in disparate ways constituting diverse individual cases. These circumstances and conditions exist in a continuum of contexts that range from individual to family, society, nation-state, and the global community.

The study of transnational migration between the United States and elsewhere generally has not included families and individuals from non-working classes. This research corrects that omission, focusing on the impact of transnational migration on women where husbands remain in Taiwan, the country of origin, and send remittances to support their wives and children in the United States, the country of destination. This pattern presents notable exceptions to cases more represented in the migration literature that focus on working class women, men, and families where remittances flow from the United States to the countries of origin. Current scholarship on transnational studies concentrates on connections between the United States and Latin America or the Caribbean, on working class women left behind by husbands, and on men and women who migrate to the United States for primarily manual productive labor (see, inter alia, Ahern, Bryan, and Baca 1985; Rouse 1991; Georges 1992; Hondagneu-Sotelo 1994; Kearney 2000; Parreñas 2001). My work contributes to theorizing the class and gender dimensions of migration, and provides needed comparative data for the study of transnational migration, with a special focus on women and families in the Pacific Rim.

The past is an organic part of the present, giving meanings to events that continue into the future. In this book I adopt a historical approach to search for meaningful analysis from historical processes and context (Thompson 1977; Braudel 1980; Cohn 1981; Comaroff and Comaroff 1992; Kellog 1994), with the world-systems perspective in particular to make sense of the Taiwanese American transnational family formation. Human voices that articulate lived experiences make up the focal agency of knowledge in this research. To enrich this study, I also resort to secondary sources in anthropology, economics, history, literature, sociology, and women's studies making this an interdisciplinary endeavor. Each of the above fields, plus others no doubt, has much to offer for a more holistic comprehension of the topic at hand.

AN OVERVIEW

This book consists of an introduction, ten chapters, and an epilogue. In Chapter One, I outline the theoretical considerations and the methodology employed for this study. Chapter Two incorporates my family history to illuminate the experiences of historical Chinese American transnational families forged at the intersection of class and race, and how it affects women due to their gender. Chapter Three provides a short history of immigration from Taiwan to the United States. I further argue that the nature of migration from Taiwan to southern California changed over time. In the early periods, former graduate students came to the area for economic opportunities. Investment immigrants joined them later. Beginning in the 1970s but predominantly in the 1980s and 1990s, newcomers to southern California began to arrive, using networks based on social relations, primarily kinship. Chapter Four looks at these immigrants' impact on local communities in southern California.

Chapter Five turns attention to Taiwanese American transnational families. It focuses on the causes of their migration as related by the women interviewed. Here I link the individuals' narratives to the broader socio-economic and political backgrounds as well as human agency, and make brief comparisons to transnational families split between Hong Kong and Canada or Australia. From the women's lived experiences, a concise history of Taiwan develops from its early days to its present status as a newly industrialized nation. With this foundation laid, Chapter Six situates these families in a global context. It concentrates on globalization with its underlying forces of capitalism, colonialism, and imperialism that turn these families transnational: one spouse in Taiwan and the other in the United States with the child or children. Chapter Seven explores gender relations and hierarchy as demonstrated in migration decision-making process and mechanism. I show that in addition to resource contribution and cultural ideologies, the socioeconomic status of a woman's natal family and legal as well as social forces influence power relations and hierarchy in a marriage. Chapter Eight discusses some effects of the international migration on women from transnational families as mothers and workers. I also note comparative references to some Korean American and Filipino American women from transnational families. Chapter Nine focuses on the impact of the transnational family strategy on women as wives, attending to a range of circumstances that delineate such impact. Then I summarize and conclude this study in Chapter Ten. I have also included an Epilogue. I hope that these chapters will contribute to the field of anthropology, Asian and Asian American studies, migration as well as women studies, and sociology.

Chapter One
Theoretical Consideration and Methodology

OTHERS' THEORIES

Before 1980, immigration to the United States from China, Hong Kong, and Taiwan fell under the same undifferentiated category within the Immigration and Nationalization Services. Until recently, scholars had also studied the people from these three places of origin collectively as "Chinese" despite their disparate historical developments and political economies.[1] Transnational families were widespread among Chinese immigrants in North America from the nineteenth to the early twentieth century. Hsu (2000: 99) calculates that between 1890 and 1940, forty percent of the Chinese men in the United States were married men apart from their families. From 1850 to 1920, few women and children were present among the Chinese in the United States (see, e.g., Lyman 1968; Nee and Nee 1986: 30–122). They remained in China while their husbands and fathers lived in America, forming transnational families.

However, sinological anthropologists generally analyze Chinese families with parents and offspring intact. Maurice Freedman discusses Chinese family with both spouses present in *Chinese Lineage and Society: Fukien and Kwangtung*,[2] and in *Lineage Organization in Southeastern China*, despite the fact that the two provinces of Fukien and Kwangtung boast the largest male emigration since at least the seventeenth century when Manchu rule extended over China. In *Chinese Society in Thailand: An Analytical History*, Skinner estimates that the total China-born immigrants in Thailand grew from 100,000 to 349,000 between 1825 and 1917 (1957: 79). They were almost entirely from Kwangtung and Fukien (ibid.: 35). "They left their wives and families behind. Their aim, rather, was to escape poverty, to acquire money with which they could return and raise the status of their

7

family" (ibid.: 97). In that era, transnational split-household families were prevalent between China and Southeast Asia, as well as the United States after 1848 when the gold rush and railroad construction drew an influx of Chinese men mostly from Kwangtung.

Discussing early emigrant communities in China, Daniel Harrison Kulp II (1966) posits that the effect of emigration is most fundamental on the family. Many of the emigrants died overseas, some failed to return or to send remittances, while others returned destitute. In many cases, "the women are forced to take up the work of the men and, for the support of the families, to work out of door" (ibid.: 53). Ta Chen (1940) relates a "dual family system" where Chinese immigrants in Southeast Asia support wives and families in China, but establish second families with local women where they reside. Despite financial security, often the wives back home find themselves deserted. Some Chinese also maintain transnational families between Hong Kong and Europe. Watson delineates linkages between Hong Kong and London kept by Chinese emigrants from San Tin. He notes that local eligible females abhor marriage to an emigrant from San Tin "who would be absent for years at a time" (1975: 174). Watson fails to consider the experiences of the wives who stayed behind. Studies on Chinese family and women have consistently neglected the impact of spousal separation, including works that deal with the period of heavy male emigration (e.g., Ono 1989).

Likewise, academic literature on Chinese American women largely ignores this split-family pattern and eclipses women's experience under such circumstance (see, e.g., Ling 1998). The few exceptions (Glenn 1983; Glenn and Yap 1994; Yung 1999; Hsu 2000) attend to the split-household strategy among stoop laborers from China in the late nineteenth and early twentieth century, the historical Chinese American transnational families like mine as discussed next in Chapter Two. Few works exist that deal with contemporary transnational families split in the United States and Taiwan.

On the other hand, transnationalists have studied such impacts on women in other populations. Unlike the unilineal and bipolar patterns that study migration to country of settlement from that of origin (Uzzell 1976), transnationalists study the social relations sustained between two or more countries by transmigrants. They sustain connections that defy geographical distance and political boundaries, and develop relationships that may be familial, economic, social, cultural, religious, and political (see, among others, Glick Schiller, et al. 1992; Basch, et al. 1994). Transnational ties are maintained regularly and over time (Portes, et al. 1999: 219). Often political territorial demarcations remain significant and consequential despite some claims of nations unbound (Basch, et al. 1994), because "transnational processes are anchored in and transcend one or more nation-state," (Kearney 1995: 548) implying the presence of nation-state and their concomitant power.

Scholars dealing with working class transnational families split in the United States and Latin America or the Caribbean argue that husbands' migration away from home affect women in multiple fashions. Women left behind, even against their will, endure long spousal separations that strain their emotions and bodies. In the absence of their husbands, they need to assume tasks and care formerly performed by the now departed husbands. This is particularly physically demanding in rural area where they engage in agricultural work. Mothers contrive to feed the family when remittances from the husbands in the United States fail to make ends meet. Some women experience abandonment by the husbands who find other women for extramarital affairs or even marriage. Women shoulder added burden as effective heads of households and make decisions regarding children's education and disciplinary measures. Some live as solitary persons in the in-laws' households under their watchful eyes (Ahern, Bryan, and Baca 1985; Georges 1992: 91–92; Hondagneu-Sotelo 1994).

Despite the negative effects and difficulties encountered, some women who are left behind gain autonomy as well as economic independence (Hondagneu-Sotelo 1994). Other studies demonstrate that female migration away from the home country frees them from local ideological and practical constraints, and allows them to negotiate power (Grasmuck and Pessar 1991; Kibria 1990, 1993). Pessar (1995) also shows that after a period of productive labor in the working class, some Dominican immigrant women in the United States choose to honor traditional ideology that confines women to the home in order to elevate social status for their families. These studies examine working-class women left in the home countries in Latin America and the Caribbean by husbands who go away to work as laborers in the United States, and women who initially come to the United States as productive laborers for the express purpose of making a living, including domestic workers who come to work in order to support their own children back home (Hondagneu-Sotelo and Avila 1997; Parreñas 2000). What about non-working class women who migrate to the United States not for economic survival? What about Taiwanese American transnational families split across the Pacific Ocean?

Out of the anthropological literature on Taiwan, there emerge two distinct views on family organization and women's position in the family. One perspective holds that family unity is influenced by external factors including property rights and economic advantages, ecological factors such as rainfall and irrigation systems, and the state (Pasternak 1972; Ahern 1973; Cohen 1976). Based on her research conducted in Taiwan, Margery Wolf (1968; 1972) argues that the Chinese family is a result of internal dynamics, with women playing a major role in order to defend their own interests and goals. Both viewpoints merit consideration. Structural factors are manifested in the daily life activities and relations of families and spouses, and transnational people negotiate with the forces that emerge from the interaction of processes at both the micro and macro levels (Mahler 1999: 692). While transnational relations extend beyond more than one nation-state, "at the individual level, transnational practices and discourses are those which are a habitual part of the normal lives of those involved" (Guarnizo 1997: 9). With migration, women as mothers and wives are often situated in family forms constructed in one context yet are expected to operate and remain unproblematic in another (Buijs 1994). The impact of migration on the individual necessitates the consideration of gender in the process (Pessar 1999). Transnationals are gendered, and sometimes in contradictory ways in the immediate familial milieu, as well as in a wider setting of the society and the world. This book explores the ways that transnational migration affects non-working women due to their gender given the domestic, national, international, and global contexts with historical specificity.

MY WAYS OF KNOWING

In order to learn about the actual lived experiences of the women and men targeted, I employed a range of methods that includes survey questionnaires, library research, interviews, and participant observation. These multiple methods helped to set individuals in the wider contexts of sociopolitical, economic, and cultural forces beyond the individual's control. "Multiple methods are used by many feminist researchers because of our recognition that the conditions of our lives are always simultaneously the product of personal and structural factors" (Reinharz 1992: 204). To generate primary data, I utilized questionnaire survey, in-depth semi-structured interviews, and the snowball sampling technique. Secondary sources in English were mostly obtained from the library at the University of California, Riverside and its inter-library services. Materials in Chinese were predominantly collected in Taiwan.

Survey

One of the first methods I used was survey. Surveys were necessary to identify subjects for my study, to establish baseline data on social economic status, household composition, age of family members, causes and time of migration, and length of spatial separation between husband and wife. Data on the length of separation were correlated to current marital relations to see if they redefined spousal relations. Survey responses also provided empirical data to determine respondents' choice of southern California for destination and residency. The survey questionnaire was written and typed in Chinese since most of the respondents were more proficient in this language than English. One of the questions asked if the respondent belonged to a transnational family, another question asked for the number of transnational family that they knew.

I conducted two separate organization-based questionnaire surveys resulting in a total of 162 responses from different individuals. The first survey was held at a Taiwanese married women's retreat from southwestern United States in April 1999. I was first referred to the event manager of this retreat to gain entry. She declined several times on the ground of a very tight schedule. Finally I requested to talk to her supervisor, the organizer of this event. The organizer was a woman who held a bachelor degree in psychology. She understood my need and agreed to my survey. On the day of the retreat, she spoke to the audience and encouraged the attendees to cooperate with my research. I collected a total of 110 responses at this occasion, the total yielded a usable sample of 88. The next day I wrote the supervisor a thank you note.

In July 2000 I personally monitored a second survey with female students in all the classes of English as a Second Language (ESL) at a community adult school in southern California, in an area known to have a high population of residents from Taiwan. I had taught ESL for nine years in adult schools prior to my doctoral program in anthropology. This experience seemed to have helped at this stage of my research. I knew of the existence of adult schools and that many immigrant adults attended such ESL classes. I contacted the school principal at this adult school, told him where I had worked before, and spoke of my need for his assistance. He readily consented to help and we made an appointment on a school day that was convenient to both of us.

On the day of my visit, he personally accompanied me and introduced me to his students in the various classes. I explained in Mandarin the purpose of my survey to the adult students. I mentioned that organizations including the Chiang Ching-kuo Foundation had awarded funds for my project, and that the Academia Sinica would be hosting me during my next ten months in Taiwan. The above two institutions were well known and prestigious in Taiwan; many students recognized the names and nodded their heads. The students became cooperative and enthusiastic in filling out the surveys. I collected a total of 52 responses at this site. The next day I immediately wrote a thank you note to the school principle.

Snowball Sampling

In addition to surveys, I utilized the snowball sampling technique to identify additional interviewees. Snowball sampling is also known as chain referral sampling. In this method, the researcher locates some individuals and asks them to refer others who are likely candidates for the research (Bernard 1994: 97). I started with two acquaintances who were wives of transnational families. Then in February of 1999 I visited a pastor in a church whose members came from Taiwan. This pastor gave me the name and telephone number of a woman to visit. In the summer of 1999 I contacted two churches with a large followings from Taiwan. Investigation on private matters in the family necessitated rapport and trust between the researcher and respondents. The church pastors whom I contacted considered my project worthwhile. They introduced me to their members known to be women in transnational families split in Taiwan and the United States. After each interview, I asked the woman interviewed to refer me to other women in Taiwanese American transnational family. Most women agreed to contact their friends on my behalf. I would follow up within a few days, and some would call me after contact was made.

Within one week of each survey and snowball, I telephoned the subjects thus identified and interviewed those who agreed to talk to me. I called the people within one week because I was afraid that if I waited too long they might forget me; or that they might move away or go away for vacation. I thought that I must catch it while it was hot. I also called ahead to reconfirm each interview, one or two days before the scheduled appointment. It was a good thing that I did because one woman had completely forgotten about our appointed meeting, and made other arrangements for the same time slot. My telephone call reminded her of the occasion and we had to reschedule for another day.

Some women were highly helpful and enthusiastic. For example, one morning I talked to a woman for approximately two hours. After the session concluded and I asked her to refer me to more women, she immediately called one of her friends in the neighborhood, and personally took me to that friend's house for an interview. On one good day, I started with an early morning appointment, got snowballed to a second one in the late morning, yet to a third one in the early afternoon. I wised up after that one good day.

I learned to stock several survey forms, needed stationery and forms, as well as token gifts for the interviewees in the trunk of my car so that they were always available where ever I went and whenever I needed them. I also dashed away a few bottles of water and some snacks in the car in the event that I had no time for lunch. Essentially, I built a mobile office and kitchen out of my automobile for the sole purpose of going from interview to interview. From the survey and the snowball sample, I identified a total of thirty-five women for semi-structured interviews which I would discuss in the following section.

Semi-Structured Interview

Semi-structured interviews resemble oral history interviews. They allow flexibility and freedom for the narrators to relate their experiences in their own words on their own terms (Anderson and Jack 1991: 11), and on complex issues not easily explained in questionnaire surveys. They provide details in the context of the person's life, and augment information obtained from questionnaire surveys and participant observation. I found survey questionnaire insufficient to satisfy my need and curiosity for more information—many questions remained. After my initial surveys and conversations with a few women, I also realized that at times discrepancy existed between questionnaire answers and their verbal feedbacks. The stories told in the comfort of their homes and at their own paces provided much more elaborations and innuendos. Sometimes the details thus obtained even differed completely from their survey answers.

Further, I wanted to hear some authentic voices. Dissatisfied with the "muted" voice or the complete lack of voice from the subject of study in such classics as Evans-Pritchard's *The Nuer,* I determined that my work would be polyphonic and dialogic so that the subjects' words would flow from conversations as they spoke, as in Shostak's ethnography titled *Nisa.* With due respect to their ability and intelligence, I also wanted the women to speak on their own behalf, just like the working class lads who comment on their own situations in Willis' *Learning to Labor.* In essence, I anticipated an engaging and engaged process for the participants of this research, including the people who were the subject of my inquiry, I the researcher, and the audience. I aspired to precipitate a direct connection between the speaker-subject and the reader of this book.

And if I wanted to learn about women in Taiwanese American transnational families, I must hear directly from them their comments on their own circumstances, their feelings and emotions. I needed a method that maximized that possibility. The research method of semi-structured inter-view met my requirement. "The use of semi-structured interviews has be-come the principal means by which feminists have sought to achieve the active involvement of their respondents in the construction of data about their lives" (Graham 1984: 114–15). Semi-structured interview is a method that generates qualitative data. I had listed twenty-five items in advance to make sure that the subjects covered my areas of concern during our conversations. The questions were open-ended. Open-ended questions give interviewee the opportunity and freedom to explore and to speak her mind. It is subject-centered with the person speaking out on her or his own term. It also permits interaction between the researcher and the interviewee (Reinharz 1992: 18) for clarification and discussion. Hence, in this project women became the agents of knowledge for their own experiences (Harding 1987: 7), and perspectives originated from their own standpoint (Hartsock 1983).

Reinharz (1992: 259) points out that the involvement of the research-er's personal experience and the research project takes the form of starting from one's own standpoint. Indeed I became attracted to the topic because I have been a member of transnational family, and for five generations at that. I am Chinese American and fluent in Mandarin, the official language and the language of educational instruction in Taiwan. Thus, all interviews were conducted in Mandarin, mostly in the private homes of those interviewed. I consider myself somewhat of a "native anthropologist" (Narayan 1997). Migration research also recognizes the significance of "the researcher's po-sitionality, as this will affect the research approach, the interactions with people participating in the research and the data analysis" (Willis and Yeoh 2000: xiii). I belong to similar class background and generation, more or less, of the women interviewed. I am also a woman, and that facilitates as well as hinders my research. In general, the women interviewed and I enjoyed a certain rapport and comfort in each other's presence. The interviews with women went more pleasantly and smoothly than I had envisaged. Those with men, however, proved to be a rather different story due to my gender. I related that story in a later section.

To a great extent, I felt the female subjects' sense of trust in me and of solidarity with me as a woman. I would recount a few examples below for illustrations. For my first interview obtained from the initial survey, I drove some ninety miles to meet a woman called Jin at her home. I brought a small box of candies as was appropriate since this was my first visit with her. In the first twenty minutes of our conversation, her husband lingered in the house.

During that whole time Jin behaved very politely but stoic and we carried on with small talks. Then Jin's husband excused himself to leave for a game of golf with his friends. Jin went to the window to watch her husband. As soon as his car sped off, Jin became animated and very talkative. She took me to the sofa, kicked her shoes off, threw herself into one end of the sofa, and told me to get comfortable in the sofa so we could talk. She immediately started to divulge how her family began the transnational family arrangement and what happened subsequently to her marriage. Another woman, Sue, talked to me in her house when her husband and teenage children were home. She took me to her son's bedroom in order for us to talk in some privacy when the son was out in the backyard. As soon as he asked to come in to his bedroom, Sue took me to another unused bedroom so we could share things between us alone. During that interview, she took me from room to room to maximize our privacy.

On one occasion, I was put to test on my relationship as a researcher with the subject of my study who were educated and very much my equal. After almost two hours of baring her soul to me about her transnational experience, Jin then propped up from the sofa where she had been crouching. She looked right into my eyes and asked me, "And what about you? Are your married?" My first reaction was indignity and discomfort. I felt that she was intruding on my private life. In split second, I arrested myself from getting more defensive. I immediately remembered that this woman had just given me a full account of her personal affair at my request to help me with my research. It would only be fair for me to share my life with her. So I started to tell her, "Well, I . . ." From the interviews, I came to feel immensely privileged to have been so entrusted by the women with their personal affairs. I also felt both touched and humbled.

Overall, I do not profess to provide generalization in this study about the transnational families. Rather, through the subjects' articulations I learnt about their particular lived experiences. I interviewed women in southern California where they lived (except one woman interviewed in Taiwan), and men in Taiwan where they worked for a living (except one man interviewed in California). These interviews generated qualitative primary data on the range of conditions that affected the women and men, their marital relations, and why they were affected in such ways. I interviewed all the women and men alone to maximize privacy, confidentiality, and fuller disclosure. I did not use a cassette recorder so that they would not feel uncomfortable about being put on the record. In addition, all the personal names used herein are pseudonyms to protect the anonymity of the people involved.

Participant Observation and World Ethnography

Another method I used in this study was participant observation. This is a basic method in cultural anthropology whereby, in a community setting, the researcher collects data in a relatively unstructured manner to learn the explicit and tacit aspects of the lives and relations being studied. Such data complement and supplement information obtained from oral history interviews and other more or less formal methods. However, my project differed from a traditional community-based study. I followed my subjects to wherever they lived in urban metropolitan areas that stretched from various parts of California to Taiwan. I interviewed wives of transnational families who lived in California. In order to locate husbands of such families to hear their voices, I followed them to Taiwan where these people resided and worked.

Increasingly, anthropologists study people and phenomena that are no longer confined to a bounded community (Abu Lughold 1991: 149; Appadurai 1991: 119). They attend to the migration of people and objects connected to a political economy that transcend the territorial boundaries of nation-states. This transformation is by no means an innovation in itself. Rather, it simply reflects the interconnectedness of our lives in the world. According to Marcus (1986: 171–72) as well as Marcus and Fischer (1986: 91–93), two textual strategies are articulated to construct "world ethnography." The first is to accommodate multiple locales within a single text. The second, and more manageable one, is to concentrate on a selected locale against the background of a world system. Yet another way is to follow the movement of a specific object or commodity in a single text through space and time (e.g., Mintz 1985; Steiner 1994). As Lewellen (2002: 24) points out, "What can no longer be ignored is that, for even the most remote of peoples, there are global inputs that form some part of the environment and that must be reckoned with." I combined all of the above approaches in this book. I focused on my topic and followed the subjects of my research to multiple cities and then across the Pacific Ocean from California to Taiwan; I integrated their lived experiences in familial, societal, national, international, and global dimensions with temporal specificity.

In the course of my research, two colleagues in the United States had asked me the same identical question, "Which community are you studying?" I answered, "Taiwanese American transnational families." Then they inquired further, "Where is it?" I replied, "All over." They looked puzzled, but my answer stood to be a statement of fact. Hannerz (1998: 246) comments as follows:

> How to delineate the field often appears less obvious in transnational studies than in classical local ethnography. There may be no more or less bounded territory here; a village, town, or neighborhood with a reasonably settled population, available to acceptably comfortable ethnographic surveillance.

In my interviews with the women in California, I covered an area over one hundred miles (one way) stretching from east to west, and over sixty miles (one way) from north to south. The subjects made up a community that transcended localized territorial confinement. The common denominator that defined their community was membership in transnational families split in the United States and Taiwan. To borrow Benedict Anderson's term (1985), this was an "imagined community."

However, I was able to join some women and participate in their activities within this community of transnational families. Some women invited me to dinners at their homes, and I invited some to dine at mine. Sometimes I helped them by translating documents or official letters from English into Chinese at the end of interviews. When a woman's daughter had to leave home for college, I got involved with both mother and daughter to locate lodging and roommates for the youngster. I also started to help search for a used automobile for her. Later I assisted the mother in her search for a new job. One couple found out that I was a former state-certified teacher of English as a second language. They requested that I tutor their teenage children who had just immigrated. They persisted on trying to pay me, but I insisted on volunteering. I explained that if they paid me I would feel too pressured. I drove to their home once a week to tutor both teenagers for an hour. Then I stayed for dinner with them and the mother. The time spent in this fashion and the conversation exchanged during such dinners gave me additional insight and information not obtainable in a task-oriented interview. The tutoring lasted three months, after which I became too busy to continue.

I also lived five days with a family in Taiwan when both husband and wife were together there. The couple was in their late fifties, older than most subjects in my sample. I first met them in the United States. Then the husband flew back to Taiwan and the wife remained in California where I interviewed her. I kept in touch with her by telephone after I went to Taiwan. The wife eventually returned to Taiwan. At a time convenient for both of us to meet, I took a five-hour train ride to visit them for five days. During those five days I became one of them in their home, cooked and ate with them, visited their grown children, and went out with them together. I also talked with the couple and their adult daughters, sometimes until midnight. The time thus spent gave me a glimpse into their home life, interpersonal interactions, and their marital relationship.

Library Research

One of the most productive endeavors during my time in Taiwan was library research. I collected materials relevant to my topic published by local scholars. These publications were mostly articles written in Chinese (e.g., Lu 1982; Wang 1993a, 1993b; Lu and Yi 1999; Chang and Wu 2000). I was also interested in the conditions that induced emigration from Taiwan so I gathered publications on Taiwan's recent political economy and educational system, and Taiwanese Americans in the United States. These sources in English were obtained at the Thomas Rivera Library of the University of California, Riverside or through its inter-library services.

THE SAMPLE: THE SUBJECT OF INQUIRY AND OBJECT OF GAZE

From September 1999 to August 2000, and then again from July to September 2001, I interviewed a total of thirty-five (35) women, with thirty-four interviews conducted in California, and one in Taiwan with someone who had returned for a brief period from the United States when I met her. My criterion for selecting interviewees was that they must be members of Taiwanese American transnational families, that is, they originated from Taiwan and were wives of transnational families whether in the past or the present. Almost everyone I interviewed also knew at least one other transnational family. At the time of interviews, the women's age ranged from forty to the sixties, with the mode in the forties to early fifties. The educational level of these women fell on the high side. Of the thirty-five women, one person possessed a doctorate while another received a master degree. Sixteen women held a bachelor degree from accredited universities in Taiwan, two in the United States, and eight graduated from junior colleges in Taiwan. Only seven women completed senior high school education without further schooling. The table below shows their educational level.

Besides their generally high level of education, those who participated in the labor market in Taiwan had engaged in professional or non-manual occupations, with the exception of one woman who worked as a nurse's aide. Before the start of their transnational family arrangement or before

Table 1.1 Educational level

Advance degree	Bachelor degree or college diploma	Technical or vocational school	High school
2	18	8	7

their departure for the United States, eighteen women stayed at home as full-time homemakers and seventeen were labor market participants.

The vast majority of these women came from at least middle-class background. The following paragraph illuminates the economic status of these people. I conducted twenty-five of the thirty-five interviews at the women' private residences.[3] Homeownership often reflects one's financial standing. For example, it takes a lot more economic strength to own a house in Beverly Hills than in South Central Los Angeles, Echo Park, or Lincoln Heights in Los Angeles County of southern California. Most of these women lived in relatively affluent neighborhoods. At least three women (and their husbands) resided in homes valued in the range of $500,000 or above in market value of the time. One of them owned a house immediately in front of a man-made lake about ten steps down, in an upscale suburb. The woman walked her dog around the lake every day. Another lived across from a house that went up for sale when I visited her. I went over to that house to check the asking price: five bedrooms, three bathrooms, 3-car garage, and about 3,000 square feet all for US$549,000. That was the year 2000 and housing prices had soared since then. They almost doubled between 2000 and 2004. Not every one of them owned such magnificent homes; but most lived in well-kept neighborhoods where the cost of single-family homes ranged from the $250,000 to $350,000 in market value of that year.

One woman named Chen lived in a house bought with all cash.[4] Her husband worked in Taiwan and the children attended universities or worked out of town in the United States. She said, "The five of us live in four separate cities." She continued to tell me about the purchase of her house,

> The first time my husband came after I bought this house I was shaking because I was afraid that he might not like it. It did not come anywhere near the houses that he liked when we were looking together . . . but I practically live by myself . . . and this street is quiet yet within walking distance to all conveniences. When he came he said that anything I bought would be good as long as I liked it. We bought this house with cash, only one hundred ninety something thousand, just a few dollars under US$200,000. It is a good price for this convenient location.

That same house would command US$400,000 in 2004. Most of the women seemed to have come from at least middle-class economic background. The only exception was a woman who worked as a nurse's aide in Taiwan. She also owned her house, but the houses in her neighborhood were less expensive, in the range of $150,000 at the time. She rented out two bedrooms to supplement her income. Two women lived in rented apartments but they also owned houses elsewhere.

One of these two women indicated that it cost approximately US$30,000 per annum to maintain her apartment household in southern California. A husband I tried to interview[5] in Taiwan indicated that it took approximately US$5,000 per month to pay the mortgage, feed his family of four, and cover all expenses and so on. They lived in a half million-dollar home in southern California and owned a house in an exclusive residential area in Taipei. He ran a very successful business in Taipei. I visited that business during my stay in Taiwan. Another husband said that he gave his wife US$4,000 every month to manage the purchased home and household in the United States, while he worked in Taiwan and lived in a home that they owned. A couple that used to have transnational arrangement was retired at the time of the interview. The wife said, "In 1999 we both retired and we came back here . . . this house is paid off. Now we vacation all over. We took an Alaskan cruise twice. We will be going to Europe next month, and we have vacation plans for the next three months." Such information helped to shed light on their financial standing. Two women were less financially sound by comparison, but they also lived in their own houses and they were university graduates in Taiwan. The above data demonstrate that, like the general immigrant population from Taiwan, these women came predominantly from middle-class background and above.

Besides interviewing the wives, I also wanted to hear from the husbands, but they were living and working in Taiwan. On two occasions I learnt that the husbands were visiting from Taiwan. I telephoned the wives and asked to visit them while they were in the United States. The wives indicated that the family was too busy with the husband back in town. On one occasion the husband was home when I interviewed the wife. With both husband and wife together, I did not get many private and personal talks from either spouse. However, the wife gave me the husband's business card in Taiwan and suggested that I call him in Taiwan. At first I had wanted to contact the husbands of those women I already interviewed in California, to get a more comprehensive understanding of the marital relation between the couple. On second thought, I was afraid that this might create unnecessary problems for the men and women interviewed, and for me as well.

What if unpleasant information were divulged to me, and then I related such information in my dissertation, and later the wives or husbands read about them? This was highly likely since they were mostly educated people who could access my work. Even though they would not know who had given me what information, knowing that I interviewed matching husband and wife meant that anything I mentioned could potentially have come from their own spouses. I discussed this issue with one of the women interviewed. She concurred with my cautionary tale, and commented that I should not intentionally seek out both spouses for interviews. With that resolved, I decided to go to Taiwan in search of any husbands of transnational families originated from Taiwan, making my fieldwork a transnational project that spanned two countries across the Pacific Ocean.

I interviewed a total of twelve husbands, with eleven in Taiwan and one in California. I met ten of the twelve husbands in public places for the interviews, and two of them at their private homes. These two were my personal friends, and I had known their families for some time before I started this project. The twelve transnational husbands I interviewed ranged in the forties to sixty in age. Save for the one man who had retired early, all the others were active participants in the labor force with ten in Taiwan and one in the United States. They were skilled professionals or business owners. Of the twelve men, only one obtained a high school education without further schooling. He became a successful business owner. The remaining eleven completed university undergraduate training in Taiwan. Of these eleven men, one furthered his studies in England and five received their doctoral degrees in the United States.

A WOMAN IN THE FIELD

I lived in Taiwan from August 2000 through the end of June 2001 on a Fulbright scholarship and a Pacific Rim Research Program Grant from the Office of the President, University of California. I was hosted by the Institute of Ethnology at the Academia Sinica in Taipei. Before my departure from the United States, I had met a woman historian who taught at a university in Taiwan at a conference in San Diego. She had offered to introduce me to her friends who were candidates for my interviews. A personal contact had also returned to work in Taiwan. He promised to introduce me to his colleagues who were transnational husbands. While I was able to interview women by the snowball technique with relative ease in southern California, locating men willing to talk to me in Taiwan proved to be testing. First, I was a grown woman looking for married men to talk about their marital relations. Second, I was doing fieldwork in an urban area where people lived and worked in high-rises. I was also an outsider to this place, with much less extensive networks than in North America. Third, I was pursuing a sensitive topic: what did they do living alone away from wife and children? Perhaps if I were a man I could have associated with them for social activities and become privy to their private life outside of work, but I was a single and matured woman totally unattached in Taiwan. Gender mattered in research fieldwork. It would appear that my gender had hindered my professional work in this case, but I continued to pursue my goal.

At the beginning I arranged for a press release looking for interview candidates to appear in the weekly newsletter of a large research institution. No one responded despite the putative existence of several persons with the requisite attributes. I called the man whose wife had given me his business card when I was in California. I told him I was doing this research, that I was affiliated with the Academia Sinica with a scholarship from the Fulbright Foundation and another one from the Chiang Ching-kuo Foundation the following year, that I wished to learn the experiences of husbands with transnational families. None of my symbolic capital impressed him. He did not want to talk. He said that he indeed had several colleagues with transnational families. "But," he said, "they wouldn't want to talk to you either." I begged again, he bellowed out an audibly big yawn. I felt rather indignant—there was a limit to my ability to stay humble. It was about nine-thirty in the evening. Maybe he was just too tired after work. Maybe I was too tactless or direct?

Then one day I was strolling around at the five-star Grand Hotel. One well known civic organization was holding its monthly meeting on the second floor. I recognized the name immediately and took some brochures from the booth just outside of the meeting room. At another occasion I also came upon an established business organization with a large number of male professional members. I tracked down the managing officers of the above two organizations, and called them to tell them about my need. I said that I was studying migration, specifically Taiwanese immigrants in the United States; I was in Taiwan to learn from husbands of transnational families. Both declined to connect me to their members because it was not the concern of their organization. They also said that as officers they could not refer me to members who fit my profile, because that would impinge upon the privacy of their members.

Then I met an officer of a business organization at an expatriate community center. Through his help I sent a press release in that month's newsletter to its members. One man wrote to me in response. This effort produced one interview. My local advisers at the Academia Sinica connected me to a few people to interview. I called another lead at least four times. Every time I called he was unavailable. I finally explained the reason of my call to the secretary. I left my name and cellular telephone number. He never returned my call. I also telephoned the woman historian whom I met in San Diego, who had offered to connect me with people to interview. When I talked to her in Taiwan she said that these people were out of town. Fortunately, my personal friend and contact introduced me to his colleagues for interviews. A local friend I met in Taiwan suggested two candidates. As a result of her effort, one granted me an interview while the other declined.

One Tuesday afternoon in February I was humming in my office, full of hope and excitement. I was singing and whistling in front of a mirror as I put on my lipstick and eye shadow. Why? At an academic conference in Taipei I had met a government official who wanted to help with my project. One day she called me and said, "Maria, I received an invitation to this organization's annual banquet. There should be several possible candidates for your research. Would you like to come?" To that I immediately replied, "Oh y-y-y-es!! Please, please, please. Thank yo-u-u-u." I tagged along, uninvited, with this official in her official limousine to a large annual banquet of a prestigious business organization at a five-star hotel. The whole night I had only one mission in mind: I told everyone I met about my research, and asked if they knew anyone whom I could interview. The businessmen sitting next to me at the dinner table said he did indeed know two people and promised to check with them. I followed up in about a week. He said that one person was not willing to talk to me. I thanked him and said I would call again in a week about the other person. When I did call he said he could not get in touch with the other. I thanked him and said that I would call again to follow up. He said that was unnecessary. Later I met a young lawyer at a cocktail reception; directly and indirectly because of him I interviewed two more husbands

After I returned to California, a former interviewee told me about a man who was once a husband of a transnational family. "He might be willing to talk to you!" She said. She gave me the telephone number of a Mrs. Chang to locate him. Mrs. Chang gave me his number. I called but it was disconnected. Through the effort of two more women I finally got to talk to him. He now lived about five hundred miles away from me. I offered to fly there to interview him. "Just wait." He suggested, "I might be going to Los Angeles area at Thanksgiving, we can meet then." We exchanged email addresses to touch base. He did not make it at Thanksgiving. Finally, during Christmas break in 2001, he and I met at the front door of a restaurant. He treated me to lunch at the restaurant where he shared with me his experiences.

Relying on this hodgepodge of sources, I managed to talk to twelve husbands of transnational families to solicit their experiences, and one person whose friends were such husbands. But then the interviews were mostly dead ends in themselves. They mostly declined to snowball.

The snowball sampling and various ad hoc techniques to locate men and women for my interviews biased my sample. They did not provide a generalization of the population studied. However, this bias did not affect my findings. I had not professed to advance a representation of men and women in transnational Taiwanese American families. Instead, I aimed to look at a range of conditions that they experienced. Although most of the women contacted were cooperative and helpful, not everyone that I approached consented to talk to me. This was particularly the case when they encountered unfortunate circumstances. Women with friends in misfortune would relate the situations to me but they would refuse to snowball. Hence, discussion on negative impacts on marital relations relied on only a few cases.

SUMMARY

Transnational families are widespread on the Pacific Rim, as well as between the United States, Latin America, and the Caribbean. Little work has been done on non-working families astride the Pacific Ocean between the United States and East Asia. With interviews conducted in California and Taiwan, this study generates primary data from wives and husbands of Taiwanese American transnational families. Unlike fieldwork in a territorially delineated local community, I followed my subjects from place to place in southern California in North America, and then to Taiwan in East Asia. This study situates micro processes involving these people in interaction with kin and the public, against the macro factors of sociocultural elements and political economy, within their countries of origin and destination across national borders. It used qualitative as well as quantitative methods that include surveys, snowball sampling, semi-structured interviews, participant observation, and library researches. It does not profess to provide a generalization of the Taiwanese American transnational families. Rather, it seeks to analyze a range of conditions and circumstances associated with the phenomenon. The interview sample mostly came from non-working class background and tended to be highly educated. A researcher's gender and network as well as the research topic affected fieldwork. Being a woman, I encountered relative ease snowballing women for interviews in southern California, but difficulties locating men willing to be interviewed in Taiwan.

The next chapter looks at historical transnational families split in North America and China in the nineteenth and early twentieth century.

Chapter Two

Historical Chinese American Transnational Families

MY TRANSNATIONAL HERITAGE

The foregoing chapter outlined the theoretical framework and methodology used in this project. This chapter turns to the historical Chinese American transnational families split in North America and China in the nineteenth and early twentieth century. Regarding nineteenth century Chinese immigration to the United States, Takaki (1998: 126) states that "for the overwhelming majority of Chinese men, the future would not include the possibility of a family in their new land." Yanagisako (1995) comments that such view reflects an America-centric perspective. This perspective is reflected in *Eat a Bowl of Tea* by Chinese American writer Louis Chu. This novel captures the bachelor life of a Chinese immigrant father and his grown son in New York. Although the book details the father's trip to China in search of a wife for his son, and the life of the newly wed in the United States, little is written to depict the experience of the mother left behind in the ancestral village, or any connection between the wife in China and the husband in New York. Many Chinese immigrants in Hawaii and the United States in that era were married men with wives and children in China, maintaining trans-Pacific families.

Indeed, my great-great-grandfather first left his family in China for California as a prospector in the mid-1800s, infected with the fever for gold like many other forty-niners. I learnt about him from my First Uncle, my father's elder brother. Following family tradition, First Uncle went to Hawaii as a young teenager in the early 1920s. He started junior high school there and worked as an editor at a Chinese newspaper after school. He took interest in family history. He told me the following:

> Your great-great-grandfather was a tall big man. He first went to
> Sacramento to dig gold with some thirty people from our village. He felt
> that the local environment over there wasn't too friendly, so he moved
> on to Hawaii. He retired back to China and lived to a ripe old age!
> Your great-great-grandmother stayed home in China during the whole
> time. Your great-grandfather also went to Hawaii. He ran businesses in
> Honolulu and Australia. He died in his middle age, near Manila en route
> from Australia back to China. Your great-grandmother lived all her life
> in the home village till her 70s.

First Uncle remembered that at the age of five, together with my great-
great-grandfather already in his 90s, he waited at the entrance to our village
and greeted my great-grandfather's casket as it carried him back home in
the 1910s. Great-grandfather was only in his 40s. As the first-born grand-
son in the patriline, First Uncle donned full mourning costume all in white
burlap with a white band tied across his forehead. He also held a gear that
reputedly would attract great-grandfather's soul back to the home where
he could rest.

I have pictures of my great-grandparents, he as a young man in a three
piece suit, and she in her twilight years in a black Chinese tunic with a pair of
gold earrings. The photographs evidently were taken at discrete time in different stages of their lives. In the 1980s, my Third Uncle, my father's younger
brother, went from Honolulu to the ancestral village for the first time since
he left as a teenager prior to the Second World War. He was the first in my
entire clan to lay eyes on the village since China lifted its iron curtain. He did
not get to see the house in which he grew up, my grandfather's house. It had
been left vacant for decades since none of the family returned to China after
1949. A distant relative kept an eye on the house and cleaned it from time
to time. I remember we got news in the 1960s that it was demolished during
a typhoon, along with Grandfather's calligraphy and books in his study on
the second floor. First Uncle said that his father, my grandfather, wrote "a
hand of good words," meaning that he was an accomplished calligrapher. I
also learnt that he wore a queue.

Although Third Uncle could not revisit his childhood home, he went to
check on his uncle's house. This uncle was his father's younger brother who
also went to Honolulu as a teenager. He owned a business in Honolulu, sent
money to his wife in China, and built this house in his absence. Two large
portraits hang on the high wall in the middle of the living room. Third Uncle
recognized that they were his grandparents, my great-grandparents. Third
Uncle took pictures of these two photographs on the wall. The portraits
already looked yellowed from the years. They were also a little torn. Upon

Third Uncle's return to Honolulu, he made prints of these two pictures and sent a set to each of the Chee families descended from the same progenitors, my great-grandparents. My mother in Toronto then made duplicates, and sent two sets to me in Los Angeles. I kept one set and gave one to a cousin who shared the same great-grandparents. I gave them to this cousin because I knew he would treasure the memento. The descendants of my great-grandparents now live in three different countries. We keep in touch by email, long-distance telephones calls, and occasional visits. Funerals and weddings mobilize the most traveling and induce the largest gathering of the clan.

HISTORICAL TRANSNATIONAL FAMILIES

As a consequence of capitalism, imperialism, and colonialism, thousands of Chinese in the nineteenth century left home for North America, and elsewhere in the world, in search of better livelihood (Cheng and Bonacich 1984). In the United States they numbered a little over 40,000 in1850, and grew to approximately 120,000 by 1879 (Ng 1995: 238). They were predominantly male. By 1889, the ratio of Chinese males to females swelled to 2,100 per 100 (ibid.: 247).[1] This high ratio reflects the fact that many husbands arrived alone while the wives stayed home in China, forming split-household families that transcended political and territorial boundaries, although many single men came as well. Glenn (1983) as well as Glenn and Yap (1994) consider such splitting to be a result of the economic, legal, and political constraints encountered in the United States. Other indications suggest additional causes. In the following section I discuss the socioeconomic, political, cultural and subjective elements for the formation of Chinese American transnational families. Some of these elements stemmed from the issues of gender, class, and race (see Chan 1991a: 103–4, 1991b; Peffer 1986, 1991; Takaki 1998: 37; for a summary see Chee 2003: 31–35).

First, these early immigrants left due to the lack of economic opportunities at home. Their initial intention was to sojourn: to work for a few years and then return with saved money (see Siu 1952–53). The high cost of the trans-Pacific passage also prevented wives from joining their husbands. However, Takaki (1998: 37–41) notes that Chinese laborers in Hawaii were likely to bring their wives with them, more than those who went to California (see also Peffer 1999: 18–21). This is due to the demand of differed local economy. In order to increase labor output from a stable work force, the sugar plantation managers in Hawaii took interest in a worker's family life. They encouraged the arrival of women, including wives. In contrast, employers in California wanted temporary migrant workers for seasonal and mobile farm work, mining, and railroad construction (Cheng and Bonacich 1984: 153). Hence, California's different work style and employers' attitudes toward workers contributed to the formation of more Chinese American transnational families on the mainland.

In addition, women's agency was a factor. During all the years that my great uncle lived in Hawaii, my great aunt remained in China until 1949 when the Communist regime took control. After that she moved to Hong Kong, then a British colony. From family oral tradition, I learnt that this great aunt did not want to leave for Hawaii. Glenn (1983: 29) describes a woman who preferred to stay in China for a more comfortable life. In that era in China, man and woman married by family arrangement rather than romantic love. Living a good life in a familiar environment near family and friends would appear far more appealing than a hard working life in a foreign country with a husband by arranged marriage. Chinese Canadian writer Denise Chong provides a vivid illustration of such situation from her family history in *The Concubine's Children*. Although the novel is about her grandparents' transnational family between western Canada and China, the lived experience yields glimpses on some families astride the United States and China in that era. In the early twentieth century, Denise Chong's grandfather named Chong Sam left his wife in Chung Shan, China to sojourn in the western province of British Columbia, Canada. He later brings over a concubine from China to work with him. The money that this concubine earns as a waitress goes to support his wife and children in China. He also uses her hard earned dollars to build the grandest looking house in the village for the family.

My great aunt also lived in the new house built with remittances from my great uncle in Honolulu. In addition, she took in a poor young woman to help around the house and to keep her company. "So what did she do at home?" I asked Uncle Jeff. Uncle Jeff is the son of my great aunt who passed away in the early 1960s. He is in his eighties now. He spent his childhood in the village, but joined his father in Hawaii as soon as he was a teenager. He remembered the life in China. He said, "My mother spent time with your grandmother. The women kin visited one another a lot. They often played mahjong and other tile games to kill time."[2] Mahjong aside, I remember that during my early childhood in Hong Kong, my own mother, my aunt, my grandmother, my great aunt, and other women relatives often spent days together to prepare appropriate food items for different festivals. There was a festival almost every other lunar month. The women stayed in our house for the preparation. After every supper they made the dough and fillings from scratch, while chatting and enjoying one another's company.

Cultural tradition further contributed to spousal separation. In nineteenth century China, Confucian ideology confined a woman's place to the domestic sphere caring for children and parents-in-laws (Chan 1991a: 103–104). For a woman, working outside of home and wandering afar was considered a misfortune. Further, a "hostage theory" also emerged. Parents kept the daughters-in-law and children behind to ensure their sons' eventual return and remittances (Takaki 1998: 37; Nee and Wong 1985: 289). Despite cultural tradition, comparative studies reveal that Chinese women continued to arrive Southeast Asia and Hawaii until its annexation by the United States in 1894 (Peffer 1999: 12–27). Such revelation indicates the existence of other factors. The following section demonstrates that the conscious design of U.S. legislations based on "race,"gender, and class assumed a significant role in the formation of historical Chinese American transnational families.

RACE, GENDER, AND CLASS

One of the early legislations that affected these families was the 1790 naturalization law. In 1790 the U.S. Congress limited alien's right of naturalization to "a free white person." In 1870 and after President Lincoln ended slavery on American soil, Congress extended the right of naturalized citizenship to "persons of African nativity, or African descent." Neither African nor white, Chinese immigrants were excluded from American citizenship on the basis of "race." Not being citizens, they could not legally bring over family members, such as wives, to live in the United States. Some husbands also left their wives in China for safety (Chan 1991a: 104). In the 1854 People vs. Hall case, the white defendant George Hall was convicted of murdering a Chinese man based on the testimonies provided by one Caucasian and three Chinese witnesses. Citing an existing California statute, the California Supreme Court reversed the guilty verdict. It declared that "Chinese and other people not white" could not testify against a white (Takaki 1998: 102). After this court decision, physical assaults and murders of Chinese escalated. Without legal protection, they became easy prey. Local whites chased out and killed Chinese in Rock Springs, Wyoming. They hanged Chinese to death in Los Angeles Chinatown. More examples exist. The same law can prohibit or incite wrongful actions. Law makers and interpreters alike must be conscious of the very power they hold over the many lives of ordinary people, and the myriad ways they can impact on their fellow human beings. To protect their women from danger and hostility, Chinese men took the risk on the Mainland United States and kept their women in safety at home.

Transnational families were also formed due to legislations reflecting biases on gender and class. In 1875, the U.S. Congress passed an immigration act commonly known as the Page Law. It prohibited the entry of Asian female prostitutes, laborers, and felons. Vigorous application of this Act and intimidating interrogations greatly inhibited the entry of Chinese women, whether prostitutes or not (Chan 1991b). Despite earlier claims that the Page Law had little or only short-term impact (Coolidge 1909; Sandmeyer 1991: 13), Peffer (1986, 1991) and Chan (1991b) provide evidences that corroborate its effectiveness. The Page Law targeted Asian woman. It denied Chinese wives the opportunity of joining their husbands on American soil. While this Page Law was based on gender and race, additional legislations were based on class and race.

In the nineteenth century, inexpensive Chinese male laborers were at first welcome. They contributed much in American nation building. However, the economic downturn in the latter part of the century caused severe competition in the labor market in California. Not being citizens and thus unable to vote, the Chinese immigrants lacked political ammunition to guard their interests. Their distinct physical traits and customs marked them as conspicuous targets and scapegoats. White labor leaders and politicians in California actively rallied to exclude Chinese workers. Their effort succeeded. Congress passed the Chinese Exclusion Act of 1882, followed by several amendments (McClain 1994; Miller 1969; Sandmeyer 1991; Saxton 1995).[3] This legislation forced many laborers to live in the United States separate from their families, while others returned to China. Once laborers left the States, they were barred from re-entry (Chan 1991b). This 1882 Chinese Exclusion law was based on race as well as class. It prohibited the entry of laborers but exempted "merchants, diplomats, students, clergymen, and travelers" (Chan 1991b: 97). To expand American trade in the Chinese market, the United States and China signed the 1868 Burlingame Treaty to allow reciprocal free travel and trade. Chinese merchants served as links in between. This merchant class was able to come, to bring wives and children. They could also afford to send family members back and forth (see Liu 1992). "To the vast majority of the Chinese living in the United States who were laborers, American laws made family life an impossibility" (Chan 1991b: 97).

IMPACT ON WOMEN

Dependent on one's economic background, the life of women left in China varied. My Aunt Ping remembered such women in her village childhood during the 1930s. My Aunt was born into a family with a transnational tradition. Both her father and grandfather worked in America like many others in the village. In her village, the woman neighbor across from my Aunt's house had three children, two sons and one daughter. This woman's husband and one son worked in Hawaii and the other son in Vancouver, Canada. Only the daughter stayed home. The mother and dauaghter lived comfortably on the remittances from the three men. My Aunt recalled another relative whose husband worked and died in Vancouver. The husband's family owned no land, but the wife came from a wealthy family with several men who worked overseas. Her natal family supported the woman, her one-year old daughter, a newborn son, and her mother-in-law. Another woman's husband went to San Francisco. He never sent remittances to support his wife and two children. The wife's father and brothers also went to San Francisco. Their remittances supported the woman and her children. Her family even bought her a maid. She played mahjong all the time, but lived a widow's life.

Some women fared less well. My aunt remembered a young woman named Mei. Mei married at the age of eighteen. Four months later her husband went abroad to work. Later she gave birth to a daughter. The daughter and mother lived with her blind mother-in-law who wobbled on bound feet. My aunt said, "Mei was known to take good care of the old lady. She even washed the stinky cloth that bound the old lady's feet." The villagers knew that the husband remitted hardly any money. Worse, he never returned. The villagers did not know how the family survived since they did not own any land. They only knew that Mei had men in her husband's absence. However, my aunt recalled, "She wasn't a prostitute. It wasn't a different man every night. There would be a steady man who visited her house regularly, for around five or six years." She remembered one such single man who lived in his own house. My Aunt said, "They did not live together."

Aunt Ping remembered Mei as an attractive young woman, and that several men had their eyes on her. Once, the old man living next door climbed over the backyard wall to enter her home one night. Without a husband or male kin at home, women fell prey to sexual assaults. Yet the villagers despised Mei and the women ostracized her. They considered her promiscuous. Fouron and Schiller (2001:556) also relate that poor women in Haiti trade sex for resources including jobs and necessities. Although these women can better survive than poor men, they lower their social standing in their own community. In other cases in China, male partners were also scorned (Hsu 2000: 107–108). In retrospect, my Aunt sympathized with Mei:

> She needed men to help her family survive. There was no such thing as wage work in the village. The men probably gave her money or food and necessities. How was she going to take care of the blind mother-in-law and daughter? Money aside, she had emotional and physical needs. She was so young! They spent four months together then the husband left. He never returned once. No one knew what happened to him. He probably died.

Long-term spousal separation affected women differently. One man left his newlywed of two months to work in the United States in the 1930s. He dutifully sent back money and letters to his wife in China until his death. They never once reunited. Some abandoned women remarried with consent from the husband's family (Hsu 2000: 105–21). Happier endings also existed. One couple committed to each other for life reunited in China when the husband retired from the United States, after a long absence of sixty years (Hsu 2000: 112).

I do not mean that women alone endure in these circumstances. Some men also suffer from loneliness and sorrow well preserved in folk rhymes written by Chinese sojourners in San Francisco Chinatown. They lament on their down and under life, hardship of work and so on. For example, one man agonizes as follows:

> I have walked to the very ends of the earth,
> A dusty, windy journey.
> I've toiled and I'm worn out, all for a miserable lot.
> Nothing is ideal when I am down and out.
> I think about it day and night—
> Who can save a fish out of water?
> From far away, I worry for my parents, my wife, my boy:
> Do they still have enough firewood, rice, salt, and cooking oil? (Hom 1987: 99).

Another man anguishes thus:

> Men on the remote frontier, all terrified:
> In autumn, north winds begin to blow.
> Sojourners from faraway places share the same thought:
> O, how can this little bit of clothing be enough in deep frost and heavy
>   snow?

Once winter comes—
A fur coat is needed all the more in the freezing cold.
I can buy one at a clothing store,
But it's not the same as the one sewn by my dear wife or my mother
   (ibid.: 105).

These stranded sojourners articulated sentiments that are intensely haunting, private, and intimate. Estranged wives and husbands trod on along life's path, destined to perch on either side of the vast fathomless Pacific Ocean.

Besides separation, some transnational families also dealt with polygyny and abandonment. Yung (1999: 113–23) relates a woman in China whose husband stopped writing and remitting. She later learned third hand from relatives that he had remarried and raised a family in America. In her old age, she exclaimed, "If only I could just see him one more time." Similar experiences abound (see, for example, Yu 1989: 37). One of my great uncles in Hawaii supported his first wife in China, and kept a second one in Hawaii with whom he lived till his last days. Kin of the extended family embraced both women as relatives. I met the first Great Aunt when I was a young child. I remember her melancholic expression the most. Her eyebrows seemed terminally knitted together. She seldom smiled. Her sons also left China to join the father as soon as they reached teenage after the First World War. She passed away alone in Hong Kong in the early 1960s.

Contrary to the above passive acceptance of such fate in real life, Chinese American novelist Maxine Hong Kingston dramatizes a victim of desertion with heroic womanhood and female solidarity to resist this destiny in *The Woman Warrior*. After a separation of thirty years, the protagonist Moon Orchard reunites with her sister named Brave Orchid in San Francisco. Brave Orchid has found a Chinese American husband for Moon Orchid's daughter to come to San Francisco from China for marriage. After five years, this daughter sponsors her mother Moon Orchid to immigrate to the United States, all without the knowledge of Moon Orchid's husband who has become a medical doctor, married a second wife, and started a family in Los Angeles. This husband has sent money for thirty years to support Moon Orchid and her daughter, but he has never sent for the wife nor inquired about her. Urged and plotted by her sister Brave Orchid, Moon Orchid looks up the husband to confront him in Los Angeles. He proclaims that she does not fit into his present life, that she must stay away, and that he will send money to support her. He then leaves. Moon Orchid soon becomes mentally ill and ends up in an asylum.

In addition to transnational polygyny like the examples above, some men kept two wives in China. My maternal grandfather, an American

citizen, worked most of his adult life in Hawaii while my grandmother lived
in China with his second wife. "Why two wives?" I asked my mother. She
explained, "My father only returned home a few times in his life. After bearing three daughters for your grandfather, your grandmother handpicked a
second wife for him in hopes that he might have a son to pass on his family
name. The second wife was not pretty." As it turned out, both my grandmother and this second wife gave birth to a son. Unfortunately, the son
of the second wife died a rather young man. This second wife presumably
did not have high status either. I hardly heard anything about her. I never
knew of her existence until I was an adult, when my maternal aunt and her
children came from Honolulu to visit me in Los Angeles and mentioned this
woman.

    Not all husbands in transnational families turned into polygamists. My
Aunt Ping's father also went away to work in America as a hired hand in agriculture. He returned home every two or three years, sometimes every other
year whenever he could come back with some savings. When all savings
evaporated he left again to earn more. According to my aunt, he came back
so frequently that there were hardly any savings left. My Aunt's grandfather
also went away like her father. Her paternal grandmother died two years
before my Aunt was born, so her mother was left all alone at home. "Every
time my father returned he left behind a child," Aunt Ping continued,

> My mother gave birth to thirteen babies. That means that my father
> came home at least twelve times. Only the first son, the middle daugh-
> ter and the youngest daughter survived. There was no midwife so my
> mother delivered all her own babies. After birth there was no nutritious
> food or enough rest, and she had to work. There were some remittances
> when my father stayed away, but my mother was hard working so she
> worked anyway.

We kids called my aunt's mother Ah Po, which meant "granny." According
to Aunt Ping, Ah Po was hardworking and peripatetic. She single-handedly
took care of the family land and the children. Nine lychee trees stood in one
of the family plots. Ah Po grew yams and taros on the ground under those
trees. She planted peanuts and vegetables in another plot. The family also
owned one acre of rice paddy, so Ah Po grew rice and all the food to feed the
children and collected wood for fuel. When there was more than enough to
eat, my Aunt and her brother peddled the excess food for cash in the village.
My Aunt remarked, "Normally, when the husband was home, husband and
wife would do all the above together for a living. But my father was gone, so
my mother did all the work. When she came home after outdoor work she

would sit down to do sewing and mending." In her old age, Ah Po eventually joined her daughter in Honolulu. She lived to her 90s.

SUMMARY

As demonstrated in this chapter, the transnational families split in America and China from the late nineteenth to the early twentieth century resulted largely from the forces of racial antagonism and class distinction, although cultural and personal preferences also played a part. Excluded by American laws and inhibited by lack of money, working class Chinese men labored in the United States while women remained at home in China. On the other hand, merchant class men brought their wives and children to live in the United States, and well-heeled families crossed the Pacific Ocean frequently regardless of costly journeys. This transnational family arrangement affected women in gendered ways, but such impact was also related to one's economic position. Those who received remittances could lead lives of leisure in their husband's absence. Some women relied on family support even if abandoned. In the absence of wage work, those without remittances and family resources depended on liaisons with other males, at the risk of social sanction. Long spousal separation could also influence marital relationship, hence women's welfare in the case of abandonment or polygyny. Indeed, culture, "race," class, and agency affected women in historical transnational Chinese American families, often in varied and gendered ways.

Chapter Three
Immigration from Taiwan: From Early Arrivals to Concentration in Southern California

The last chapter discussed historical transnational Chinese American families of the nineteenth and early twentieth century. This chapter turns attention to contemporary migration from Taiwan to the United States. It looks at the changing nature of immigration from Taiwan, and why the immigrants had concentrated in southern California. I argue that in the early period professional immigrants initially pioneered to this region for occupational reasons, followed by entrepreneurs seeking business opportunities. Later, early immigrants started to sponsor their relatives who came to the area on kin sponsorship. Overtime, kin sponsorship became the dominant pattern. In the sections below I discuss this changing process.

In the first major research on immigrants from Taiwan in the United States, anthropologist Hsiang-shui Chen (1992) conducted one hundred interviews with Taiwan immigrants in Flushing, New York. These one hundred individuals arrived in the United States between 1954 and 1985. The earliest arrivals were four persons working as professionals at the time of his interviews. They had come for graduate studies between the years 1954 and 1966. Then there were two sailors who jumped ship in 1967 and 1969, and one woman sponsored by an American company in 1967. "In all, 10 out of the 14 who came before 1970 were students, and two were the sailors who jumped ship. Only two were sponsored by relatives" (ibid.: 60). By the time I conducted my interviews between 1999 and 2001, the majority of the women in my sample and their families were sponsored to immigrate to the United States, mostly by siblings and occasionally by parents, forming what is called chain migration that is an unexpected outcome of the 1965

American immigration policy (Reimer 1983). In 1991, "a total of 106,914 Taiwanese immigrants were residing in California" (Tseng 1995: 38). After 1982, a large percentage of them went to the San Gabriel Valley area of Los Angeles County in southern California (Horton 1995: 23). The majority of them worked in professional, executive, and teaching occupations before migration (Immigration and Naturalization Service, Public Use Sample, from Tseng 1995:40). Such information points to a largely non-working class socioeconomic status, and a concentration in southern California.

EARLY ARRIVALS

Unlike the stoop laborers who came to the United States from China in the nineteenth century, the earliest comers from Taiwan were mostly graduate students. By Taiwan government policy at the time, no male students were allowed to leave until they had completed their military service. After its completion, students might apply for Taiwan's government scholarship to pursue graduate studies in the United States. Selections of students were strictly enforced, and only the top candidates who passed stringent examinations were considered. When I stayed in Taiwan from September 2000 to the end of June 2001, I encountered quite a few scholars and professors in their forties or early fifties who had completed their doctoral programs on such scholarships. Although some pursued their interest in social sciences, most of these early students majored in science and technology as part of the trend to contribute to nation building and the modernization of their country.

In times past, Taiwan students pursued higher education in Japan and Europe, particularly in England. Since the Second World War, the United States became the nation that received the largest number of international students (Cheng and Yang 1998). According to the Educational Statistics of the Republic of China maintained by Taipei's Ministry of Education, students studying abroad began to rise as of 1963, jumping from 216 persons in 1950, to 2,125 in 1963. The number kept steady throughout the late 1960s, reaching 2,711 in 1969, and the United States received approximately 2,000 students per year, far exceeding the 144 to Canada and other countries, and the ninety to Europe (Chang 1973: 52). As these graduates completed their advance education with a master degree or doctorate, many of them remained. While the number of students reached 1,995 in 1965, and 2,925 in 1969, the rate of return stood at only 2.9 percent and 2.8 percent for the respective years (ibid.: 53). These individuals stayed, worked, and contributed to the local economies in the United States.

These highly educated individuals were able to remain due to changing immigration policies in the United States, as well as development in Taiwan. Even in the age of globalization, capital and labor flows are not totally deregulated (Sassen 1988), nor are nations completely deterritorialized as posited by Basch, Glick-Schiller and Szanton (1994). The power of the state to a great extent controls and disciplines the body (Foucault 1991), such as bodies that cross national political borders.

The development of migration theory has long recognized the controlling power of the state that defines international migration (Zolberg 1989). U.S. immigration policies profoundly affect Asian immigration to this country (see, among others, Hing 1993; Ong and Liu 1994). In October 1965 the U.S. Congress passed the Immigration and Nationality Act that facilitated the entry of these people from Taiwan. Until the 1965 Immigration Act, the majority of the immigrants to the United States had been Europeans from the Western hemisphere, especially Canada and Mexico. In 1965 the United States liberalized its discriminatory immigration policy in an attempt to portray itself as a leader of the democratic world, and to bring skilled and educated labor to fill needs in certain prosperous sectors of the economy. During this period, little labor resistance existed because of a strong domestic economy, on-going civil rights movement, and the perception that the liberalization would not lead to a major increase of immigration from Asia (Ong and Liu 1994: 51).

This 1965 Act proved to shape future Asian America including the development of Taiwanese American transnational families. Immigration from China (including Hong Kong and Taiwan—the three were not treated as separate categories until after 1980) rose from approximately 110,000 in the 1960s to 390,000 in the 1980s (U.S. Immigration and Naturalization Service 1989). Chinese immigration to the United States was first halted by the 1875 Page Law that inhibited the entry of women, then by the 1882 Chinese Exclusion Act and its amendments that barred the entry of laborers. In recognition of China as a U.S. wartime ally, in 1943 the Congress repealed all previous Chinese exclusions and restriction laws, extended naturalization rights to the Chinese, and granted a token quota of 105 entries per year to immigrants of Chinese origin. The 1965 Act also abolished the 1924 quota system that denied entries to practically all Asians. More important, this Act established the preference system, including preferences for family reunification, professionals, and skilled labor.

The preference system gave rise to a duality of Chinese immigrants (Liu and Cheng 1994). On the one hand, low-skilled laborers with little human or financial capitals arrived as family members of old time Chinese stoop laborers. They came primarily from Hong Kong. After 1979 they also hailed from Mainland China (People's Republic of China) when the United States and China normalized diplomatic relations. On the other, the brain drain of highly educated and skilled professionals originated primarily from the Republic of China, commonly known as Taiwan. The majority of the immigrants in the early period were grown adults, with the assumption that they would join the labor force. Taiwan's graduate students who completed their training in the United States benefited from this 1965 immigration act, as did professionals trained in Taiwan. These engineers, scientists, and skilled professionals acquired their permanent residency status under this provision. The brain drain professionals and the beneficiaries of the family reunification provision began the continuous and steady flow from Taiwan to the United States.

Four of the thirty-five women in my interview sample were married to these former graduate students who had completed their advance education in the United States. They then obtained employment that qualified them for legal permanent residency. Of these four women, the first went to the East Coast from Taiwan for university education in 1971. Her name was Dana. Dana's older brother and sister had come to the East Coast before her as graduate students on scholarship in 1967. The second woman, Kate, also went to the East Coast as an undergraduate in 1975. Both met their husbands in the United States and subsequently got married. The husbands were already working when they met. The third woman, Joan, was already married in Taiwan. She came with her husband for his graduate studies in the Midwest in 1975. Although she had already finished her undergraduate education in Taiwan, she completed a second bachelor degree program with a different major while her husband was studying for his doctorate. The husband obtained employment upon his graduation and they became legal residents in 1980. The fourth woman, Shi, received her bachelor degree in Taiwan and came to work for a relative in 1980. She got married shortly there after. Her husband had received a master's degree earlier in the United States and was already working when they met.

All these four husbands had specialized in science and technology: Two in electrical engineering, one in industrial engineering, and one in biochemistry. Except for the biochemist, all of the others later moved into the computer industry. All of the above graduates subsequently obtained American citizenship. They represented the early comers who arrived for advance education. In addition, one woman in my sample obtained her master's degree 1990 in the United States. She later joined her sister who had settled in southern California. A friend referred her to an employer who sponsored her for legal residency. Many of these American citizens in turn sponsored their family members to immigrate to the United States, including their parents, children, siblings and their spouses and children, who then could sponsor other family members once they qualified. Of the eleven husbands whom I interviewed in Taiwan (the twelfth and last husband was interviewed in California), five had received their doctorates in the United States. One of the five completed his program in the 1990s, the other four belonged to the early student population who came in the 1970s and early 1980s. Three returned to Taiwan upon their doctoral graduation. One remained in the United States to work, obtained his citizenship, but eventually returned to Taiwan in the 1990s while his wife and children continued to live in the United States, forming a transnational family.

For his study on Taiwan immigrants in Flushing, Chen (1992) conducted eighteen months of research between October 1984 and May 1987 (absent between1985 and October 1986). His sample shows that before 1970, ten out of fourteen interviewees came as students, two were sailors who jumped ship, and only two individuals came on kin sponsorship; while only twenty-nine out of 115 respondents cited kin sponsorship between 1955 and 1985 (1992: 60–63). When I completed my interviews between April 1999 and August 2001 (with absence from August 2000 to July 2001 when I conducted fieldwork in Taiwan), nineteen of the thirty-five women in my sample had come on kin sponsorship. This high number presents a stark contrast to Chen's interviewees who arrived prior to 1985. As he correctly comments, "In terms of their immigration history, the Taiwan immigrants are still in a pioneering stage, so chain migration in future years will play an even larger role" (ibid.: 63).

KIN SPONSORSHIP

The difference in number between 1985 and 1999 partly reflects the significance of kin sponsorship initiated by earlier pioneers, including the early graduate students. These pioneers settled to work in the United States, subsequently acquired their permanent residency and then American citizenship that qualified them to sponsor their relatives to immigrate legally to the United States. In her study on working-class Mexican migrants in the United States, Hondagneu-Sotelo (1994) posits that access to migration network is gendered. Male and female members of the same household resort to discrete social network for their own migration assistance. From other migrant women already in the United States, single women in Mexico receive encouragement, job contacts, accompaniment, and social connections to go north. When their husbands oppose to their migration north, married women and their children obtain encouragements and assistance from women and kin of the wives to reach the border. Husbands, sons, and brothers build their own social networks to migrate, and these networks are often not shared with women (ibid.: 92–95). They are undocumented migrants. "As more women migrated to the U.S. [sic], they developed female networks of their own, so that it is now not uncommon for family and household members to use different social networks" (ibid.: 95).

I argue that their situation of gendered and disparate network access is largely due to the undocumented nature of their migration to the United States. In my sample of nineteen individuals who came on kin sponsorship, such access was shared instead of separate, due to the legal or documented status of their immigration. Save for one woman who was sponsored by her parent as a single woman, eighteen came on kin sponsorship by siblings of either the husband or the wife: nine by the wife's sister or brother, and nine by the husband's sister or brother. Husband and/or wife migrated with children as a family unit on available kin sponsorship via either the woman or man's social relations, even though the decision to migrate might have involved conflicts within some families

Such kin sponsorship appeared direct and simple at times, other times it turned into a complex chain migration that involved multiple ties of social relations. The following examples from my sample demonstrate this continuum from simplicity to complexity. One woman recounted her sponsorship links as follows:

> My sister sponsored us to come here. She came to the United States in 1983 for graduate school in computer science. After graduation she worked at a school that sponsored her for the green card [legal permanent residency]. She then sponsored my parents and then me as her sister.

Another woman gave the following information:

> My husband's younger brother sponsored us as siblings. His wife's younger sister married an American. She later became a citizen and then sponsored her sister and the sister's husband, my husband's brother.

Other women came after a round about chain of sponsorship. One woman's experience spoke to this chain effect:

> My husband's brother came and lived here and sponsored us. How did he come? His wife's brother was the first to immigrate. This brother A became a citizen and sponsored his sister B (my husband's brother's wife). Sister B and her husband C (my husband's brother) became citizens and C sponsored his parents D (my husband's parents). These parents D then sponsored my husband E and I am the wife of E.

When the U.S. Congress passed the 1965 Immigration and Nationality Act extending the right and privileges to citizens of Asian descent, it had not at all calculated or predicted this extent of Asian kinship ties. These ties in turn enabled several families to legally immigrate to the United States sponsored mostly by the siblings of the husband or the wife. For these people, the access to migration networks was shared in the same family, unlike some Mexican undocumented migrants.

Mostly related to the former graduate students and skilled professionals, many of these subsequent immigrants from Taiwan were also educated and came from non-working class backgrounds. Likewise, the thirty-five women in my sample appeared to have come from that sector of society. And like many others from Taiwan, they chose southern California as their point of destination. But why southern California? In the following paragraphs I discuss these people's reasons for their choice.

CONCENTRATION IN SOUTHERN CALIFORNIA BY CHANNELING

Immigrants from Taiwan disperse in urban areas, mostly on the East Coast (such as New York and Maryland), in the south such as Texas, and in California. Southern California became a favored destination only in the past three decades. One woman named Lily recounted the Taiwanese immigrants' choices of destination in the early years. I identified Lily in the survey at the school for English as a second language. She appeared very enthusiastic in sharing her experience with me and invited me to her home. She was once a wife in one of the transnational families that I studied. She was in her sixties and already retired when we met. She said,

> I came from a big happy family. My parents would have been one hundred years old if they were alive. Imagine, my mother already went to

English school in her days. She attended the same high school as Madam
Chiang Kai-shek.[1]

Lily met and married her husband in Taiwan. He completed his grad-
uate work in science and technology on the East Coast and returned to
Taiwan where he worked as a professor as well as a corporate executive.
Lily's several brothers also came to the United States for graduate studies in the 1960s. One majored in accounting and attended the University
of Washington that was reputable in that discipline. Another went to the
University of California, Berkeley. The others all went to the East Coast.
Lily explained why hardly anyone studied in southern California in those
early years,

> In those days graduate students from Taiwan did not come to south-
> ern California. They considered Los Angeles a cultural desert without a
> good enough university. They looked down upon Los Angeles.

However, southern California later came to hold the largest concentration of
residents from Taiwan. Why had they chosen this location?

In a comparative study of Chinese ethnic economy in New York and
Los Angeles, Y. Zhou (1998) argues that the mild climate and the relative short distance between Los Angeles and Taiwan, as well as the favorable local and international economic cycles, attract well-educated and
well-endowed people from Taiwan. I contend that Yu fails to recognize the
diachronic and qualitative specificity of migration. I propose that early pioneers indeed reached the region for economic opportunity, but over time the
nature of immigration changed. Social relations later channeled Taiwanese
newcomers to southern California. In a well-researched study of Mexican
migrants to the United States by an interdisciplinary team of sociologists
and anthropologists, Massey, et al. (1987) demonstrate that as migration
from the point of origin to the point of destination continues and develops
over time, the qualitative nature of migration changes. Earlier migrants go
to more diverse destinations. While these pioneers venture to areas that offer
work opportunity and establish themselves, subsequent migrants begin to
arrive via their network of social relations, whether kin or friends. The findings of Massey, et al. support their core argument that "migration is a social
process with a strong internal momentum that reinforces itself over time"
(1987: 319). They explain as follows:

> The channeling of migrants occurs as social networks focus increas-
> ingly on specific communities. As daughter settlements of Mexican

out-migrants develop, the social infrastructure linking them to the parent communities becomes more directed and reified and the network becomes self-perpetuating. More migrants move to a particular place because that is where the networks lead, and because that is where the social structure affords them the greatest opportunities for success. As more migrants arrive, the range of social connections is further extended, making subsequent migration to that place even more likely (Massey, et al. 1987: 153).

As a few families settle in initial destination, they serve as magnets that attract additional migrants to work sites in particular cities. The early pioneers can provide assistance in work referral, living accommodation, necessary information, financial assistance, social outlets and emotional support. When the settled community reaches a critical mass, socioeconomic organizations takes place and a channeling of migration develops as social networks concentrate from the same point of origin to the same point of destination over time.

As cited by Hugo (1981: 201–208), several studies in the 1960s and 1970s on internal migration in Africa, Asia, Latin America and elsewhere all point to the assistance and information flow from social relations as the deciding factor in the decision to migrate and the choice of destination. Existence of kin, friends, and associates in the destination alleviate or remove the uncertainty and cost associated with moving to a new environment. They help to provide allocation of employment, housing, social interactions, and mutual aid. Scholarship on international migration also demonstrates the centrality of social network in directing and sustaining migration (Boyd 1989; Findlay 1990; Gurak and Caces 1992; Massey 1990; Massey and Espana 1987; Massey, et al.1993, among others). On the other hand, Wilson (1994) modifies the network mediated migration theory, and demonstrates that Mexican wage labor migrants join friends and relatives at various locations throughout the United States at their first and subsequent crossings of the border. Rather than only going to locations with network aid, they disperse to multiple destinations where they can find network aid and work opportunities. Wilson's study illustrates wage labor migrants who move around in search of "the most congenial labor and residential companions, or alternatively, availing themselves of whatever work opportunities they become aware of through contacts" (ibid.: 276). Essentially, these wage migrant laborers "follow the crops," so to speak.

Contrary to Wilson's Mexican migrant wage workers, the non-working class Taiwanese immigrants did not have to "follow the crops" due to their superior financial background. Instead, they were channeled to southern California via social network. This development occurred with the Taiwanese immigrants' concentration in southern California. The transformation had not happened suddenly or abruptly. Rather, the arrivals of pioneers and kin/friend overlapped in the transitional period until the pioneer arrivals tapered off. Graduate students predominated among early arrivals from Taiwan between 1960s and 1970s. After the completion of their advance education, many remained in the United States to work and subsequently became American citizens. Some of these pioneers came to southern California for work opportunity. The 1965 Immigration and Nationality Act entitled them to sponsor their parents and siblings for family reunification. This Act started a chain migration on kin sponsorship in the late 1970s and 1980s, along with other new comers who arrived as investment immigrants. Human agency enhanced their choice for southern California. In the 1970s, a real estate agent named Frederick Hsieh actively promoted in Taiwan the availability of appealing housing in the City of Monterey Park located in southern California. Several immigrants bought into this area. Over time, the nature of their migration to southern California changed from pioneers who reached the region for economic opportunity to channeling via social network, primarily through kinship. The data collected from my interviews and questionnaire surveys supported my argument.

In addition to the thirty-five women interviewed, I conducted two separate surveys resulting in a total of 162 responses from different individuals. In April 1999 I collected 110 responses at an organization-based regional women's retreat with attendees from different counties in southern California and from out of state. I personally monitored the survey during the entire time. Eight of these individuals came from out of state and their responses were excluded. Seven answered less than half of the questions in the questionnaire. They were also discarded. Five did not answer the questions on why they elected to live in southern California, and two were included in my interview sample. For the above reasons, a total of twenty-two were removed from the 110 survey questionnaires collected, leaving a usable sample of eighty-eight. In July 2000, I again personally conducted and monitored a second survey for an entire morning at an adult school in an area known to have a large population of people from Taiwan. In this survey, I was trying to identify subjects to interview, so I announced to them in Mandarin and English that only women originating from Taiwan needed to participate. I collected a total of fifty-two responses. Two individuals did not answer the questions on why they chose to live in southern California and five were subsequently interviewed, leaving forty-five individuals in the final sample. The two surveys thus yielded 133 different persons as my final sample used for discussion herein. In the following section I present and discuss the responses from both surveys, but first the smaller sample of forty-five individuals from the adult school. The data in Table 3.1 below list the reasons provided by the respondents.

The table shows that twenty-six out of forty-five respondents indicated climate as the main criterion for their choice of southern California. At first glance, climate appeared to be the most cited reasons for choosing southern California, but further look into the matter revealed other correlations. In the survey questionnaire, I asked two more related questions: 1) any kin in southern California prior to arrival; and 2) any friend in area prior to arrival. Many gave a positive answer to both questions: out of the forty-five individuals, seventeen had kin and sixteen had friends in southern California prior to arrival. The number of kin for these people ranged from one person to many people including grown daughter, son, brother, sister, parents, and in-laws. The following table gives a composite of these variables showing local social network for the twenty-six individuals who answered that they chose the area due to its climate.

In Table 3.2, only two out of the twenty-six women who indicated climate had neither kin nor friend in the area prior to arrival, naturally they had not come here because of them. The first woman aged forty-one was a housewife who came in 1997 for her children's education. She cited the good environment and climate. The second woman aged forty-three arrived in 1999. She chose the area because of its environment and climate. She was a business owner in Taiwan as well as southern California. She left Taiwan

Table 3.1 Reasons for choosing southern California. Survey at a school for English as a second language. Sample total = 45

Reason	No. of Responses*
Climate	26
Kin in Area	13
Presence of Many Asian/Chinese/Taiwanese	7
Proximity to Taiwan	6
Good Air Quality	4
Good Environment	4
Friends in Area	3
Food Availability	3
Following Husband	3
Husband's Work Location	3
Husband's School Location	1

*The total number of responses exceeded 45 since each individual gave as many reasons as applicable.

Table 3.2 Social network in southern California prior to arrival for the 26 respondents who chose climate

English as a second language school survey. Total = 26.

Year		Local social network prior to arrival		Reason for choosing southern California		
Age	Year Came	Kin in Area	Friends in Area	Kin in Area	Friend in Area	Climate
32	2000	x	x			x
44	1999	x	x			x
43	1999					x
60	1999	x	x			x
55–60	1999	x				x
42	1999	x				x
57	1998	x	x			x
43	1998	x	x	x		x
41	1997					x
74	1996	x	x			x
52	1995	x	x	x	x	x
72	1995	x	x			x
40	1991		x			x
43	1990	x	x			x
39	1990		x			x
55	1990		x			x
48	1989	x	x			x
64	1988	x				x
67	1985	x				x
60	1984		x			x
68	1984	x	x	x		x
73	1983	x	x			x
57	1983	x	x			x
56	1966		x			x
75	19?5	x				x
62	?				x	x
Total		18	16	3	2	26

for this area because of business opportunity, seasonable climate, convenient local transportation, good air quality as well as law and order compared to Taiwan, and stable merchandise market price.

Table 3.3, age distribution, shows the importance of climate to people in certain age groups. The table reveals that respondents over the age of fifty-five tended to consider climate as a factor. Age is a factor when climate is a consideration. However, I argue that climate is important but not the

Table 3.3 Age distribution
for individuals choosing
climate as a criterion.
School survey.

Age	No. of Persons	
30–34	x	1
35–39	x	1
40–44	xxxxxxx	7
45–49	x	1
46–49	x	1
50–54	x	1
55–59	xxxxx	5
65–69	xx	2
70–74	xxx	3
75–79	x	1

most critical deciding element for these senior people, proximity to kin care would be the major factor. Indeed, two sons of the seventy-five-year old woman lived in southern California prior to her arrival, and she had been living with one of them since she arrived.

The sample from the retreat is larger, with eighty-eight individuals. The results are presented in the following table.

Table 3.4 Reasons for coming to southern California.
Survey at organization-based women's retreat, April 1999
Sample total = 88

Reason for Choosing Southern California	No. of Response*
Kin in Area	36
Climate	27
Husband's Work Location	12
Friends in Area	11
Work Opportunity	8
Proximity to Taiwan	7
Presence of Asian/Chinese/Taiwanese	6
Good Environment	4
Own School's Location	2
Food Availability	2
Kid's School	1
Husband's School Location	1

*The total number of responses exceeded 88 since each respondent gave as many reasons as applicable.

Out of the eighty-eight individuals in this survey, thirty-six chose southern California due the presence of kin, eleven due to the presence of friends, twenty-seven for its climate, and seven for its proximity to Taiwan. Elsewhere in the questionnaire indicated that prior to their arrivals in southern California, fifty-four already had kin and fifty had friends in the area. Other answers in the questionnaire uncovered that the majority of the kin ties were brother, sister, spousal sibling, and cousin. In the 1980s, parents and a grandmother had lived in the area prior to some respondents' own arrival.

Although twenty-seven women said they chose southern California for its climate as indicated in Table 3.4, all but three already had friends or kin in the area. Of these three individuals, the one (aged 49) who came in 1974 reported that she chose the area for its climate and the large members of co-ethnics. It was her husband who decided to come with their four children to invest in the motel business. They were the entrepreneurs. The second woman, aged fifty-seven, arrived the United States in 1977 with her husband and child. She indicated that her husband made the decision to immigrate, but no further relevant information could be extracted. The third woman left for the United States in 1969 with her husband and children for a medical residency (likely her husband's). This was a graduate student. She chose southern California for its climate and availability of Chinese food.

Out of eighty-eight women, twelve came to California because of their husband's work location. Two reached the area in the late 1960s, three through the early, mid- to late-1970s, and four in the early 1980s. After this period the trend started to taper off, with one more in 1995, and another in 1997. All but two of these wives possessed a university degree. It could be surmised that their husbands were more likely former graduate students who remained to work in the United States, especially in the 1960s and 1970s, although it is also possible that they were entrepreneurs in the 1970s and 1980s. One of the two women with only a high school education worked as a civil servant before departure from Taiwan. She and her family came to the United States because her husband decided to further his education. Husband, wife, and two children came in 1982. The husband was a graduate student. The other woman with only a high school education was the wife of a church pastor who worked in southern California. They arrived in 1997. The twelfth woman was thirty-three years old. She moved to southern California in 1995 due to her husband's work location. She possessed a master's degree. Her husband was likely a professional. They had friends and a sibling in the area before their arrival.

All the twenty-eight women who reached California after 1987 had either kin or friends in the area. Only six had no kin (but friends) and also only six had no friend (but kin) in the area prior to arrival. In the period after 1987, fourteen out of the twenty-eight women said they chose southern California because of kin in the area, nine said because of climate, but eight of these nine also had kin in the area. In fact, all nine respondents had either friends or kin in southern California prior to arrival. These twenty-eight women arrived in each year from 1987 to 1998 except 1990 (this survey was conducted in April 1999). Their kin were close family members that included grandmother, mother, father, sister, brother, spouse's siblings and parents, uncle, aunt, cousin, and grown sons and daughters. The information above demonstrates that proximity to Taiwan consistently ranked low as a criterion for choice, and climate as a factor often accompanied kin ties and sometimes presence of friends in southern California. Social network played an increasingly important role in attracting immigrants from Taiwan to southern California.

The above data support my contention for the changing nature of immigration from Taiwan to southern California over time. In the 1960s and 1970s, former graduate students came to this region for employment opportunities. A few other entrepreneurs also arrived for possible business ventures. Through the 1980s former graduate students and entrepreneurs continued to reach this area. At the same time, others started to come to the area where their kin and/or friends lived. This occurred particularly after Taiwan began its liberalization policy, granting more exit permits and outward capital movements in 1987. Additional residents in the area supported more business establishments that catered to the residents' needs and wants. Increases in businesses and conveniences attracted yet more arrivals. In a feedback loop residents and businesses fueled each other. Large concentration of these people provided the ecology for the formation of larger business firms (Sanders and Nee 1996), such as Chinese American banks (Li, et al. 2000). Such financial institutions in turn contributed to the development of the area where these people lived (Li, et al. 2002). Eventually, some suburban areas of metropolitan Los Angeles transformed into "ethnoburbs" (Li 1998).

In the late 1980s and 1990s, the flow of graduate students who came for work in the area had largely ceased. Entrepreneurs still came in the 1990s, but many more started to arrive in southern California via kin sponsorship, mostly by siblings and chain effect under the Fifth Preference of the 1965 Immigration and Nationality Act. Such sponsorship by siblings usually took ten years to process for approval. One woman's sibling filed the application in 1980 and they got approved in 1990; another applied in 1982 and approval was granted in 1992. Two others filed in 1983, one got approved in 1993 and the other in 1994; two women's families applied in 1987 and both received the green light in 1997. It took so long that often the women said they had all but forgotten about it when the notification came from the American immigration office. It appeared apparent that in the 1990s, many new arrivals had been channeled to southern California by their network of social relations in this area. Most of these were kin relations. Some entrepreneurs without kin sponsorship entered under the business investment provisions. The United States' 1990 Immigration Act permitted the immigration of foreigners who were willing and able to invest US$1 million in a U.S. business that would create employment opportunities for local residents. Many applicants from Taiwan and Hong Kong took advantage of this provision. This too declined when more and more entrepreneurs in Taiwan directed their manufacturing investment to Mainland China and Southeast Asia in the 1990s. As shown above, the pattern of who came, how they came, as well as why these people converged on this area altered with time.

Even the interview sample with the thirty-five non-working class women in transnational Taiwanese American families corroborated that trajectory. The following section presents the data from this sample.

In Table 3.5, eighteen cited kin in the area as their reason for coming to southern California. Only eleven out of thirty-five women considered climate to be a factor. Proximity to Taiwan accounted for only seven. This is noteworthy, considering the fact that these women were members of transnational families and their husbands (and occasionally the women) flew back and forth between southern California and Taiwan. As the respondents could give multiple reasons for their choice, four out of the eleven women cited both climate and kin in the area, and two cited both climate and friends in the area. When considered with two other questions, the correlation between social network and concentration in southern California became significantly higher. These two questions asked, 1) if they had any kin in the area prior to arrival, and 2) if they had any friends in the area prior to arrival. Out of the eleven women who cited climate, seven had kin and five had friends in the area while four had both kin and friends before arrival. One woman had six families members plus her mother and more than ten families of friends before her arrival, as she chose kin link, climate, proximity to Taiwan, and a multi-cultural environment as her criteria.

A net of merely two of the climate respondents had no kin or friend prior to their arrival in southern California. Naturally they had not come to the area via social relations. Both women were business co-owners with their husbands, and both came to open a branch office for their company

Table 3.5 Reasons for choosing southern California as destination

Interview sample = 35

Year came	1970–74	1975–79	1980–84	1985–89	1990–94	1995–99	Total*
Kin in area		x	x	x	xxxxxx	xxxxxxxxx	18
Climate		x		xx	xx	xxxxxx	11
Friends in area				xxx		xxxx	7
Proximity to Taiwan			x		x	xxxxx	7
Lots of Asians/Chinese/Taiwanese				xx	x	xx	5
Convenient Transportation						xxxx	4
Business/work Opportunity			x	x			2
Husband's job location	x		x				2
Language convenience				x		x	2
Multicultural Environment						x	1

*Although these data came from 35 women, the respondents gave as many responses as applicable. Some respondents gave multiple responses, thus making the total reasons for all categories above 35.

in Taiwan with the visa that entitled them to become permanent residents after their business showed proven record of success. They were the entrepreneurs. Interestingly, neither cited proximity to Taiwan as a criterion for choosing southern California. In addition to climate, one of these two entrepreneurs cited the presence of many ethnic Chinese and daily living amenities that resembled those in Taiwan. She came in 1989. The other woman said that she just chanced upon Los Angeles. The very first time she joined a tour to the United States in 1975, Los Angeles was the first stop so she felt more familiar with this city. On the other hand, the most cited reason for choosing this region was the presence of kin in the area, responded by eighteen out of thirty-five women. At this time it would help to look at the ways these women and their families immigrated to this area, as indicated by visa category in Tables 3.6 and 3.7.

The tables break down the thirty-five women and their families' entries to the United States by decade and by method of immigration. The figures in Table 3.7 reflect the increasing number of immigrants sponsored by kin, more than doubling by the decade, as does the category for business investment or branch expansion. Most revealing is the number of individuals who came on visitor's visa, jumping from zero in the seventies to one in the eighties and then fourfold in the nineties. Prior to the liberalization policy in Taiwan in the late 1980s, it was extremely difficult for Taiwan residents to obtain an exit visa from the Taiwan government for tourist/visitor purposes. Although this is a small sample of only thirty-five women, the increase appears to be indicative of the trend in the larger population. The lack of response in the category "marriage to graduate students" between

Table 3.6 Immigration by visa category.
Interview sample = 35

Kin Sponsorship	19
Business Investment/branch	6
Visitor's Visa	5
Married former Graduate Students	4*
Self as former Graduate Student	1
Total	35

*Two women first came as undergraduate students and one came to help a relative right after university graduation in Taiwan. They later met and married former graduate students from Taiwan who were already working at the time when they met. One woman arrived with her husband to begin his graduate studies in the U.S.

Table 3.7 Immigration category by year. Interview sample = 35

	1971–80	1981–90	1991–2000
Kin sponsorship	2	5	12
Business investment or branch	1	2	3
Visitor's visa	0	1	4
Marriage to graduate students	4	0	0
For graduate study	0	1	0

1980 and 2000 speaks for the age of the women interviewed. The thirty-five women would have been married prior to the decades between 1980 and 2000, yielding the zero entry for those years. On the other hand, there were indeed fewer female than male graduate students coming to the United States in the early years, although many females came from Taiwan for advance education in more recent periods. The lack of numbers for the decades between 1980 and 2000 again reflects the age of the women, as by then they would have long completed their university education. In fact, the only woman who came for graduate training in the 1980s had been working and married for several years after her undergraduate education in Taiwan before she arrived for her graduate school as a mature student. For those who came on kin sponsorship in the 1990s, their applications were initiated in the 1980s, taking approximately ten years to process. These women's sponsorships were by siblings or occasionally parents, after the first wave of pioneers who had obtained their citizenship.

SUMMARY

Immigration from Taiwan to the United States started in the 1950s. The earliest arrivals came for graduate studies on the East Coast and the Midwest. Many of these students remained to work in the United States after the completion of their training. The 1965 Immigration Act established preferences for family reunification, professionals, and skilled labor, and several of these early arrivals sponsored their family members to immigrate to the United States. Immigration from Taiwan began to rise in the 1980s. Most of them came from non-working class background. In the early period, graduate students came to southern California for work opportunities; later, entrepreneurs also arrived. Attracted by active real estate promotion, they settled in the suburban areas in the San Gabriel Valley of southern California. Over time, more immigrants started to come on kin sponsorship. Immigrants from Taiwan increasingly concentrated in southern California by the effect of channeling migration via social networks. They chose to live in southern California primarily due to the presence of kin and friends already present in the region.

The rapid influx of immigrants from Taiwan also changed the characteristics of some local communities in the United States. The next chapter discusses the impact of Taiwan immigrants on the City of Monterey Park and nearby areas in the San Gabriel Valley of southern California.

Chapter Four
Taiwanese Immigrants' Impact on Local Communities

The previous chapter provided a historical development of Taiwan's immigration to the United States, tracing the early arrivals of graduate students to concentration in southern California. This chapter looks at these immigrants' influences on the region. Their increased presence in large number altered the landscape and socioeconomic as well as political characteristics of some local communities. The first area most affected by these immigrants is the City of Monterey Park, California. It is nicknamed Little Taipei. This name Little Taipei alone demonstrates the extent of influence from Taiwan, whose capital is indeed Taipei. Monterey Park has been labeled the first suburban Chinatown. It boasts a majority of Chinese residents and occasional mayors of Chinese descent. Incorporated on May 29, 1916, it is situated in what is now called the San Gabriel Valley, an area originally inhabited by Shoshonean Native Americans.

THE CITY OF MONTEREY PARK

When the Spanish missionaries arrived with a party of soldiers in 1771, they established a mission in the San Gabriel Valley and tried to convert the Native Americans. The area later became part of a land grant to Antonio Maria Lugo from the King of Spain. In 1866, an Italian immigrant named Alessandro Repetto bought 5,000 acres in this area. Prior to the Civil War, an Irish immigrant Richard Garvey passed through the area as a United States army mail carrier. He later prospered, bought 5,000 acres, and started developing the area that included the present Monterey Park. To pay for the development and his debt, Garvey sold portions of his real estate. The first subdivision was developed and named Ramona Acres (75th Anniversary Book Committee 1991).

By the 1920s, white, Asian, and Latino residents began farming and started flower nurseries in the Monterey Highlands area. Monterey Park experienced population growth between the Second World War and 1960. The local population steadily increased through the forties and fifties. New housing tracts sprang up throughout the 1950s. Japanese Americans, Chinese Americans, and Latino Americans as well as Euro Americans bought into the area. Monterey Park is only about twelve miles from downtown Los Angeles via the San Bernardino Freeway (Freeway Ten). The city is well served by the Freeway Ten and Freeway Sixty running east and west, and by the Pasadena Freeway going north and south. More and more Asian Americans moved into the area from 1960 to 1970. The city was fast becoming a middle-class suburb. By 1970, the total population of Monterey Park was 49,166. It consisted of thirty-four percent Latinos and fifteen percent Asian Americans, the rest being of European extraction. "Japanese Americans at this time outnumbered Chinese Americans in the city, 4,627 to 2,202" (Fong 1994: 26).

In 1952, the developer of the Monterey Highlands Subdivision refused to sell a house to an African American physicist and his wife. The subdivision's homeowners association abstained from involvement with the matter, while a few residents assumed a segregation attitude. The City Council unanimously passed a resolution to endorse existing state statutes that prohibited discrimination. Most of the public supported the African American couple to purchase their home by letters of support, and civic organizations such as the Chamber of Commerce offered to mediate the dispute. When the couple filed a lawsuit against the developer, he finally consented to sell a house to them (ibid.: 23–24). By 1960, Anglo residents made up eighty-five percent of the total population, Latino 11.6 percent, Asians 2.9 percent, and Blacks 0.1 percent, out of a total population of 37,821 (Monterey Park Community Development Department, cited in Fong 1994: 22).

This area remained relatively quiet prior to the 1970s. Few of the Taiwanese immigrants had come in these early years, but my cousin and his family were already living in Monterey Park. When I came to visit and stay with them in the summer of 1978, only two mediocre Chinese restaurants existed in the vicinity. We always drove to Chinatown in Los Angeles for Chinese meals and groceries. However, beginning in the 1970s, Monterey Park already started to experience an influx of immigrants from Taiwan. The influx was due to geopolitics, changes in U.S. immigration policy, and liberalizing economic policies in Taiwan. It was also brought about by purposeful human agency. In the following section, I first discuss the national and international political economy before I continue with human agency.

NATIONAL AND INTERNATIONAL CONTEXTS

In 1971 the United Nations ousted Taiwan and extended membership to China (The People's Republic of China). In the same year, United States and China signed the Shanghai Communique agreeing to re-establish diplomatic relations between these two countries. This agreement was consummated in 1979 when the United States terminated diplomatic relationship with Taiwan and normalized it with China. In addition, The United Kingdom and Mainland Chinese government signed a Joint Declaration in 1984 for the retrocession of Hong Kong to Chinese rule by 1997. International politics triggered uncertainty about the future stability in Hong Kong and Taiwan. Such uncertainty generated waves of immigration to the United States. While people from Hong Kong mostly emigrated to Canada or Australia, large number of Taiwanese came to the United States.[1] These immigrants were mostly people who possessed the financial, social, and human capitals that benefited the local economy, including the Chinese American banking sector (see Li, et al. 2001; Li, et al. 2002; Chee, et al. 2004). They were among the group of new immigrants who by-passed Los Angeles Chinatown all together to settle directly in the San Gabriel Valley area (Wong 1989; Tseng 1994, 1995). Their settlement in southern California partly stemmed from internal developments in Taiwan, in response to external forces at a more global scale.

Prior to June 1987, the Taiwan government had adhered to a draconian capital movement policy. Its Central Bank of China (CBC) imposed strict maximums on outward movement of financial capital by Taiwan's local residents, notwithstanding certain formal and clandestine channels for flows. In July 1987 the CBC liberalized its control on outward and inward remittances. The liberalization initially permitted outward remittances of US$5 million per annum per person or company, and inward remittances of US$50,000. The ceiling for both kept fluctuating, until July 1990 when both ceilings stabilized at US$3 million. This policy led to US$7.4 billion non-bank outflow in 1988, US$8.2 billion in 1989, "and an average bank capital outflow (mostly trade-related financing) of about US$3.9 billion during 1988–1990" (Liu 1992: 169–175). Much of this flight capital landed in southern California, as customer deposits and capital infusion to Chinese American banks in the area, amidst relaxation of American banking regulations in the 1980s. Recent Taiwanese immigrants have primarily been well-to-do with substantial financial resources. For example, according to one estimate, at least 1.5 billion dollars were deposited with Chinese American banks in Monterey Park in 1985 (Tanzer 1985: 68–69). According to the 1990 Comprehensive Annual Financial Report issued by the Monterey Park Management Services Department, "by 1989 the combined deposits in Monterey Park . . . had swelled to over $1.9 billion . . . roughly $30,000 for every man, women, and child in town" (Fong 1994: 49).

U.S. domestic economic development also aided this monetary gain. The U.S. crisis with savings and loan associations in the 1980s destabilized the domestic economy. Federal budget deficit caused interest rate to rise to attract foreign investment. A strong foreign exchange rate also favored Taiwan capital movement to the United States. Taiwan's Ministry of Foreign Affairs estimated that US$349 million moved to the United States during the first eight months of 1989, up from $70 million in 1987. This money followed Taiwan's business and residential concentration most notably in San Gabriel Valley in southern California. Meanwhile, the 1986 Immigration and Reform Act of the United States increased the limit of Hong Kong immigrants to the United States from six hundred to five thousand. In addition, the 1990 Immigration Act included an employment-creating provision: one could immigrate to the United States by investing one million U.S. dollars in a business concern that would create employment opportunity for local residents in the United States. Many applicants from Hong Kong, but especially those from Taiwan, took advantage of this provision. Several of these immigrants worked as entrepreneurs in southern California. Besides legislations, national and international developments in the countries of origin and destination as well as human agency brought about further immigration to southern California from Taiwan.

HUMAN AGENCY

The influx to Monterey Park was also induced by purposeful human business strategy. The choice of Monterey Park as these immigrants' destination was through the effort of one real estate agent named Frederic Hsieh. In the 1970s, Hsieh invested heavily in real estate in Monterey Park. He purchased several properties and developed them into new housing. He aggressively promoted these homes in Taiwan and Hong Kong, through advertising in newspapers and magazines, hailing Monterey Park as the "Chinese Beverly Hills" (Tanzer 1985). New immigrants from Taiwan favored this Chinese Beverly Hills. Unlike early nineteenth century Chinese immigrants who were laborers, most of these newcomers were professionals, business executives, or business owners from non-working class backgrounds. Wong (1989: 117) notes that at first Taiwanese entrepreneurs attempted to launch their businesses in Los Angeles Chinatown, but its Cantonese-speaking old-timers resisted these Mandarin-speaking new arrivals.[2]

Attracted by a suburban life style and by the business potentials, the Taiwanese newcomers leapfrogged to the nearby City of Monterey Park in San Gabriel Valley. Developers purchased land and existing properties in Monterey Park, and turned them into new houses as well as high-density condominiums. When the new immigrants arrived, many of them came to buy their homes in Monterey Park. It was a residential community with newer housing facilities in a suburban environment, and centrally located just outside of downtown Los Angeles. Beginning in the 1980s, Monterey Park started to offer such conveniences as restaurants, markets, and stores that catered to East Asian and Southeast Asian needs. Like a chain reaction, increased population stimulated the growth of more businesses to serve co-ethnics, and more businesses provided additional convenience for local residents. This in turn attracted more homebuyers and renters to the area. Kaplan (1998) argues that residential clustering correlates with business concentration. As Sanders and Nee point out, "a concentration of small ethnic firms may be critical to generating an institutional environment that promotes ethnic enterprise and provide ecological conditions favorable to the growth of larger and more profitable firms" (1996: 246). This chain reaction acted as a feed-back loop and supported further growth and clustering of what Li (1998) has called the ethnoburbs of southern California

CHANGING "ETHNOSCAPE"

I lived in Monterey Park from July 1984 to April 1996 and worked as a real estate broker in the area from 1987 till I moved away. Residential real estate prices almost doubled between 1984 and 1988. I witnessed, and still remember vividly, the changing landscapes of Monterey Park and adjacent cities due to the growing Asian population. Ethnic businesses sprang up to serve co-ethnics in the 1980s. Prior to that, there were two major grocery stores (Hughes Market and Alpha Beta) both located on the east side of Atlantic Boulevard just south of Emerson Street. They catered to a Euro American clientele.[3] In the 1970s, a group of Taiwanese established the first Chinese supermarket in a strip mall on South Atlantic Boulevard, south of Newmark Avenue. The market was called the Di Ho Market,[4] named after a well-known shopping area in Taipei. This market touted the many different kinds of Chinese vegetables that were not available at the Hughes Market: *Jie lan* (Chinese broccoli), *yu cai* (a cruciferous green), *mao gua* (hairy squash) and the like as well as oyster sauce, five spice powder, and fifty-pound bags of rice. In the same mall right next to the market, there were many mom and pop eateries that sold noodles and dishes as found in Taiwan, including *dan bing* (Chinese omelette), *yu tiao* (fried dough twists), and *yu fan* (glutinous rice). These eateries were owned and staffed by immigrants from Taiwan who spoke Mandarin and the Minnan language.[5]

Many more Chinese shops started to open for business. They included fast food stores that sell wanton noodles, barbecue ducks, and barbeque pork as they replaced the old coffee and doughnut shops that catered to the long-time resident Euro Americans. Later, additional Chinese supermarkets appeared: the Hong Kong Market at the interesection of Garfield and Garvey Boulevards, and the Quang Hua Market on Garvey Boulevard and Nicholson Street. Local shoppers crowded these businesess. When I went to shop there on the weekends, I invariably encountered difficulty in finding a parking space at their parking lots. As the local population grew in size, its demand for services drew more businesses to spring up. The dense concentration of immigrants from Taiwan brought forth a diasporic convergence of ethnic Chinese in Monterey Park and its vicinity in the San Gabriel Valley. Except the Di Ho Market, the immigrants from Taiwan did not own these supermarkets. They were owned and run by ethnic Chinese from Vietnam.

In *The First Suburban Chinatown*, Timothy Fong brings up the issue of intra-ethnic diversity in Monterey Park. In his discussion on the political contention for city offices in Monterey Park, Fong points out such diversity among the Chinese American candidates. His discussion is limited to the difference between American-born and foreign-born Chinese politicians in their competition for public office. Fong neglects to investigate the complex intra-ethnic diversity among foreign-born Chinese (Chee 1995/96: 238). In *The Politics of Diversity*, John Horton (1995: 21) correctly points out that "not all Chinese are from China." With statistics from Public Microdata Samples, he shows that Chinese immigrants in the United States were born in various parts of the world, including China, Vietnam, Taiwan, Hong Kong, Thailand, Cambodia, Burma, Indonesia, Latin America and other countries (ibid.). Many of these people also immigrated to the United States in different time periods for dissimilar reasons, and they came from disparate socioeconomic and cultural backgrounds (Chee 1995/96).

As stated by L. Abu Lughod, "anthropologists are increasingly concerned with national and transnational connections of people, cultural form. . . . They study the articulation of world capitalism and international politics with the situation of people living in particular communities" (1991: 149). Monterey Park is a microcosm of macro-dynamics. To borrow Appadurai's term, its "ethnoscape" comprises groups that are "no longer tightly territorialized, spatially bounded, historically unselfconscious, or culturally homogeneous" (1991: 191). Such intra-ethnic diversity is reflected in the commercial arena in Monterey Park. In her article "Chinese Ethnic Economy: San Gabriel Valley, Los Angeles County," Y. F. Tseng (1994) alludes to the impact of dialectal and cultural differences on Chinese ethnic economy. She also mentions that the Chinese immigrants from disparate Asian countries facilitate international trade between the United States and their countries of origin. While the article addresses the overall ethnic economy, it offers little on the diversified intra-ethnic backgrounds of the Chinese business owners. The section below looks at the convergence of intra-ethnic diversity brought about by the demand for goods and services by immigrants predominantly from Taiwan.

DIASPORIC CONVERGENCE

My thesis of a diasporic convergence was partly based on the data collected from the fieldwork I conducted in 1996 and in the summer of 2000. During these two periods I collected information on the businesses on site, from employees of the business establishment selected for the survey and from interviews. The businesses surveyed were banking institutions, supermarkets, and large restaurants with formal banquet facilities. They were located in the downtown area of Monterey Park along two major commercial thoroughfares: Approximately 2.3 miles along Atlantic Boulevard that runs north and south, and roughly 1.3 miles on the intersecting Garvey Avenue that stretches east and west. This area is bounded by Atlantic Boulevard to the west, New Avenue to the east, Hellman Avenue to the north, and Harding Street to the south. This is the business section in the City of Monterey Park.

Only the banks, restaurants, and supermarkets owned or managed by ethnic Chinese along these two roads were included. The ethnic Chinese who owned the businesses surveyed here had come from disparate countries of origin. The following table shows the types of business and intra-ethnic diversity of ownership.

As shown in Table 4.1, there appears to be a clustering of intra-ethnic ownership in the three categories of businesses. Six of the banks show ownership by immigrants from Taiwan, four by ethnic Chinese from Indonesia, one from Japan, and three by old-timer Chinese Americans, but none from Vietnam and Hong Kong. On the other hand, all of the three large

Table 4.1 Types of business and owners' countries of origin

Types	Hong Kong	Indonesia	Japan	Old-timer	Taiwan	Vietnam	Total
Bank	0	4	1	3	6	0	14
Restaurant	3	0	0	0	0	0	3
Supermarket	0	0	0	0	1	3	4

(From Chee, et al. 2004: 214)

restaurants indicate ownership by immigrants from Hong Kong, none from Taiwan and Vietnam; while three out of the four supermarkets are owned by Sino-Vietnamese. One of the three restaurants surveyed, the Harbor Village Restaurant (now closed), was owned by a restaurant chain from Hong Kong. The Ocean Star Restaurant and NBC Restaurant were owned and managed by immigrants from Hong Kong who had come to the United States in the last few decades. They were Cantonese speakers. Most of them had immigrated here as a result of the 1965 Immigration Act for family reunification. They were often offspring and relatives of former stoop laborers who had come to the United States from southern China. "Some observers, who note fewer professionals among Chinese immigrants, for example, contend that after the initial influx of professionals in the late 1960s and early 1970s, poorer, working-class Chinese began entering" (Hing 1993: 131).

Most of these immigrants from Hong Kong had worked in restaurants before as owners, waiters, or cooks either in Hong Kong or in the United States. The restaurants were typically owned in partnership. The partners usually worked hard for a few years to accumulate capital, pooled their resources for the start-up, and worked in the restaurants that they co-owned. It was a way to earn a monthly wage, as these immigrants did not have adequate skill or English proficiency to compete in the professional sector. I asked one of the restauranteurs the following question, "Why do you all go into the restaurant business?" He answered,

> When we were still in Hong Kong before we came here, our relatives in the United States told us that we better learn how to work in the restaurant, either as cooks or as waiters. Those were the kind of warnings we got from them. Also, when we arrived here and looked for jobs, we relied on family network. Old Chinese immigrants' job network *IS* the restaurant business (emphasis his).

While Cantonese speakers from Hong Kong operated high-end large restaurants in the above table, Sino-Vietnamese owned three of the four supermarkets. When I lived in Monterey Park, I frequented these super-markets for my grocery shopping. The cashiers conversed in Vietnamese among themselves, but they also switched code to Cantonese or Mandarin with an accent that betrayed Vietnam as their former country of domicile. Sometimes they changed from Vietnamese to Cantonese and back again in one single sentence. Chinese had lived in Vietnam for generations, and Vietnam was part of the Chinese empire from 111 B.C. to A.D. 939 (Wilmott 1980: 59). Before the Vietnam conflict, ethnic Chinese in South Vietnam were barred from participation in civil service. Therefore, they tradition-ally engaged in entrepreneurial enterprises, in trading and business. Chinese prominence in Vietnamese economy before the fall of Saigon can be seen as follows:

> The large Chinese trading firms in Saigon dominated rice export, small-goods import, and most of the small-scale manufacturing. This is not to say that all Chinese were wealthy businessmen . . . and even among those in trade the vast majority were poor, perhaps owning no more than a portable stall and a few dry goods to sell in an open market. Nevertheless, even these small businessmen had a commercial mentality that differed markedly from the peasant culture of the majority of the indigenous population (ibid.: 72).

Long the minority dominated by ethnic Vietnamese, many Sino-Vietnamese left Vietnam for the United States as refugees after Saigon fell to the Viet Cong in 1975.

The American Congress passed the 1975 Refugees Act that allowed 125,000 refugees to come to the United States. Between 1978 and 1981 more than 400,000 refugees arrived, and about ninety percent of them came from Vietnam. In 1984 another 40,000 entered the United States. The 134.8 percent growth rate of Vietnamese Americans between 1980 and 1990 (261,729 to 614,547) makes them the fastest growing Asian Pacific group (Hing 1993: 132). A large number of refugees from Vietnam settled in southern California. These Vietnamese Americans included a high percent-age of ethnic Chinese. The ethnic Chinese also brought their skill and spirit in commerce. The growing Asian population in Monterey Park, fueled by immigration from Taiwan, provided both a demand for goods and services as well as an excellent niche for entrepreneurs. One of the long time commu-nity insiders who owned businesses in the area told me the following, "You know, one of the supermarkets in Monterey Park is owned by the people who used to provide food supply to the American military bases in Saigon! They are experienced and they have the know-how of this business."

On the other hand, immigrants from Taiwan engaged in business and banking.[6] The immigrants from Taiwan led to a sharp rise in entrepreneurship in the local communities. As Evans (1989) suggests, a large ethnic group whose members are linguistically isolated from mainstream society provides a favorable environment for immigrant entrepreneurship. Indeed, the self-employment rate among Taiwanese immigrants has been estimated at twenty percent while that for immigrants from Hong Kong at ten percent (Tseng 1995: 41), both higher than the percentage in the average American population. Further, Kaplan (1998) argues that residential clustering correlates with business concentration. The large number of immigrants created a demand for goods and services, drawing businesses to spring up in the community. The availability of such goods and services in turn attracted additional newcomers from Taiwan. The 1990 Immigration and Naturalization Services data show that twenty-two percent of all Taiwanese immigrants indicated their intended destination to be Los Angeles. These newcomers were also highly educated and professional. In addition to a strong educational background, a large number of these were business-owners in Taiwan, and "Taiwanese immigrants to the United States were disproportionately drawn from the bourgeoisie class" (Tseng 1995: 44). In 1986, "executives and professionals comprised sixty-three percent of all Taiwanese who intended to reside in Los Angeles" (ibid.: 41).

Light (1979) theorizes that minority immigrants go into self-employment due to the disadvantages that they suffer in the host society, including language barriers, unfamiliarity with local custom and culture, and non-transferability of their human capital. However, this theory does not explain the varied rate of self-employment for different immigrant groups, such as the high rate of self-employment for Taiwanese and Koreans, and the low rate for Mexicans. While Light (1984) earlier demonstrates the necessity of sufficient resources, Waldinger, Aldrich, and Ward (1990) further point out "the interaction of opportunity structure and group characteristics." A large number of co-ethnics from Taiwan were mostly well-to-do, and many of them came with adequate financial capital.

Tseng (1995) argues that the demand opportunity and entrepreneurial capacity contribute to the rapid growth of Taiwanese businesses. These co-ethnics from Taiwan with sufficient purchasing power provided a ready market for the goods and services offered by those with entrepreneurial capacity. In their study of the Chinese American banking sector in Los Angeles County, Chee, et al. (2004) further advance a diasporic convergence thesis: the robust performance of this local economy was made possible by the sizable convergence of ethnic Chinese from the diaspora. This diasporic convergence of Chinese with financial, human, and social capitals created a critical mass for the supply and demand that fueled the local economy embedded in the regional as well as global contexts, with interactions that were intra-ethnic, inter-ethnic, and international in nature across ethnic boundaries for profit maximization.

EASTWARD EXPANSION

As the immigrants bought up Monterey Park, the shopping spree spilled over to neighboring areas in the San Gabriel Valley. The newcomers' presence spread out to the cities of Alhambra, San Gabriel, Temple City, South Pasadena, and the affluent San Marino where $500,000 would purchase only a plain house in a "poor" neighborhood in the late 1980s. When housing prices became saturated in the West San Gabriel Valley, buyers ventured eastward where the same dollar amount brought a nicer and bigger house. In the East San Gabriel Valley, homebuyers first moved to the unincorporated area of Hacienda Heights located approximately fifteen miles east of Monterey Park and easily accessed via the Pomona Freeway (Highway Sixty). Next they populated brand new tract homes built by such developers as Shea's Home in the rolling hills south of the Pathfinder Road in the unincorporated area of Rowland Heights, and in the cities of Diamond Bar or Walnut.

The early ethnic Chinese buyers in Hacienda Heights primarily came from Taiwan. Hacienda Heights houses the largest Buddhist temple in North America, the Hsi Lai Temple, which attracts a large congregation of Taiwanese. The Hsi Lai Temple exemplifies transnational cultural projects in a religious dimension. It was established by the monk Master Hsing Yuan who founded the Fo Guang Shan Buddhist temple in Taiwan. The multi-million dollar temple was financed with donation largely amassed in Taiwan. When the temple first opened its doors, it offered vegetarian lunches to the public and charges were by donation. In those early years before the existence of vegetarian Chinese restaurants in San Gabriel Valley, this temple remained the only public establishment that served vegetarian meals in the San Gabriel Valley. Once in a while my friends and I made special trips to Hacienda Heights from Monterey Park for the food alone. In the early 1990s, I also took classes at the temple—Buddhist scriptures on Sunday, acupressure and vegetarian cooking classes during the week. I even taught English as a Second Language for one quarter as a volunteer at the Temple.

The suburban sprawl spread to the unincorporated Rowland Heights located immediately east of the unincorporated community of Hacienda

Heights. According to the 1996 State of the County Report, total population for the unincorporated Rowland Heights was estimated to be 40,000 in 1995. Asian Pacific constituted the largest group with slightly over 14,000, followed by approximately 13,000 Latinos, and approximately 10,000 Caucasians. By year 2000 census, the population of Rowland Heights totals 48,553 with 24,432 of Asians (50.3 percent), of which 14,053 (29 percent) are Chinese. Whites number 14,206 (29.3 percent), followed by 13,748 (28.3 percent) of Hispanic or Latino. In the 1980s and until the very early 1990s, Korean businesses predominated in the area. As more residents bought into Rowland Heights, mostly from Taiwan, Chinese businesses also sprang up to meet the demand of the market. In the commercial areas of Rowland Heights, ethnic Chinese and Korean businesses co-exist. Three large Korean supermarkets, named the Greenland Foods, the HK Market, and the World Market attract a large patronage of ethnic Chinese because of its competitive prices especially in produce. HK Market is the anchor tenant of a strip mall evidently developed by Korean Americans—almost all the other tenants in this strip mall are Korean small businesses.

By the mid-1990s, Rowland Heights became the most visibly Asian community in the East San Gabriel Valley. The Pacific Square and the Hong Kong Market Square are two large food and shopping centers along the main commercial thoroughfare called Colima Boulevard that goes east and west. There are also the Diamond Square food and shopping malls on Fullerton Boulevard just south of Freeway Sixty, and the 99 Ranch Market north of Freeway Sixty just off the Nogales exit. Chinese had developed all of these four shopping malls. Most of the stores and restaurants in these malls were owned and operated by ethnic Chinese, many of whom originated from Taiwan, offering goods and services to their co-ethnics, mostly speaking in Mandarin.

Besides the residential and commercial explosion from West San Gabriel Valley to East San Gabriel Valley, industrial growth also expanded eastward. Many of the immigrants from Taiwan are entrepreneurs, including traders, manufacturers, distributors and importers. As they bought residential homes in Monterey Park, Arcadia, and San Marino, they also purchased warehouses in industrial zoned areas such as in the cities of El Monte and Industry. A Chinese American bank executive indicated that warehouses in El Monte are typically smaller sized, in the range of five thousand to ten thousand square feet. As their businesses grew, the small warehouses could no longer support their space need. They moved east to the City of Industry where they could find 50,000 square feet to 100,000 square feet warehouse space.[7]

In addition to the growth and development of small businesses in the San Gabriel Valley, the ethnic Chinese banking industry also prospered mostly due to the influx of immigrants from Taiwan. As a result of new housing development and purchases, the local ethnic Chinese residents in Monterey Park increased. The high concentration of Chinese residents created supply and demand for various business enterprises. A large population also provided a ready deposit base for banking institutions (see bank deposits cited above). With increased deposits, banking institutions amassed additional capital base to loan out to more borrowers or a larger amount of loans. More businesses opening and growing led to needs to borrow additional funding from banks for working capitals, and continuous real estate construction created demands by developers to borrow from banks to finance their construction projects.

Taiwanese immigrants provided human and financial capital in both the demand and supply side. Indeed, banks backed by Taiwanese or Chinese American capitals mushroomed in the 1980s. For example, two former students from Taiwan started the General Bank after they received their graduate training in the United States. Their capital was pooled from a group of Taiwanese immigrants, and further supported by the Unipresidential Enterprise, a very large food manufacturer in Taiwan. In the 1980s, several banks opened their doors for business in the San Gabriel Valley area. Many of them were funded and managed by immigrants from Taiwan (Li, et al. 2000).[8]

Unlike an ethnic enclave such as Chinatown that is part of a larger city and dependent on certain public city services, these suburban communities are self-contained that encompass an entire city or unincorporated county areas in the suburb. The many businesses large and small, and the development of these self-contained communities minimized many of the potential difficulties encountered by new immigrants in their country of destination, especially in terms of language barrier and daily living. The initial difficulty frequently mentioned by several of the women interviewed was the need for driving. In Taiwan, frequent services of the subway trains, taxies, and buses provided convenient public transportation. After they mastered their driving skill, the women all reported the convenience and ease of living in southern California. Lily said, "We came to southern California because of its seasonable climate. We also have many former friends living here. We knew these friends back in Taiwan. There is no language problem and there is plenty of Chinese food available." The many amenities found in Chinese ethnoburbs eased these women's transition to life here as new immigrants. Ching claimed, "There was no language problem. In fact, I have lost my

English after moving here. There is no need to use English, you go anywhere or do anything you can just speak in Mandarin. I don't feel like I have left Taiwan." Susan remarked, "As for daily living, all I need is Chinese. You have Chinese supermarkets, Chinese banks, Chinese organizations, Chinese churches. It is a Chinese community." Janet confirmed as follows: "Here everything is convenient. Supermarkets, banks, everyday necessities could be met by Chinese businesses. It is a Chinese community." Jan alluded to the availability of Chinese media, "I am not lonely here. Here there are Chinese cable television programs all day. You can also rent videos in Mandarin."

The television channels (with viewer's choice of Mandarin or Cantonese) feature daily news on the United States, Taiwan, and China. Radio stations in Cantonese as well as Mandarin broadcast programs all day. The video stores rent out the latest soap opera series and movies popular in Taiwan. Several magazines and newspapers in Chinese line the counters of many bookstores situated next to Chinese supermarkets and restaurants. The Chinese World Journal, the Chinese newspaper with the largest circulation in southern California, contains sections specifically on news from Taiwan and China. They are all owned, funded, and run by Chinese immigrants as well as by headquarters in Taiwan. They have been termed transnational media (Fong 1996; Leong 1996). In addition, two major directories of yellow pages circulate in southern California: 1) The Chinese Yellow Pages/ Southern California, and 2) Chinese Consumer Yellow Pages. Both measure approximately 2¾ inches thick for their year 2000 editions. However, the present convenience and ease for these immigrant women mask a more tumultuous development in the past. The following section discusses the turmoil that this development had weathered.

A TUMULTUOUS URBAN AND ETHNIC/RACIALIZED RESTRUCTURING

The rapid influx of these immigrants from Taiwan altered the residential and commercial landscape of Monterey Park, the first city to absorb the large number of Taiwanese newcomers. The fast growth and development of the physical structures of the environment that accompanied their arrivals, and the burgeoning of ethnic businesses catering to the new residents contributed to a hasty transformation of the local community. Such transformation unsettled local long time residents who were mostly Euro Americans. For example, the new immigrants' investment in local real estate drove up housing prices. Multi-family units such as condominiums replaced old single-family residences. The business section of Monterey Park also underwent a change of appearance. Old buildings were torn down and replaced by new ones. The six-storied Lincoln Hotel stood out in the middle of two-story older structures. Although the new businesses and buildings revitalized the declining shopping businesses in Monterey Park, the new businesses and multi-unit family housing also escalated population density and traffic congestion. Chinese stores sprang up to replace former businesses that catered to old-timer Euro Americans' palate. The many Chinese businesses also displayed signage in the Chinese language, a measure that helped to change the physical appearance of Monterey Park, a once quaint and quiet town. This urbanization process was brought on by the influx of immigrants and real estate developers from Taiwan.

The arrival of the newcomers also restructured the class feature of this suburban community. Old-timer Euro American residents had long enjoyed a higher status in Monterey Park. In the past, Japanese American residents had become assimilated and worked their way up the social scale, following the pattern theorized by Gordon (1964). Contrary to that, the Taiwanese immigrants broke from the traditional immigrant mobility fashion. Immediately after their arrivals, most bought luxury homes and drove expensive European cars such as Mercedes. Established local Euro American residents complained about these affluent newcomers as follows:

> Before, immigrants were poor. They lived in their own neighborhood and moved into ours after they learnt English, got a good job, and became accustomed to our ways. Today, the Chinese came right in with their money, and their way. We are the aliens (Horton 1992: 223).

This rapid influx of Taiwanese homebuyers started a cycle: more buyers led to the development of yet more new homes, which in turn attracted additional residents and businesses. The prevalent and prominent presence of the Taiwanese immigrants created tensions in the city. In the public political arena, the conflict stood between the slow growth and fast growth factions, and the contention for public offices among candidates from different ethnic backgrounds. At a community level, it was the delineation of boundaries drawn by local long time residents. The sudden influx of residents with different phenotypic appearances presented immediate visual boundaries for long-time residents who were mostly Euro Americans. Local Euro American residents resented the change in their community. The *Los Angeles Times* reported remarks such as "I feel like I'm in another country. I don't feel like at home any more," and "I feel like I'm a stranger in my own town. . . . I don't feel like I belong any more" (Arax 1987). "The romantic image of a carefree small town held by long time established residents were given a rude awakening by all the dramatic restructuring taken place in the city" (Fong 1994: 213). Urbanization and the problem associated with the process became racialized, and spatial restructuring led to a class rupture of the old community.

The issues of class and race compounded urbanization. Euro American old-timers started to feel an "intrusion of their community." The rapid growth of the city and the massive arrival of the Taiwanese immigrants combined to set off a series of racialized anti-immigrant actions. An example is the English Only movement in the early 1980s. I moved to live in Monterey Park in July 1984. Once when I went to buy groceries at the Hughes Market on Atlantic Boulevard, two Euro American males and one female were standing by the entrance to gather signatures for the English Only referendum. One of the males approached me and asked me to sign. I shook my head. In an attempt to counter the impending Asian dominance in the neighborhood, long time residents organized an "English Only" movement, trying to make English the only official language of the city. Proponents gathered 3,200 signatures, and formally petitioned to the City Council in November 1986 (ibid.: 316–327). It was passed by the Monterey Park City Council, although the movement never came to fruition. It was illegal.

Besides political economy, an important factor in such anti-immigrant feeling is ideology. Miles (1989: 132) comments on ideology as follows:

> Ideologies are never only received but are also constructed and reconstructed by people responding to their material cultural circumstances, in order to comprehend, represent and act in relation to those circumstances. Ideological reproduction is therefore a historical legacy and individual and collective attempts to make sense of the world.

The presence of a large number of these newcomers from Taiwan presented perceived differences to American local residents, created by visible phenotypic traits, the sight, sound, and smell of conspicuous concentration, and the tone and non-meaning of an unfamiliar language. Ousted in the local socioeconomic hierarchy by the new immigrants, confronted by their large number, and demarcated by their visual and cultural differences, Euro American local residents constructed their own version of the United States and their community, to make sense of such rapid and extensive presence of these unfamiliar people from Taiwan. The notion of community and nation lives only in one's imagination:

> It is imagined because the members of even the smallest nation will never know most of their fellow-members, meet them, or even hear of

> them, yet in the minds of each lives the image of their communion. . . .
> In fact, all communities larger than primordial villages of face-to-face
> contact (and perhaps even these) are imagined. Communities are to be
> distinguished, not by their falsity/genuineness, but by the style in which
> they are imagined (Anderson 1991: 6).

The restructuring did not fit local residents' imagined community according
to the style they had constructed. Many of them cashed out on their home
and benefited from the sales. It was a seller's market. The high demand on
single-family housing had driven up real estate prices. They sold their homes
and left for other communities that perhaps more resembled their imagination. By 1990, Euro American residents constituted only twelve percent of
the city's population, down from eighty-five percent in 1960 (Fong 1994:
193–94).

Movements such as the "English-only" movement are exclusionary
constructs manifested in exclusionary actions. Some Euro American local
residents excluded other people to protect their imagined culture, community, and nation based on an imagined mainstream, Euro American image.
Indeed the newcomers were legally admitted members of this nation, "but
even where entry is granted, their distinct cultural profile has the potential to
be signified as a measure of their membership of another" (Miles 1989: 117).
To these Euro American residents, the perceived "intrusion" of members
from another nation upon the United States and upon the local community
aroused sentiment to protect their community and nation. Of course, these
people had forgotten that the United States was a country of immigrants,
and that their forebears had also originated from elsewhere. Their image of
an American was further informed by the centuries of governmental policies, legislations, and actions that actively and consciously excluded people
of color. The Civil Rights Movement had brought us forward somewhat,
but far more needs to be done and at all levels. This responsibility falls on
all members of this nation-state, from the power elite in particular to the
everyman/woman on the street.

There were also political contentions for power in the Monterey Park
city government among Anglo, Chinese, and Latino Americans in the 1980s.
Candidates from the three ethnic backgrounds competed for the position of
city mayor. Monterey Park went through an extremely tumultuous decade
amidst ethnic strife.[9] Given the rapid pace of urbanization, the city was
divided into the pro-growth and the no-growth factions. The pro-growth
group consisted of mainly Euro American and Taiwanese real estate developers and investors. The no-growth group was made up primarily of local
long time residents who were Euro American nativists. When the no-growth

faction successfully defeated the pro-growth members of the City Council, they quickly put a moratorium on both residential and commercial development. This moratorium affected the Taiwanese immigrants who invested in, purchased, or developed real estates. At the end, a compromised group that favored managed growth was voted into city offices. The two elected officials were two Chinese Americans who drew support from mostly Chinese voters, but also voters of other ethnic backgrounds. "Consequently, Monterey Park entered the 1990s with a Chinese American mayor and a city council that had taken a neutral stance towards the development issue that previously divided the city" (Waldinger and Tseng 1992: 109).

In the later part of this period, many Euro Americans took off in a white flight, and Asians became the majority residents in town. In the 1990 census, the total population in Monterey Park was 60,738, while Asians comprised fifty-six percent of the total, a 104 percent change from 1980. Chinese made up sixty-three percent of the 34,898 Asian residents counted. Chinese became the majority. According to the 2000 census, the population of the City of Monterey Park totals 60,051, with 37,125 (61.8 percent) Asians, 17,358 (28.9 percent) Hispanic or Latinos, and 12,786 (21.3 percent) whites. Among the Asian residents, Chinese constitute 41.2 percent with 24,758. Nowadays, business establishments from commercial banks to "mom and pop" stores are mostly owned and operated by Chinese. Tiny Naylor's was the only family-style restaurant offering old-fashioned American fare until the completion of the Atlantic Square shopping mall, which housed such establishments as the Boston Market and Starbucks, on the southern edge of Monterey Park. Monterey Park is self-contained with its own governmental agencies and services, social, cultural, and economic organizations. Speaking only the Chinese language, whether Cantonese or Mandarin, one can function very well through practically the entire city. Chinese dominance was evident: City officials and employees at the City Hall, be they Anglo, Latino, or Chinese, all have Chinese transliteration of their names on their business cards.

SUMMARY

Unlike the single working-class immigrants of the nineteenth century who came from China to the United States to perform stoop labor, those from Taiwan in the past few decades are largely educated and professionals from better socioeconomic backgrounds. They also came with their families. Many of them became entrepreneurs or skilled professionals in corporations. Their economic power contributed to a regional economy, dominated the entire

San Gabriel Valley area in southern California, and transformed the local community where they lived. The 1965 Immigration and Nationality Act facilitated Taiwanese immigrants to the United States, giving them legitimate entry. Economic power brought on resentment from other long time residents against the Taiwanese immigrants, but economic and political power also helped these immigrants to counter nativistic attempts to dominate and exclude them.

In recent decades, some of these immigrants formed transnational families: the husbands worked in Taiwan to support the wives and children who lived in the United States. Why did they immigrate to the United States from Taiwan in the first place? The next chapter answers this question from the women's standpoints.

Chapter Five

Migration from the Women's Standpoints

The transnational family phenomenon is widespread among Taiwanese Americans. It is also prevalent between Hong Kong and Canada, Australia, and New Zealand (the last three being part of the British Commonwealth, as was Hong Kong before 1997). These families from Hong Kong are referred to as "astronaut families" in the literature (see, for example, Pe-Pua 1996; Man 1993; Ho 2002). The return of Hong Kong to Chinese rule in 1997 triggered an exodus of Hong Kong residents (see, among others, Skeldon 1994, 1995).[1] While geopolitics stood as the quintessential cause of emigration for the people of Hong Kong, women in the Taiwanese American transnational families that I interviewed reported various reasons for their departures. This chapter examines the forces that impel these families to migrate from Taiwan to the United States from the standpoints of the wives and mothers interviewed. These women appeared keenly aware that their lives were intensely intertwined with macroscopic forces in and beyond their society. As they reflected and commented on their situations, a brief history of Taiwan emerged that twined ethnicity, class, and gendered perspectives.

CAUSES OF MIGRATION FROM TAIWAN TO THE UNITED STATES

Most migration studies privilege the economic and sometimes political causes of migration. The women in my sample related several different reasons for their migration to the United States, a complexity that included a gender dimension. Some came for a single reason, others out of multiple motivations. A few women migrated to avoid parents-in-law issues. By comparison, postulating one single economic or political reason for migration appears to simplify and essentialize the situation.

While a few women reported individual personal motives, most apparently had reacted to processes within Taiwanese society, and to national as well as international geopolitical dynamics. These women's reasons for migration corresponded to those found among a larger sample of immigrants from Taiwan, albeit in different proportions. In a study commissioned by Taiwan's Ministry of Overseas Chinese, Hsiao and Smith (1994) report that among the immigrants from Taiwan, the major motivation for emigration was business and employment opportunity. The second motivation was educational opportunity for children. A supposed inferior quality of life in Taiwan ranked the third. In comparison, political factors such as threat from China did not appear important (ibid.: 23). Out of the 373 people surveyed, Hsiao and Smith (ibid.: 31) tabulate that 206 men and 167 women considered career development as the major motivation for their emigration from Taiwan to the United States.

Compared to the Hsiao and Smith survey, the thirty-five women I interviewed indicated that their families migrated to the United States for the following reasons: national ethnic strife; regional political tensions, social or natural environmental problems; business or work opportunity in the United States, children's education; to avoid military service or in-law obligations; self-education, marital problem, and family reunification. The table below lists the frequency for the above reasons as reported by the interviewees. Since they reported as many reasons as applicable, the total exceeded thirty-five.

A significant factor emerged from the above responses: children's education ranked by far the most frequent reason given by twenty-one respondents. It differed from the information in the survey by Hsiao and Smith (1994). This discrepancy could have been caused by the biased nature of our samples: theirs concentrated on business owners, and their survey responses came from individuals who sought assistance from Taiwan's government office for their business endeavors. On the other hand, my study focused on women with transnational family experiences. In addition, gender, educational level, and sampling technique possibly contributed to the difference. I obtained my interview samples by the snowballing technique, and I sought only women in transnational families. These women also tended to be highly educated. Hsiao and Smith (1994: 23–27) indeed point out that in their survey, respondents with a university education considered children's education as the main reason for emigration, and that more men than women emigrated for career development especially in the age group between thirty

Table 5.1 Causes for migration

For children's education	21
Taiwan's national political tension	6
Political threat from China	6
For business or career opportunity	5
To join family members	5
Deteriorating social environment in Taiwan	4
Deteriorating natural environment in Taiwan	4
To avoid son's military service	2
To void in-law problems	1
Marital problem and self education	1

and fifty. Although Hsiao and Smith provide rather comprehensive general information, it lacks background details on the causes of emigration. In the following section, I situate the reasons of migration, as elaborated by the women interviewed, in the context of Taiwan and East Asia to demonstrate the interaction between larger socioeconomic and political dynamics and individual agency. I start with politics, children's education, followed by business opportunity, and then the rest in the order of frequency as numerated in Table 5.1 above.

NATIONAL ETHNIC STRIFE

To varying degrees, twelve women cited Taiwan's political climate as the impetus that had sent them away. The unsettling political situations included both regional threats in East Asia and internal instability in Taiwan. Six women related the national political tension that arose from the intra-ethnic conflicts in Taiwan. To better understand this situation, a brief early history of Taiwan is in order.

Austronesian (Malayo-Polynesian) peoples had inhabited Taiwan. Later, Chinese and Japanese pirates and fishermen visited the area. Dutch, Portuguese, and Spanish also passed through the island. In 1624 The Dutch East India Company colonized Taiwan and set up an entrepot near the present day city of Tainan on the southwestern coast. It recruited laborers from China to cultivate sugarcane and rice. Elsewhere in China the Manchus overthrew the Han ruler of the Ming dynasty and established the Qing dynasty.[2] In 1661 the Ming loyalist Zheng Cheng-gong (also known as Koxinga) failed in his effort to resist the Qing government. He retreated to Taiwan with his troops and expelled the Dutch. Later Zheng's heirs surrendered to the Qing government and Taiwan came under Chinese sovereignty in 1683.

During China's political turmoil in the seventeenth century, Han immigrants and other pioneers came to Taiwan. They eventually transformed it into a settlement, and Taiwan became a Qing prefecture. Local scholars entered the imperial civil examinations in China and inherited the Chinese scholar-gentry tradition. Beginning in the seventeenth century, the indigenous Austronesian inhabitants of Taiwan were joined by Han immigrants from the coastal Fujian province of southern China, from a region called Minnan. They spoke Minnan hua (Minnan language). Another Han people, the Hakka, arrived from the coastal Guangdong province of southern China. They spoke their own Hakka hua (Hakka language). The Minnan and Hakka spoke mutually unintelligible languages and tended to self-group. In the early years, feuds often broke out between these two groups (see Lamley 1981).

In 1895 China lost the Sino-Japanese War, started in 1894, and ceded Taiwan to Japan by the Treaty of Shimonoseki. At first there were resentment and outcry of Chinese abandonment by local Taiwanese residents. For about five months a few resisters organized and supported an independent island regime called the "Taiwan Republic." Despite Japan's military occupation, other armed resistance and guerrilla warfare continued for the ensuring seven years throughout the island. Casualties were high on both sides. As permitted until 1897 by the Treaty of Shimonoseki, an officially estimated twenty-three percent of Taiwan's population repatriated to China (Lamley 1999: 208).

The contemporary ethnic tensions involved the descendants of the early Minnan and Hakka immigrants to Taiwan, referred to as the ben sheng ren (people of this province, i.e. the province of Taiwan), versus the Mainlanders referred to as wai sheng ren (people of other provinces) who came to Taiwan from China after 1945 as well as their offspring born and/or raised in Taiwan.

My sample of thirty-five women included both ben sheng ren and wai sheng ren. The sub-ethnic differences sometimes affected their perspectives. Out of the six women who considered Taiwan's internal political tensions as one of their reasons of emigration, two were ben sheng ren and four were wai sheng ren. The two ben sheng ren both talked to me about an incident called the Two-Two Eight (February 28). One of these two women was Kai. Kai's grandfather was a high-ranking official in a city government of Taiwan during the Japanese colonial era. Her father was educated in Japan. She thought that the Japanese did a good administrative job and took good care of the people with law and order. Kai remarked that the thief would get caught right away if some one reported even just a petty theft. She continued as follows:

> Sure it's colonial rule but it was good administration. The Japanese in
> Taiwan were all well dressed and impressive. At the time my father was
> a university student in Japan along with lots of others. When Japan lost
> the war he and his friends were jubilant. They figured they could return
> to Taiwan and contribute to nation building. But the mainlander KMT
> came with their own officials and implanted them in the government in
> Taiwan. The Taiwanese had not a chance despite their superior educa-
> tion and training. Those soldiers were ugly in tattered clothes and were
> undisciplined.

During its colonial rule, Japan utilized Taiwan as a market for Japanese
products, and extracted Taiwan's rice, sugar, and other raw materials for
home use. It instigated primary education, and later industrialized Taiwan's
infrastructure, economy, and technology as a strategic base for Japan's military southward advance into south China and Southeast Asia. To a greater
or lesser extent, the various Japanese governor-generals implemented assimilation policies, enforcing the adoption of Japanese customs, culture, and
language. They also set up a strict panopticon type of surveillance system
by civilians for disciplinary control to stamp out rebels. Some Taiwanese
residents became local chiefs and officials such as city mayors. Assimilation
effort intensified during the 1930s preceding the Second World War period,
mandating "imperialization" of Taiwanese in an attempt to turn them into
loyal Japanese, suppressing local Taiwan culture, customs, clothing, and
language. War-time rule in Taiwan was totalitarian: "Strict household registry, constant surveillance by the police and special security agents, and
the presence of local paramilitary units along with the large Japanese military contingents stationed in the colony" (Lamley 1999: 239), together with
compulsory military conscription in June 1945.

Beginning in the early 1900s, Taiwanese elites also attended educational institutions in Japan. Kai's father belonged to this group educated
in Japan. These students, professionals, and Taiwanese residents in Japan
might have numbered approximately twenty to thirty thousand (ibid.: 231).
Like the young early Indonesians who learned about democracy and fostered
nationalism in their colonial education (Anderson 1991), the Taiwanese students, professionals, and intellectuals likewise were influenced by modern
ideas then prevalent in Japan, China, and the West. Some of the intelligentia
mobilized political and cultural movements to advance Taiwan's home rule
and self-governance. When Japan lost in the Second World War, the Cairo
Declaration handed Taiwan to the Guomindang (Kuomintang or KMT,
the Nationalist Party) of China headed by Chiang Kai-shek (Kerr 1965:
23–27). At the time, "the Taiwanese people more eagerly anticipated the

inauguration of Chinese rule over their island homeland . . . On October 25, widespread public celebrations were held" (Lamley 1999: 247).

The provincial administration headed by Chen Yi of Chiang Kai-shek's KMT arrived from China. It replaced Japanese administrators and workers with personnel from the Mainland even though they might be incompetent. It confiscated assets such as real estate left by Japanese residents, and monopolized state enterprises. The administration prevented the participation of most Taiwanese businessmen, professionals and the educated in the new government. Taiwan's resources were used to support the war effort in China. "Inflation, grain shortage, lack of military discipline, unemployment, corruption, industrial collapse, and cultural conflict led to simmering discontent in the towns and cities of Taiwan" (Phillips 1999: 293). When the KMT was collapsing in Mainland China in 1945, refugees from the Mainland fled to Taiwan by the thousands.

An event in Taiwanese history known as the 228 Incident[3] magnified the tension between the local Taiwanese residents and the arriving Mainlanders. On February 28, 1947 in a public park, some Mainlander Monopoly Bureau officers harassed and beat a local Taiwanese woman allegedly selling cigarettes without license. A crowd gathered in anger, an officer fired into the crowd and killed one person. Unrests erupted in Taipei and spread to other urban centers. Among other demands, Taiwanese representatives negotiated with Chen Yi for representation and reform in the provincial government of Taiwan. Armed troops arrived from the Mainland on March 2 and started a massacre, killing local civilians, students, teachers, organization leaders, and people who had previously offended KMT personnel. When the Communist Party finally took control of China in 1949, Chiang Kai-shek's regime evacuated to Taiwan and established the Republic of China (ROC) on the island. Chiang strengthened his control over Taiwan, and became the president for life with one-party rule. Wai sheng ren and ben sheng ren alike were killed, imprisoned, and intimidated to suppress dissidence and communist activities culminating in what is now termed the "White Terror." Chiang's White Terror extended its reach to Chinese Americans. His secret agents assassinated an university professor and a journalist who were American citizens formerly from Taiwan (Wang 1995).

Omi and Winant (1994) opine that racial projects in the United States can be analyzed in a minimum of three perspectives: the political spectrum from the right to the left, the macro level and micro level of lived experience, and history. Likewise, one can view ethnic relations in Taiwan through at least the lenses of the political, the macro and micro levels, and in historical time. Contemporary Taiwan scholarship categorized the people of Taiwan into four major ethnic groups: the wai sheng ren referring to the mainlanders and their offspring even if they were born in Taiwan; and the ben sheng ren who were further divided into the Austronesian aborigines, the Hakka, and the Minnan people.

The classification of the four major ethnic groups revealed that it was politically informed—the criteria were inconsistent. Ben sheng ren consisted of the Minnan, the Hakka, and the aborigines each distinguished according to such cultural attributes as languages, customs, and origin. All those who came after 1945 were categorically lumped into one group as the wai sheng ren (the Mainlanders), despite their disparate provincial origins, local customs, and dialects from the vast area of China. However, the wai sheng ren themselves recognized their differentiations even in the early years, establishing their own provincial or hometown associations for mutual aid, as early as in 1946. According to Zhong (1999: 70), "up to December 1995 . . . there exist a total of 296 home town/province associations" in the city of Taipei. These associations exist unto this date.[4] Present day ethnic tension arose between the wai sheng ren and ben sheng ren.

Writing in the late 1970s, Gates (1981: 267) notes that "recovering the Mainland is the principle on which the legitimacy of the present government rests." Based on that principle, Chiang Kai-shek's KMT regime took several measures to command patriotism and loyalty from wai sheng ren and ben sheng ren alike. It acted to build a national tradition, "as part and parcel of the state's project to define itself and rationalize its continued existence" (Chun 1996: 54). The state purged Japanese influence and imposed Mandarin as the official language at the exclusion of local dialects in public places. Mandarin also became the language of education. Students were forbidden to use their mother tongues at school, whether Minnan or Hakka. The state also legitimized Mainland Chinese cultural symbols and undermined local Taiwanese ones in the public. Chang (2000: 65) reports as follows:

> Taiwan's traditional customs, folk religious practices, opera and music were soon systematically defined as local, backward, superstitious, and either harmful to national unification and/or national modernization. The traditions of Chinese officialdom were upheld as the high culture of Taiwan.

The state promoted traditional Chinese culture and symbols to distinguish it from Communist China, and to claim itself as the legitimate representative of China. The state's policy resulted in "a perception in Taiwan of

Mainland superiority or advantage and Taiwan inferiority or weakness"
(Gates 1981: 273).

When Chiang's regime first took power in Taiwan, it gave wai sheng
ren special quota in government employment; and many wai sheng ren obtained positions in the military, civil service, and education. Mainlander
industrialists also received state assistance. After fifty years of high-handed
policy complete with martial law by Chiang Kai-shek's government, resentment and resistance grew particularly among the intellectuals who fought
for freedom and democracy. When liberalization began to take place in the
1980s, intellectuals propagated the idea of a Taiwan identity and culture.
The Minnan dialect was openly spoken in the public arena, more local ben
sheng ren politicians began to seek political elections. Many wai sheng ren
began to fear the loss of opportunity, or even ill treatments by the ben sheng
ren (see Chang and Wu 2000).

We hold perspectives from our particular position and vantage point in
society, and from our lived experience. While Kai whose father was educated
in Japan specified that she disliked China the state because she was a ben
sheng ren, Liu, also a ben sheng ren, expressed her feelings for the nation.
She said,

> I am ben sheng ren. Some of the wai sheng ren had a hard time. When
> they first came after the retreat, there was little communication because
> in the 1940s few people in Taiwan spoke Mandarin, and the wai sheng
> ren did not understand Minnan hua. Chiang Kai-shek's government
> looked for spies and sometimes got the wrong people out of personal
> revenge. The soldiers were not all bad but some got into disputes with
> the locals, and of course they had guns and killed. Then later came the
> 2-28 incident. But not everybody dislikes wai sheng ren. I for one do not
> have family members wronged by the KMT.

Shang in my interview sample connected the ethnic difference to job
opportunity. She reflected as follows:

> I graduated from university with a major in Chinese literature. It was
> not easy to get a good job. You have to have connection for a good job. I
> am a wai sheng ren. I don't speak Minnan hua, and we lived in the south
> where there were mainly ben sheng ren.

Access to commerce and bureaucratic positions took distinct paths. Roots
and family ties in local community and public circles enhanced one's reputation and opportunity for business success. Wai sheng ren resorted to
network in bureaucratic jobs since they concentrated in the military, civil

service, and education (Gates 1981: 277). Many ben sheng ren, particularly the Minnan ren who made up over seventy-five percent of Taiwan's population, concentrated in the private sector of small to medium-sized enterprises. Since the ben sheng ren pervaded private enterprises, often the language of business was Minnan hua.

Opportunists began to capitalize on such ethnic difference for political gain. Jaye and her family left Taiwan in 1995 because they felt that internal ethnic strife was getting chaotic in Taiwan. According to Jaye, situations turned worse during election time. She said,

> It was during the Taipei mayoral election, and the politicians used divisive ploys to get votes, pitching wai sheng ren against ben shen ren. Sometimes one to two hundred taxi drivers would park their taxis together, and the drivers would be arguing against the wai sheng ren, in favor of Taiwan independence.

Another woman Faye and her family emigrated in 1997. One of the reasons for their departure was the ethnic tension in Taiwan. She told of the following:

> I am wai sheng ren and I grew up in the City of Taipei. We all spoke Mandarin in school so I do not speak Minnan hua. I was treated very rudely a few times for that. That was about ten years ago and it got worse during election time. Politicians accentuate on localization and capitalize on ethnic pride among the public in order to get more votes.

Faye offered an example to illustrate the situation. One time she got into a taxi and told the driver where she wanted to go in Mandarin. He wanted her to say the same to him in Minnan hua. She told him that she did not understand Minnan hua. When the taxi reached her destination and she was getting off, the driver said something very vulgar to her in Minnan hua, then he said, "Suppose you understand this sentence!" Faye commented, "I did understand what he said and I got very upset. This is one reason I did not want to remain in Taiwan. I didn't want to live in that environment."

While conflict arose in the public arena, close interactions occurred at the personal levels that transcended ethnic polarity accented in the public sphere. Faye mentioned that many people's in-laws were wai sheng ren or ben sheng ren because numerous men and women intermarried. Since Mandarin was the language of instruction at schools, students could get along and communicate with one another. She said, "The common people got along. Some of my sisters-in-law are ben sheng ren. When I was in Taiwan my ben sheng ren friends were good too." Another woman said, "Many people's in-laws were wai sheng ren or ben sheng ren. We intermarried. So you have everybody in the same family." Hai in my interview sample exemplified such intermarriages. She related some negative incidences:

> My father was wai sheng ren and my mother was ben sheng ren.[5] In the 1980s and 90s with the appearance of the New Democratic Party, there was a general negative attitude towards wai sheng ren. For example, my father was retired and did not drive. He rode the bus and most of the bus drivers were ben sheng ren. They were rude to my father. They often did not stop at the bus stop. Instead they drove way past the stop on purpose so my father had to walk a long way back.

A social scientist who was also the offspring of such an intermarriage said that she did not feel such animosity while she attended university in the 1980s. She then left Taiwan for graduate studies. When she returned to Taiwan in the 1990s, she began to sense the tension. A young woman in the twenties and worked as a research assistant told me that her father was wai sheng ren and her mother was ben sheng ren. While she was in university her classmates would call her a half-breed and other nasty names. She felt very hurt because these were her former classmates who used to be her friends in more innocent times. She said that her brother worked at a private firm owned by ben sheng ren. Her brother had no problem because he spoke Minnan hua. But she worried about her own future prospect since she did not speak that language.

I propose that this development of ethnic dynamics in Taiwan sees a parallel to the development of racial relation in the United States. Based on Gramsci's war of maneuver and war of position, Omi and Winant (1994) explain part of the racial dynamics in the United States as follows: forced outward from mainstream society by Whites, minority of color turned inward to form their own communities such as Chinatown and Manilatown. Minority groups nurtured themselves and obtained support and value within their own communities to combat their marginalized positions, forming what Takaki (1998) has termed ethnic islands. In 1971 the United Nation ousted the Republic of China (ROC, Taiwan) to accommodate the membership of the People's Republic of China (PRC, Mainland China). In 1979 the United States severed its official ties with the ROC, and reestablished diplomatic relation with the PRC. Several other countries followed suit. Imposed diplomatic isolation marginalized the ROC in the world political community.

The ROC reacted to the outward marginalization in the official world society by increasingly liberalizing its foreign, domestic, and economic policies including capital movements. As the state reached outward to counteract the marginalizing world politics, the nation oriented inward for value and self-worth. ROC's supposedly inferior stature in the world political order devalued its prestige, status, value, and moral worth of Chiang Kai-shek's KMT regime and its attendant cultural symbols. Cultural revitalization emerged to look for alternatives within Taiwan's local attributes including its arts, with particular emphasis on its language, literature, and history.[6] Analyzing Taiwan's contemporary literature, Hsiau (1999: 1) remarks "these humanist intellectuals try to authenticate the political assertion of identity by creating collective symbols and reclaiming a particular national tradition of literature." In this sense, Taiwan's contemporary localization paralleled Japan's enforcement of its language and customs during the colonial period, as well as the Chiang Kai-shek regime's imposition of Mandarin and traditional Chinese culture, as an attempt in the "invention of tradition" (Hobsbawm and Ranger 1983). Further, the reversal of the ethnic order in Taiwan arose when there was weakening deterioration in the state so blatantly reflected by its diminished position in the world community. The former imposed stasis gave way to spontaneous crisis, hand in glove with the opening up of the state as a result of political intervention led by intellectuals and responded to by Chiang's successor, his son Chiang Ching-kuo, during a period of liminality.

Opposition political projects had simmered under Chiang Kai-shek's regime. One well-known example was the Mei Li Dao (Beautiful Island) or Kao Hsiung incident. Mei Li Dao was an underground magazine (the Formosa Magazine) whose staff and supporters were eventually imprisoned by Chiang's totalitarian state.[7] Armed with legitimate violence, the state prosecuted, imprisoned, and assassinated dissidents including American citizens formerly from Taiwan. Ling-Chi Wang (1995) terms this extraterritorial subjugation "dual domination": the domination of Chinese Americans by dominant groups in the United States and by the state of the ROC. The tight grip of the ROC eventually loosened. "Where there is significant decay in the capacities of pre-existing state programs and institutions to organize and enforce its . . . ideology" (Omi and Winant 1994: 88), like a vote of no confidence in the old system, electoral politics and popular demands forced the state to give in to people's quest for democratization.

This opening up of the state shifted ethnic meanings. World politics as well as national forces intensified a re-articulation of local ethnic identity that focused on Minnan heritage instead of Mainland Chinese tradition. The paradigm shift was perceived or utilized by some to juxtapose ethnic dichotomy between the wai sheng ren (people of other provinces) and ben sheng ren (people of this province). In essence, a socioeconomic political development in a particular historical point of time became ethnicized. Opportunists capitalized on that ethnicized issue and magnified its significance in order to rally for votes along ethnic divide in public elections. The women's claim of politicians capitalizing on ethnic vote is not without ground. In a keynote speech to the Legislative Yuan's (Branch's) monthly meeting, a policy adviser to President Chen Shui-bian commented that politicians should not further politicize ethnic differences between ben sheng ren and wai sheng ren. He pointed out that the segregation between the two groups had mostly subsided within the private sphere, yet it persisted in the public arena as an ethnic card for political gains (Taiwan Daily 2001a).

Although politicians manipulated ethnicity as if it were a concrete reality, the concept of ethnicity is a fluid construction. Like "race," ethnicity is articulated and rearticulated by the subjective actor and by the objective world imposed upon the ego, often influenced by the forces of material conditions. In the instrumentalist mode, art dealers in Cote d'Ivoire pose as members of one ethnic group or another to facilitate their business dealings in African art (Steiner 1994). Early Jewish and Irish immigrants to the United States slowly "became white" as they advanced in socioeconomic and political gains (see Sacks 1994 and Ignatiev 1995). In the United States, I am lumped as Asian American. There are so few Asian and Pacific Islanders that further splitting would jeopardize our political representation. When I shop at the Yao Han Supermarket in Little Tokyo of Los Angeles, the cashiers speak to me in Japanese; at the Mexican mercado (market) in East Los Angeles, they communicate to me in Spanish.

One of my interviewees in Taiwan was Hakka. He assured me that I was also Hakka because my ancestral hometown was Zhong Shan, just like Dr. Sun Yat-sen, the Chinese counterpart of George Washington, whom he claimed to be a Hakka from Zhong Shan. Since many people with my surname were Hakka in Taiwan, and given the fact that none of my grandmother and great aunts had bound feet just like Hakka women, I began to think that perhaps I too was Hakka. On the other hand, a Cantonese-speaking legislator who originated from Zhong Shan, but not a Hakka, insisted that this Hakka interviewee had made a grave error, that Sun was not a Hakka and that I was also not Hakka. Several people in Taiwan also thought that I was Minnan ren because my family name was "Chee" in accordance with the pronunciation of overseas Chinese in my ancestral dialect, the same pronunciation as in Minnan hua. In Mandarin the transliteration would be Hsu as spelled in Taiwan, or Xu as in Mainland China; in Cantonese it would be Chui or Tsui as it is spelled in Hong Kong. Despite all the information, none of that mattered after I returned to the United States. I resumed my label as Asian American, Chinese American, or simply Chinese. And the issue receded.

My officemate at the Academia Sinica found out in Taiwan, after twenty two years on American soil, that she was fifty percent wai sheng ren from her matriline, twenty-five percent Minnan and twenty-five percent Hakka from her paternal family. To learn more about her newly discovered heritage, she started to read about the Hakka, and visited Hakka museums that were non-existent in the United States. Even across the racial divide predicated upon phenotypes, Japanese had been considered to be "white" in apartheid-era South Africa, where Chinese managed to increasingly share the same public spaces and facilities restricted to whites on a de facto basis since the 1950s. Chinese are also able to challenge the law that dictates racial categories:

> Although classification as a 'white' was dependent on appearance, it could also be determined by association and general acceptance. An example of this loophole in the legislation was the case of a Chinese, Mr. Song, who in 1962 successfully applied for re-classification as a "white" on the grounds that he always associated with whites and was accepted by them. The Race Classification Board lost the case, and Mr. Song was declared a "white" (Harris 1998: 293).

In the United States, Chinese immigrants also maneuvered between black and white in post-war Mississippi. As they rose in economic standing, the Chinese started to dissociate themselves with the local black underclass in social interactions and residential areas. They began to move closer to the social and physical spaces occupied by local whites in order to distinguish themselves from the black in the bottom of the hierarchy, in an attempt to blend in with the white higher up in the echelon (Loewen 1988). As Paul Gilroy remarks (1991), "It ain't where you're from, it's where you're at." Ethnicity, like race, is a social construct within a cultural context with historical specificity.

The section above discerns the tension on ethnic politics within Taiwan. Next I discuss the regional political conflicts between Taiwan and Mainland China.

REGIONAL POLITICAL FACTORS

In the regional context, China's threat affected some of these transnational Taiwanese American families as early as 1975. Yung was in the early fifties when I met her. Single-handedly she ran her own business in California. Both her natal family and her husband's family lost everything when the "communists" took over China in 1949, and her husband's family went through a purge in a northern province. The husband was only twelve years of age at the time. Yung said that when the Viet Cong took Saigon in Vietnam in 1975, her husband was very afraid that the communists would come to Taiwan. He urged her to go to the United States and find ways to set up a company so the family could eventually leave Taiwan. It was under this circumstance that she came to the United States, and eventually started the transnational family arrangement. Another woman called Yee said that the United States Immigration and Naturalization Services had approved her family for immigration for some time but they were in no rush to leave. The perception of the looming political danger was the deciding factor, referring to China's 1996 missile exercise that targeted Taiwan. They departed in 1997. Another woman Ching had the following to say,

> My husband is in the sixties. He fled the communists from China to Taiwan with the KMT. He and his family suffered a lot then. In 1996 the Mainland held its missile exercise. My husband was very worried.

The military struggle between KMT headed by Chiang Kai-shek and Mao Zedong's Red Army continued even in the face of Japanese invasion in China. When Mao established the People's Republic of China in 1949, Chiang's KMT adherents of bureaucrats and civilians accelerated their evacuation to Taiwan that began in 1945. When the first democratic election took place in Taiwan in 1996, China underscored its claims of sovereignty over Taiwan in pointing its missile exercises in Taiwan's direction. In response, the United States dispatched two aircraft carriers to the Taiwan Strait.

A woman commented, "the political prospect in Taiwan didn't look promising." Another one stated, "my husband felt that the political situation in Taiwan was very unstable. A strong movement towards Taiwan's independence had been gathering momentum." Multiple political parties existed to contend for power: there was the KMT which was the old faction from Mainland, its splinter group called the New Party that favored unification with China in time, and the Democratic Progressive Party which wanted an independent Taiwan. A woman lamented,

> If Taiwan has the ability to be independent, yes. But does it? If there be a war between Mainland and Taiwan, then only the people suffer. Why not maintain status quo now and keep our good life!

A ben sheng ren commented as follows, "The Taiwan situation was very chaotic. We of course don't want to reunite with China!—It's a communist country, properties were nationalized and living standard is still low." Geopolitical instability in Asia, political contention between Taiwan and China over the national sovereignty of Taiwan, and internal ethnic politics in Taiwan all affected these people. They saw the United States as a safe haven and started to immigrate here.

While regional and national political turmoil in Taiwan fed the stream of emigration out of Taiwan, educational disadvantages experienced by children in Taiwan caused some people to leave. Women talk about their children's experiences with such disadvantages in the next section.

CHILDREN'S EDUCATION

Focusing on Mexican immigrants, Goldring argues that transmigrants maintain transnational practices in order to claim and valorize their social status. These transmigrants keep linkages through providing tangible material concerns, such as remittances, "improved homes, consumer goods, and new services and infrastructure" (Goldring 1998: 189). The Taiwanese American families also created and maintained transnational arrangement for status attainment. However, instead of status for themselves, as is the case with Mexican transmigrants, these people engaged in transnational practices for the reproduction of the socioeconomic class position for their children by the accumulation of education.

Bourdieu (1984) posits that within the French national context, people of different social class backgrounds actively acquire cultural practices and tastes that distinguish them as members of their class. He delineates their participation and activities in great length, but fails to connect class reproduction to the larger political economy that fluctuates with time. In this section, I extend Bourdieu's concept of social reproduction of class position to the transnational space. I further demonstrate that in this case, class reproduction was connected to historical conditions with temporal specificity. I argue that these Taiwanese American transnational families purposely maneuvered migration as a strategy to reproduce or improve their socioeconomic position in society, at a historical time that such a maneuver became imperative for them in their view. Parents might have invested in children's education out of parental altruism, or they might have considered it as investment in old age support (Lin 1998; Lin and Li 1999). Regardless of motive, women from Taiwan came to the United States for social reproductive purposes in order to ensure better educational and future opportunities for their children, unlike Latin American working class women and Filipina nurses and domestic workers (see Parrenas 2000, 2001) who migrate for productive labor and money. At a dinner party that I hosted at my home for a transnational family, a woman's remark reflected this characteristic. She claimed, "If there were no children, there would be no need to make the move to come here."

Twenty-one of the thirty-five women I interviewed cited better educational opportunities for their children as the main purpose of their migration. A woman named Kai specifically indicated that she and her family did not migrate here for economic reasons, "In my case, I came for my son's education, and for a better living environment." In most cases, only those with economic ability migrated to the United States. Kai offered an anecdote that illustrates this situation:

> Let me tell you one story that tells the economic backgrounds of the people who immigrated to the United States from Taiwan. I always told my daughter to keep a low profile at school. She acted and dressed like any other in her class. Then one day when she told her classmates that she was emigrating to the United States, they all oohed and aahed and exclaimed, "We did not know that you are wealthy!" I would not say that we're so very wealthy, but we're certainly not poor. We hadn't moved here for money.

Another woman, Lily, also commented on the economic backgrounds of these people, "The adults who came have two basic qualifications: they are economically able, and they have a decent educational level. One has to have money as well as academic ability." For these families, scholastic ability and money could be transformed into capital.

Bourdieu (1986) expounds upon three forms of capital: economic capital in the guise of money and property rights, social capital consisting of social contacts and obligations, and cultural capital in such forms as educational qualification. In this case, the families stressed cultural capital. Bourdieu posits that cultural capital exists in three forms: First, in the embodied form of the mind and body; second, in the objectified form of cultural goods like books and paintings; and third, in the institutionalized form such as educational attainment. Potentially, all these forms of capital can be converted into economic capital, particularly as income and property rights. In concordance with Bourdieu's cultural capital postulated above, studies demonstrate that education is the most important factor that decides status and occupation in Taiwan. Most position openings list specific minimum educational requirement, and salary is commensurate with the highest educational degree obtained by the successful applicant. The higher the level of education achieved, the higher the rank of first job and salary (Sun and Wu 1993; Chang, et al. 1996). In turn, first jobs directly influence the kind and level of one's future occupation. Taiwan practices differential pay for equal work: an incumbent with higher educational qualification commands better salary for the same job. Tsai (1998: 466) concludes that "Taiwan's stratified educational system functions as a sorting and allocating mechanism. In conditions of excess demand, higher educational credentials confer a higher return of occupational status." These credentials are the fruits of successfully passing highly selective qualification examinations. A crucial instrument for social mobility is education (Wang, et al. 1986), in other words, the accumulation of Bourdieu's cultural capital in the form of educational qualification.

Indeed, the women I had interviewed came across fully cognizant of the correlation between socioeconomic success and educational achievement. To enhance their children's educational opportunity, Tai and her family migrated to the United States partly for the children's education. I asked her why she and her husband uprooted the whole family for the children's education, why it reigned supreme to them. She explained to me as follows:

> We were poor before . . . manual labor is hard work. It's much easier if you work with a pen. . . . It's better to be a doctor, or to have a Ph. D. to be a professor. It's not good and it's low class to be a manual laborer. So we do our best to prepare our children for a better future . . . to rise to a higher class.

I posed the same question to another woman named Ting. She answered, "In Taiwan, education determines your future, your occupation. Higher education brings higher occupational level, higher social and economic status." I asked Ting if she had suggested any particular occupation to her children. She replied,

> Medical doctor, lawyer, etc., high income! We showed my son the college report for different occupation with incomes, and the highest are usually medical doctors and lawyers. . . . We told him, to do one hour's work cutting grass would bring in less money than one hour of work as a professional.

But the educational system is highly competitive in Taiwan, like in Japan, and the channels are very limited. Across the nation, all students must sit in city-wide joint examinations after nine years of compulsory education.

The result of this examination determines their future schooling prospect in more ways than one. First, this examination tracks students into academic education or vocational education systems. Students with scores above certain level are assigned to an academic track; those with scores below particular standard are tracked to vocational schools. The academic track prepares students for regular university education in liberal arts, sciences, and professional schools such as medical school. Vocational track prepares students for vocational or technical training. Second, students with higher scores in the city-wide joint examinations are then placed in more prestigious schools known for their academic excellence.

At the end of the twelfth grade, there is another round of highly selective joint entrance examinations for university or technical college education, students also need to take examinations administered by individual colleges or universities. Although a very few gets admitted by special selection based on outstanding achievement such as excellence in sports by national standard, the vast majority compete in the highly selective entrance examinations. The level and kind of education completed greatly determine one's opportunity in the job market, hence his or her future socioeconomic status. In general society also reveres academic excellence. This reverence places the academic track and vocational track in a hierarchical order, and the academic track is considered to be more prestigious than the vocational. In order to prepare for the many examinations, students attend private tutoring schools (also known as cram schools) in the evening after regular school hours, going home only in the late evening such as nine o'clock or nine-thirty. Thus, the pyramidal selection process and rigorous entrance examinations induce severe stress and anxiety for both students and parents. Parents and local scholars alike well know the importance of education towards a financially brighter future, and the studies by scholars in Taiwan seem to support Bourdieu's thesis of cultural capital being convertible into economic capital.

On the other hand, they categorically eclipse the potentially political and hegemonic character of different educational systems. Gramsci's treatise on education (1971: 26–43) proves illuminating here. According to Gramsci, hegemony of the ruling class is achieved with consent from the people being ruled. Often such consent is naturalized in the people by cultural institutions such as education. He critiques the Italian educational system that also separates schools into classical and vocational streams, and advocates a system that allows individuals to be educated in the same classical tradition so that they may learn to think until they get a job. In Gramsci's opinion, the vocational schools are designed for the instrumentalist class, but the traditional schools that concentrate on academic subjects prepare students for the dominant class and intellectuals. Gramsci points out that "the traditional school was oligarchic because it was intended for the new generation of the ruling class, destined to rule in its turn" (ibid.: 40).

I contend that Gramsci's insight also applies to Taiwan. Its tracking system that segregates academic and vocational training indeed perpetuates the socioeconomic classes of society as shown in Taiwan's scholarly findings. Further, traditional schools educate children in the sciences and liberal arts to continue onward in universities, to prepare them to think as a person so they become able to rule, to control, or influence those who do not. This tendency is apparent in the educational characteristics of Taiwan's ruling elites. Whereas political and social movements in Taiwan had historically been propelled and spearheaded by intellectuals, policy advisers and policy makers invariably had completed academic and higher education such as a law degree or doctorate. The former president Lee Teng-hui had received his Ph. D. from Cornell University. The incumbent Chen Shui-bian is a lawyer trained in Taiwan. His Minister of Foreign Affairs since April 2004, Dr. Tan Sun Chen, received his doctorate in the United States where he had resided for thirty years before his return to Taiwan.

Taiwan's cabinet is known to be highly educated. Based on government information on cabinet members, Gerald McBeath (1998: 93) compiled the following information on their educational levels:

> Only one stopped his training at high school, four at college. Twenty (53 percent) had doctoral degrees (including three in law), and the remaining 12 (or 32 percent) had master's degrees. Most of these officials studied abroad. Of the 23 with foreign degrees, the vast majority (17 or 74 percent) studied in the United States. Three studied in Japan, two in Europe, and one in Canada.

Most legislators arose from the educated class. From the 1996 Roster of Legislature, McBeath (ibid.: 99) also found that

> 92 percent have received at least a college education. A majority has taken graduate work, and a very high percentage (27.4 percent) has completed doctoral work. Few legislatures have this degree of educational specialization. About 44 percent studied abroad after college, and the choice for most was the United States.

The above statistics demonstrate the advance academic achievement obtained by the high-ranking officials of Taiwan. In other words, unlike the vocational track that produces instrumentalist workers, the academic track prepares students in the classical tradition and groom future rulers who dominate the various state apparatus and set policies that run them.

The educational system in Taiwan makes it increasingly difficult to transcend by personal initiative socioeconomic class division as well as the great divide between the ruling and the ruled. Some parents used migration as a strategy to counteract the rigid educational system and established channels. Parents migrated to prepare a child for higher occupation and status than was possible in Taiwan given the child's scholastic aptitude and inclination, to free a child from a rigid education, to give a foundering child a second chance, to broaden their worldview for a global era, or so they claimed. All of these goals shared one feature, one hope: that their children may move up or at least reproduce their parents' social economic position in society. In the end, perhaps these children may be able to rule and influence rather than to remain subordinates.

Yen and her family had immigrated primarily for her younger child's educational opportunity. According to Yen, this son had not fared well in academic subjects. Instead, he excelled in art and had won several prizes with his drawings. Given Taiwan's pyramidal educational system and stringent examination requirements, he would most likely end up in the vocational track, with a dim outlook for high-income employment opportunities in the future. In Taiwan, this also meant a diminished social status. Yen put it this way:

> Here in the United States, students could be artistically inclined, and still be considered worthy when they continue artistic pursuits in art schools or performing arts. This is the major reason for my family's decision to come here.

Tai reported the same situation with her eldest child:

> He's artistically inclined. He had attended art classes since he was young but artistic students did not have much career future or opportunity in Taiwan. . . . He would have more opportunity in the United States.

One mother described her son's experience as follows:

> He was right in the middle rank in a class of about forty students. But he felt taunted and belittled. The teachers openly ranked the students in front of everybody. Some parents also told their children not to play and socialize with my son since he was not among the top. It hurt his self-esteem. He felt bad about himself and he did not want to return to school.

The youngster requested his parents to send him away to study abroad. After deliberation, the mother accompanied the son to begin his senior high school in the United States, and the father remained to work in Taiwan. Eventually, this son made it to an Ivy League university.

Another family also migrated to the United States for the children's education. Sponsored by the husband's sibling, the parents and two children had been approved for immigration to the United States for sometime. Since both husband and wife worked as professionals in Taiwan, they waited as long as possible to make this international move. Finally, they came in time for the two youngsters to begin their ninth grade in the States. According to a family friend, these two teenage children had always ranked in the bottom of their classes, they must go elsewhere for a second chance otherwise they would never make it in Taiwan. Another woman's two teenage daughters also needed this second chance. The parent remarked that the older daughter had always been a slow learner since kindergarten. Her performance continued to be less than mediocre in the eighth grade. To avoid being tracked into vocational school, the mother took the two girls to New Zealand so they could continue with a regular academic education, as they awaited approval for their immigration to the United States under kin sponsorship by the husband's brother. In 2000, the mother and two daughters immigrated to Los Angeles, California. Both girls were reportedly progressing well in the new environment. I asked another mother how her son performed at school in Taiwan. She commented that poor scholastic performance was not the problem,

> I wanted him to have a broader perspective. Taiwan is a small country. One easily becomes a big fish in a small pond. The United States is a big country with lots of people from many different parts of the world. It would give him a bigger window to the world, for a wider horizon.

Two women reported the perception that admission to university was easier in the United States than in Taiwan. The first woman recalled, "We came for our children's schooling. It seems easier to get admitted to universities here. It is hard in Taiwan." The second woman said, "We left Taiwan primarily for the children's education. In the 1980s it was not easy to get admitted to a university in Taiwan." However, rather than an inferior standard of education in the United States, the mothers pointed to the shortcomings of the educational system in Taiwan. Janet commented, "The educational style in Taiwan is rigid. It's better in the United States . . . Taiwan's educational system does not emphasizes comprehension, just rote memory. My children prefer the system here." Jan described as follows, "Our son was in the seventh grade. Studying got to be very tiring for him. Everyday he went to tutoring classes after regular school." This demanding schedule appeared to continue into high school according to Lily,

> The education in Taiwan was too standardized and rigid, with an emphasis on rote memory. The educational system was so competitive. For a teenager, schooling was a heavy burden. There was only studying in his life, nothing else. There was just too much homework, heavy-duty homework.

One woman's children had attended primary school in the United States before the families returned to Taiwan. Having experienced two different systems, the children reacted negatively to the system in Taiwan. The mother reported the following: "They didn't like the way teachers taught in Taiwan. There were always examinations, only rote memory. The teachers would say to students 'why are you so stupid.' My daughter started to lose confidence in herself." Another mother said, "Teachers would also criticize the students who did poorly, instead of trying to encourage them." One of the children actually took the initiative to ask the parents if he could go to school in the United States.

Mothers also compared the relative flexibility of the two schooling systems, preferring the American one to that in Taiwan. One woman pointed out the more open admission in the United States,

> Our son was not that industrious and did not care for studying too much. In Taiwan, once you miss your chance, there would be no more opportunity even if you want to catch up later when you are older. In the United States, anyone of any age can always go back to school. For example, it is easy for an adult to gain admission to community colleges. There are more opportunities here to attend college even at different stages of one's life.

Lily's words below best summed up the women's opinions,

> There ought to be opportunity to develop individual talent and potential, yet the education in Taiwan was too standardized and rigid, with an emphasis on rote memory and scholastic aptitude. . . . It was a competitive system, and teachers were strict. . . . This system set limitation to some gifted students. They could have more opportunity to develop their talents in the United States, to excel in any field in which they have an aptitude. Immigration to the United States provided an alternative, to give the talented children a different space, and to give those less inclined another chance.

While the above sounded celebratory, one woman held her reservation, "Indeed education in Taiwan is spoon feeding. It is livelier and more liberal in the United States, more freedom to develop one's talents. Yet, another reason is a third world mentality—everything American and western is better." Another woman criticized American education as follows, "Is American education that good? I don't think so. It does not teach children about respect for teachers and parents." Whether celebratory or critical, for these women, migration was primarily a strategy to counteract local disadvantage experienced by their children in education. It was an active resistance to a system that they perceived to have limited their children's possibility to succeed in Taiwan. They migrated to the United States in an attempt to accumulate children's cultural capital, in hope of the children's ability to convert such cultural capital to economic and social capitals in the future, in order to at least reproduce their parents' current socioeconomic status in society.

The migration strategy assumed a particular urgency and historical significance for wai sheng ren (Mainlander) Taiwanese American parents, in light of Taiwan's national political development in recent years. As discussed in the above section titled *National Ethnic Strife,* the Mainlander KMT regime had increasingly lost its ruling power to ben sheng ren politicians and political parties. The upsurge of localization emphasized a Taiwan identity, local Minnan language, and cultural symbols that undermined Mainland cultural tradition favored by the KMT. Many wai sheng ren perceived this transition of political power and localization movement as a threat, as possible ill treatment in the future, and as loss of opportunity in Taiwan when their children came of age. Being wai sheng ren no longer symbolized a superior and dominant social status in society, as it once did during the heydays of the wai sheng ren KMT regime. In addition, the wai sheng ren who came from Mainland China after 1945, together with their offspring, had no inheritance of land that was traditionally owned by ben sheng ren. Without land that could convert to economic capital, to the wai sheng ren parents, it would appear imperative that their children succeeded in education in order to attain future economic security and social status.

While educational opportunity for children played a paramount role in motivating people from Taiwan to emigrate, other people departed for better business opportunity. I discuss that aspect in the section below.

BUSINESS AND WORK OPPORTUNITY

Unlike the high percentage of respondents indicating business opportunity and career development as their reasons to migrate here as reported by

Hsiao and Smith (1994), only five of the thirty-five women I interviewed indicated that they had come for business or work opportunities as well as children's education and other reasons. Merely one of the women cited business opportunity as the sole reason that had prompted her and her husband to immigrate to the United States in 1989. I met this woman, Liu, when I conducted the survey at the adult school.

Liu was a ben sheng ren. In Taiwan, she and her husband owned a factory that was highly automated. No more than thirty workers were needed to run the machines. Articulate, open, and seemingly interested in politics, she asked me not to reveal her real name because of what she had to say. Liu considered Chiang Ching-kuo to be the best president they had. She said, "He built all these highways. Transportation of goods became possible and efficient. Time is money in business." Chiang Kai-shek passed away in 1975 and his son Chiang Ching-kuo succeeded him as the second president of the Republic of China on Taiwan. To facilitate and accommodate the industrializing effort, in the 1980s Chiang Ching-kuo's government implemented the "Ten Major Construction Projects" to overhaul Taiwan's infrastructure. These projects included constructions of an international airport, a highway system that connected the north and south of Taiwan, improved railway systems throughout the island, and upgraded electrical power supply and port facilities.

Labor cost was low before Taiwan's extraordinary economic performance, popularly known as the "Taiwan miracle." Liu and her husband were competitive in bidding subcontract work from overseas. When Taiwan's economy took off, surplus reserve increased and the standard of living improved. Labor cost went up, and more local people engaged in speculative activities such as the stock exchange. From the 1980s onward, Taiwan imported foreign laborers from Southeast Asia to meet demands in the manufacturing and construction industries. Liu also attributed business problems to politicians. She said,

> Lee Teng-hui . . . made policies in the interest of the big enterprises because they contributed to his political campaigns, at the expense of small to medium-sized enterprises. Most of Taiwan's businesses are small to medium-sized. Then politicians raised minimum wage to please laborers. It led to inflation, and we lost the competitive edge in labor cost. Business was just so-so but the laborers kept demanding more and more, it was getting harder for us to compete for contracts, yet the Democratic Progressive Party continued to encourage labor movements and strikes to court their votes.

When Chiang Kai-shek took control of Taiwan in 1949, he declared martial law that prohibited demonstrations and protests as well as labor strikes. As

Deo (1989) points out, beneath the Taiwan miracle stood the subordinated workers. Martial law remained effective until 1987 when it was lifted by President Chiang Ching-kuo. Chiang Ching-kuo passed away in 1988, Vice President Lee Teng-hui served the remaining term. Although a member of the KMT, Lee was a Taiwan-born ben sheng ren. In 1996 Lee became the first president in Taiwan by direct election. Large conglomerates contributed to his campaign finance. Following his term, the Democratic Progressive Party rose to power. Their political reforms gave workers the right to form their own unions and to strike. Laborers mounted 2,271 labor disputes in 1995 (McBeath 1998: 127). In response business owners organized or attempted to dominate unions, and some curb labor by threats (realistic) to relocate to less expensive sites in Southeast Asia or on the Chinese Mainland (ibid.: 127–28).

Liu continued to comment on the labor situation, "More than ten years ago I told my workers that if workers go on strike demanding higher wages, they would force the owners to relocate out of Taiwan." That essentially happened. A large number of manufacturers went to establish factories in China, Vietnam, Indonesia, Malaysia, and Thailand to take advantage of local cheap labor in order to maximize their profit margin. A large majority went to China where there were fewer language and cultural obstacles. According to a newspaper report, the unemployment rate has escalated in Taiwan to the highest level in its recent history. Taiwan lost its competitive edge—cheap labor that could not legally unionize—leading to Liu and her husband's move out of Taiwan.

Besides the above reasons, some women indicated that they had migrated for a better quality of life out of dissatisfaction with the local environment. The following section looks at the women's analyses of the social and natural environmental factors that prompted their emigration.

THE SOCIAL ENVIRONMENT

Two women expressed that the deteriorating social environment was the reason for their departures from Taiwan. Ting was in the early forties at the time of the interview. She came to the United States in 1998 with her teenage son and daughter. They chose southern California because her sister and brother were already living there. Her husband worked in Taiwan to support the family. Ting had the following comments to offer:

> The social environment was deteriorating in Taiwan. There appeared
> to be a lot of nouveau riche who got rich quick from the stock market
> and from real estate. There no longer was an emphasis on cultural and

educational cultivation, but blatant conspicuous consumption. They flaunted their wealth. Newspapers also reported major cases of bank and company embezzlements, imagined how many smaller cases not publicized? My husband is a modest person, we don't want our children to grow up in such environment.

Kai came in 1997. She talked about the rising crime rate in Taiwan that motivated her migration in search of a better living environment. She said, "I had been here before and I preferred it here." She told me what had happened to one of her friends back in Taiwan:

> He was a physician and his medical office had its doors wide open. One day he was sitting down with a new patient, and asked that patient what was wrong. That person said: "I'm a fugitive. I need some money. Can I borrow some?" Of course he did not mean to borrow. So there was this practice that physicians often stashed away NT$10,000 to 20,000 [equivalent to US$300 to $600 approximately] in their drawers for this kind of situations.

Her friend was not harmed because he had prepared money for just such an occasion. Kai also mentioned that one major crime was kidnapping that was particularly rampant from 1990 to1995, and that sometimes criminals kidnapped members from wealthy families for ransom. Although Los Angeles is a city known for its high crime rate, nestled in anonymity and in the relative safety of her suburban home, Kai evidently felt more security and protection for her family. While discontent with the social order in Taiwan sent some women and their families away, dissatisfaction remained high in Taiwan. In June 2001, the Central Police University released the result of a 2001 public opinion poll. As much as 70.1 percent of the residents were dissatisfied with the condition of law and order in Taiwan, while female respondents and those with higher education showed the most dissatisfaction (Taiwan Daily 2001b).

In addition to the deteriorating social condition, the natural environment also propelled some women and their families to emigrate. In the section below, women relate their negative experiences with the natural environment in Taiwan.

THE NATURAL ENVIRONMENT

Two women reported that their own or their children's allergy associated with poor air quality was their only reason for leaving Taiwan. By comparison, what was considered polluted air in southern California appeared to be improved quality for these people. Wei and her three children literally ran away for their lives in 1988. According to Wei, she and her son both had allergies in Taiwan. Her son's condition was particularly acute with frequent upset stomach, fever, and all kinds of symptoms. She said, "The doctors just couldn't figure out what it was. It was the air pollution in Taiwan! Whenever we vacationed here in the summer his symptoms all but disappeared, so we decided to immigrate to live here."

I met Wei at a single parent counseling service center in southern California. One of the women I had interviewed told me about this center. She suggested that I participated in some of its activities to locate additional candidates for my interviews. She offered that I could use her name as a reference to contact the organizer of the service center. I called up the organizer, Mrs. Chang, who let me attend the next monthly service gathering at the center. Wei worked at this center as a full-time volunteer. When she heard about my project, she told me that she was what I was looking for. Wei was in the fifties when I met her. The wife of a physician, she never worked for pay although she was also a medical professional by training. She and her children lived in the United States while her husband practiced in Taiwan to support them. Another woman named Tsai also pointed out air pollution problem in Taiwan that had caused them to emigrate. All her three young teenage children, a daughter and two sons, suffered from asthma in Taiwan. In 1996 she and her husband finally immigrated to California. The change evidently worked. All three youngsters had been living here without problem. While Tsai stayed here with the children, her husband flew back and forth between Taiwan and California to take care of the family business and financially support the family in the United States.

Taiwan's industrialization had not been achieved without cost. The most taxing was that of a deteriorated natural environment, and one of the resultant hazards was pollution. Such hazards were so serious that between 1980 and 1996, a total of 1,211 local anti-pollution protests occurred, mostly led by victims (Hsiao 1999: 34). Consciousness in the public mind was also heightened by the work of intellectuals and the media. Intellectuals initiated concerns for the environment. Newspapers, magazines, radio, and television reports exposed incidents to the general populace and further popularized awareness in the public beginning in the late 1970s and early 1980s (Hsiao and Tseng 1999: 104). Starting in the 1980s, anti-pollution demonstrations became nation-wide and many surveys showed acute dissatisfaction with environmental problems among the people. The public was pessimistic about the future of their environment (Hsiao 1999: 32–33).[8]

May was another woman who came to California for a better living environment. But she primarily left Taiwan with a personal motive. Women did not always accommodate others' need in their decision to migrate. They also assessed their own interests and actively maneuvered to achieve their goals. I discuss this aspect in the next section.

WOMEN'S AGENCY

Back in the late 1980s, May came to southern California for the first time to visit her relatives. She became very fond of the more relaxed life style and the living conditions in southern California. Although she appreciated the spacious housing here compared to Taiwan, it was not the main reason for her emigration. For May, the single most important factor for her decision was to avoid familial obligations toward her parents-in-law. In Taiwan, May worked as a full-time accountant, all day from Monday through Friday and half a day on Saturday morning. That was the full time work schedule for all government offices and most private offices, with office hours on Saturday morning. This schedule changed during my stay in Taiwan from August 2000 to July 2001. Beginning January 2001, office hours ran from Monday to Friday, with every Saturday as a day off.

May was the first one to marry into her husband's family, and he happened to be the eldest son. Although May and her husband lived in their own place apart from the parents-in-law, as the daughter-in-law she was expected to pick up grocery and brought it to the in-laws every week. Since they lived far away from May, she felt that her "day-off" was another kind of work day. As May recalled, she had not minded it in the beginning because she was the only daughter-in-law and there was nobody else to help the two elderly people. As time went by, one after another her husband's younger brothers got married, yet none of their wives shared with the caring for the parents-in-law. May continued to shoulder the responsibility alone. Eventually it started to annoy May. She would have liked a helping hand in the care for the two elderly. When May came to southern California to visit her relatives, she fell in love with the suburban living environment and relaxing life style. But there was more. She said,

> I also wanted to get away from the obligation to my in-laws, I figure I've done my share, so let the other wives do it. . . . I stay here with my two children who go to school here on student-visa. When my visitor visa expired, I just stayed on to care for them while my husband works in Taiwan and sends money to support us here.

Some studies show that working-class women who migrate away achieve autonomy from patriarchy (e.g. Hondagneu-Sotelo 1994). Toward that goal, this non-working class woman actively negotiate to migrate from Taiwan for her liberation from familial obligations to parents-in-law. Woman agency assumed a paramount position in May's family in their decision to depart for the United States. On the other hand, male children's military service requirement provided additional incentive for some families to leave Taiwan.

MILITARY SERVICE

Related to external political conflict was parents' concern for their sons' compulsory military service. According to Taiwan's conscription law, all male citizens of the Republic of China are obligated to fulfill military service between January 1 following the eighteenth birthday and December 31 of the forty-fifth birthday. The disabled, deformed, and persons unable to serve due to incurable diseases are exempted; anyone previously sentenced to seven years or more of imprisonment are prohibited to enlist. Military service requirement applies to persons with dual citizenship even if they enter Taiwan on a foreign passport.

Although only two women expressly pointed to Taiwan's conscription that motivated their departures, three other women talked about the service in such a way that indicated the avoidance of military service as a consideration in their decision to migrate. For Janet, conscription was the sole reason for her departure. She said,

> We decided to emigrate because our children are both boys, and boys have to serve in the military for two years. It's hard work! At the time my oldest son was fast approaching fifteen but the United States authority had not yet approved our immigration, so I took the two boys to Singapore first and they went to school there until we got approval to come here.

In 1996 Ling also brought her son to southern California before he reached fifteen years of age. She and her son first came on visitor's visas; later the son started attending school on a student visa until their immigration application was approved. Another woman also emigrated with her two sons before they reached the age of fifteen. Why did the mothers hurry to leave with their sons before they became fifteen years old? A mother provided an explanation as follows,

> Before we left, boys older than fifteen were not allowed to leave Taiwan. After we left, things changed. They could leave up to eighteen years of age if they leave to attend university, but the parents must sign to guarantee their return to Taiwan for military service. If you stay out of Taiwan until the age of forty-five then you are free from military service. If you hold a Taiwan passport, you need to apply for exit and entry permits to leave or enter Taiwan. You cannot come and go like you can in the United States.

Taiwan has been changing its restriction on exit/entry of male of conscription age. According to information released in 1998, a male who leaves Taiwan before conscription age to attend school in a foreign country may now re-enter Taiwan and then apply for exit permit again within two months stay in Taiwan, upon presentation of valid and certified school attendance abroad. However, there is an age limit on this exemption: up to the age of twenty-four for an undergraduate university education, twenty-seven for a master's degree, and thirty for a Ph. D. Under normal circumstances, violation of conscription law by delayed return or failure to return to report for enlistment is punishable by law (Overseas Scholar 1998: 8). Recently, it was announced that male children who attended schools in Mainland China would be regulated under the same category as those who went to foreign countries (United Daily News 2001a).

Why did parents not want their sons to enlist in military service? Ching provided one reason,

> My husband never regretted about sending the kids here. If the boys stayed in Taiwan, they would have to serve in the military. My husband served out his share. He thought that was not worth it. It was an extremely hard life. And if there were ever a war [with China], it would be warring with your own people. It is meaningless. He's a wai sheng ren and I'm a ben sheng ren. He was born in the Mainland and came to Taiwan when he was five years old. ... He's caught in between. He doesn't want the children to have to war in that situation, in that contradiction.

Not all parents had this view on conscription. One woman stated that her son could finish university and a master degree and then return to serve in the military. She said, "He should serve because that is his own country." This mother was a seventh generation Taiwanese who immigrated to the United States in 1993. She said, "Taiwan is my country, my home, my land." However, it appeared that most parents and males of conscription age in Taiwan held a negative attitude toward military service. A recent official survey in Taiwan reported the following statistics:

Fifty-five percent surveyed feared conscription. Thirty-seven percent objected it. . . . Twenty-one percent considered it a waste of time, and twenty-three percent indicated unwillingness to serve. . . . Seventy percent of parents adopted a negative view of the military after their sons' completion. Forty percent of parents or males of conscription age felt that one needed connection to be assigned to a good unit (United Daily News 2001b).

Negative view and avoidance of military service likely explain, at least in part, the significantly higher number of transnational families with male children. Out of the thirty-five transnational families, twenty-three families had sons. The remaining twelve were excluded due to the following reasons: six families had American-born children, two came to the United States on secondary migration from South America, two with only daughters, and two had sons who migrated after military service. Out of the twenty-three families with sons, one family migrated after one son's service but before two other sons' coming of age. All the other twenty-two families arrived in the United States before their sons reached conscription age. In addition, while only seventeen daughters left Taiwan for the United States, a total of thirty-four sons immigrated. The following tables show the age distribution of these youngsters from the twenty-three families upon arrival in the United States.

SUMMARY

The women interviewed recounted several different reasons for their migration to the United States: children's education, Taiwan's internal ethnic tension, political threat from China, business or career opportunity in the United States, joining family members, deteriorating social and natural environment in Taiwan, to avoid son's military service, to avoid in-law problems, marital problem and self education. Migration is a complex process that involved multiple causes. In my interviews, the most cited reason was children's education. Education was the primary avenue for social mobility in Taiwan, yet its educational system was highly competitive, with a tracking system divided into academic and vocational training streams that perpetuated socioeconomic classes of society. Some non-working class parents used migration as a strategy to counteract the rigid educational system and established channels faced by their children, to avoid their children being tracked into vocational streams when they fell behind in academic standing. Parents migrated to prepare children for a higher socioeconomic status than possible had they remained in Taiwan, and to give them a broader education for a

Table 5.1 age distribution at arrival, male. N = 34

Age	5	6	7	8	9	10	11	12	13	14	15	16	17	18	19	20	21	22	23	24	25	26
# of Person	1	1	0	1	1	4	2	4	5	3	5	0	3	0	1	1	0	0	1	0	0	1

Table 5.2 age distribution at arrival, female. N = 17

Age	1	2	3	4	5	6	7	8	9	10	11	12	13	14	15	16	17	18	19	20	21	22
# of Person	1	0	0	0	0	0	2	1	0	1	0	3	2	1	3	2	0	0	0	0	0	1

global era, with the hope that they might move up in socioeconomic position in society or at least reproduce their parents' current class position. For some wai sheng ren (Mainlander) parents, academic accomplishment became particularly crucial in order to succeed at this historical moment, when Taiwan's internal politics changed hand to local Taiwanese power elite that might, they feared, closed off opportunity to offspring of Mainlanders.

These people had immigrated to the United States. They were beyond migration. Why then did they choose to live out a life in the transnational space, where one spouse resided in Taiwan while the other spouse and their child(ren) in the United States? The next chapter looks at the reasons for the formation of these Taiwanese American transnational families.

Chapter Six
Global Political Economy, Local Disadvantages, and Transnational Families

In the last chapter, the women from transnational families spoke on the causes for their migration from Taiwan to the United States. These reasons arose from their standpoints. They commented from their material experiences in their lived world. Most of the women articulated the intense power of the sociopolitical and economic elements in their society. It unveiled their cognizance of such powerful forces in their daily existence. These factors led to their migrations. But why did their families become transnational after migration, split in the United States where one spouse lived with the children, and in Taiwan where the other spouse worked to support the family in the States?

In their studies on Haitian, Granadians, and Filipinos in the United States, Basch, Glick-Schiller and Szanton-Blanc (1994) provide three reasons for transnational practices: 1) family reproduction in the face of political and economic insecurity; 2) social exclusion in countries of origin; 3) racialized exclusion in the United States. Further, Goldring (1998) demonstrates that some Mexicans do it for status claiming reasons. In recent times, families that originated from Hong Kong departed for political reason. Some became transnational after migration because of certain disadvantages encountered in their countries of destination (see, e.g., Man 1993, 1996a, 1996b; Pe-Pua, et al. 1996), they are referred to as astronaut families. In Canada, some Hong Kong women and men accepted jobs below their qualifications and past work experiences, constituting what Skeldon (1994) has termed "downward displacement," because they could not obtain comparable or satisfactory employment due to non-transferable licenses, lack of local work experience required by employers, inadequate proficiency in English, or discrimination. In some Hong Kong astronaut families, husbands (and occasionally wives) returned to work in Hong Kong because of better economic opportunities, and they financially support their spouses and children in such countries as Australia, Canada, and New Zealand. However, if the Taiwanese American transnational families are to be incorporated for consideration, these reasons are only responses to immediate material conditions. They are epiphenomenal. For Marx, there is a distinct difference between "appearance" and "essence," but one is no more or less real than the other. Both are necessary in the investigation of social phenomena to give a more comprehensive understanding. "The distinction between 'essence' and 'appearance' refers to different levels of determination, that is in the last analysis to the process of cognition, not to degree of reality" (Mendel 1976: 20).

Taiwanese American transnational families indeed arose partly as a consequence of certain disadvantages encountered in the United States. More important, the transnational family formation grew out of the globalization process that imbued our era with its deep-seated and concomitant constituents of capitalism, colonialism, and imperialism, much like Asian immigration to the United States in the nineteenth century (see Cheng and Bonacich 1984). Leslie Sklair (1999) categorizes four clusters in the study of globalization, namely the world-systems approach, the global culture approach, the global society approach, and the global capitalism approach. In this chapter, I first discuss the world-systems theory used here to look at globalization, and then Taiwan's economic ascendancy in a global political economy. Next I view the kinds of disadvantages experienced as related to me by individuals in my sample, and the formation of Taiwanese American transnational families in a global context for a more comprehensive gaze at the phenomenon.

GLOBALIZATION AND TAIWANESE AMERICAN TRANSNATIONAL FAMILIES

I argue that Taiwanese American families became transnational mainly as a direct result of globalization. These transnational families actively maneuver the system for their children, to reproduce or improve their socioeconomic position in society. They used migration as a strategy to counteract local disadvantages in education faced by their children in Taiwan. After migration, the subsequent formation of these transnational families was caused by certain local disadvantages faced by new immigrants, by the glass ceiling phenomenon faced by Taiwanese American professionals who were former graduate students in the United States, and by Taiwan's ascendancy in a global political economy. They formed transnational families as a strategy to maximize returns on productive and reproductive labor. They accumulated economic capital in the country of origin, to transfer into their children's educational capital in the country of destination, in order to transfer it again to children's future economic and social capital. Their effort was made possible by the maintenance of transnational families that transcended the nation-states, at a historical moment and context favorable for their formation. Their families mediated the local and the global by living out life in the transnational space, made possible by their economic ability as members of the non-working class.

The impact of globalization on the local level is often shown to be negative (Lewellen 2002). In contrast, the local took a free ride with the global in this case. Taiwan's economic ascendance in the context of a global political economy provided a way out for the husbands who encountered hindrances in the local U. S. labor market, for business owners and professionals who continued to operate their businesses in Taiwan and/or China. The economic growth in these places gave them the opportunity to maximize their income potential. It was this economic power that enabled these men and women to maintain their transnational families with remittances from Taiwan to the United States, contrary to the usual flow from the United States to the country of origin. These Taiwanese American transnational families represent exceptions to the consistent one-sided view of negative effects on the local of globalization. Globalization has indeed caused oppression, inequality, and harmful impact in many locations, but it can also provide opportunity and liberation. The crucial factor is not globalization in and of itself. It is one's class position in society in relation to globalization that charts the difference. For these men and women, their more privileged position bolstered by adequate skills and capitals turned the effect of globalization to their advantage. Globalization became an asset rather than a liability due to their class background. That also partly explains why these transnational families prioritized their children's education above all, in order that they could move upward or at least reproduce their socioeconomic position in society.

As pointed out by Kearney (1995: 548), "global processes are largely decentered from specific national territories and take place in a global space." Simply put, globalization refers to the interconnectedness of the world (Chase-Dunn, personal communication, September 2001). Globalization is world integration (Boswell and Chase-Dunn 2000: 297). It entails the interconnections of the socioeconomic, political, and cultural aspects of our world unbinding at an increasingly planetary scale. Publication on theory and research that embraced a global view germinated in Wallerstein's *The Modern World System* (1976). In this book, Wallerstein contextualizes fifteen century and sixteenth century Europe in an integrated world economy of Europe, an economic system that traverses the then existing political and territorial boundaries. Wallerstein drew on dependency theory (Kearney 1995: 550).[1] While dependency theory conceives the world as divided into core and periphery, world-system theory breaks that bipolarity and substitutes it with a more complex paradigm of power hierarchy consisting of a core, a periphery, and a semi-periphery. In sixteenth century Europe, they were characterized by the mode of labor control: "slavery and feudalism in the periphery, wage labor and self-employment in the core, and . . . sharecropping in the semi periphery" (Wallerstein 1976: 65). In our contemporary world, the core is made up of wealthy, industrialized nation-states with advanced technology, military strength, and high-wage labor. The periphery consists of nation-states that are "undeveloped" where labor wage is low and military might is comparatively weak. The semi-periphery mediates somewhere between the core and the periphery. In the period after the Second World War, the United States exemplifies a core nation-state, India, Pakistan, and Africa the periphery; while Taiwan, Singapore, Mexico, and Brazil would be part of the semi-periphery (Chase-Dunn and Hall 1997: 2).

Wallerstein also drew from the Annales school of French historiography (Hall 2000: 5). Wallerstein (1976, 1989, 1996, 1997) argues for an understanding of historical specificities in the context of a larger general historical pattern. The world-system theory provides that perspective to look at micro and macro interactions, but scholars have taken different approaches in their researches. While Wallerstein (1974, 1976, 1979) considers a world system to be a multi-cultural network of goods exchange necessary for daily living, Braudel (1975, 1984) emphasizes commodity trade as the most significant interconnection where economic domination constitutes hegemony. Charles Tilly (1984) focuses on political interconnectedness, just as David Wilkinson (1987) concentrates on military confrontations and political conflicts. Further, Schortman and Urban (1987) points out the importance of ideological diffusion in addition to the economic aspect of intersocietal linkages. Chase-Dunn and Hall (1997: 2) aim to substantiate Wallerstein's world-system theory in a general account to explain social change by looking at the role of intersocietal interactions. They define world-systems as "intersocietal networks in which the interactions (e.g., trade, warfare, intermarriage, information) are important for the reproduction of the internal structures of the composite units and importantly affect changes that occur in these local structures" (ibid.: 28). Chase-Dunn and Hall also consider the world-system concept useful in the study of stateless and classless societies. To them, world-system refers to "the whole social context in which people live and the material networks important to their daily life" (ibid.). The whole system includes "individuals, households, neighborhoods, firms, communities, cities, and so on, as well as states and interstate system" (ibid.: 15).

It is in this latter framework that I adopt the world-system approach to look at the global political economy that ultimately caused the families to become transnational between Taiwan and the United States. No matter how dire the conditions might be in Taiwan, transnational families would not have materialized without the global historical conditions that induced and favored their eventual formations. These families began to form due to the socioeconomic and political forces in national as well as globalized contexts that involved several nation-states. First, some families became transnational because of certain disadvantages experienced by some new immigrants, and because of internal colonialism practiced within the United States based on socially constructed racialized boundaries. These constructions are legacy of a world hierarchy from a colonial era. Other husbands or wives continued to conduct their business in Taiwan to benefit from a more favorable environment for their businesses. Second, the breadwinners in these families were able to support the families in the Untied States with income generated in Taiwan due to its economic ascendancy, made possible by geopolitics, in a globalized world economy with increasingly integrated production systems.

In the following pages I first view Taiwan's economic ascendancy in a global political economy beginning in the 1950s from a world-system perspective, next I discuss the disadvantages faced by the husbands/fathers of transnational families.

GLOBALIZATION AND TAIWAN'S ECONOMIC DEVELOPMENT

Taiwan's industrialization and its economic miracle enabled the Taiwanese immigrants to support two households, forming their transnational families in Taiwan and the United States. Normally, industrialization is an end result of purposeful planning. According to Dicken, there are three general types of industrialization strategies: 1) Local processing of raw materials; 2) import-substituting manufacturing; and 3) export-oriented industrialization (1992: 177). With both Chinese expertise and American assistance, Chiang Kai-shek's KMT (the Nationalist Party) regime adopted all three strategies.

However, Taiwan's economic success in the last few decades was more than the outcome of industrializing strategies. Taiwan's economic development was tied to the interconnection of geopolitics and economy affecting different nation-states, in sum, the globalization of political economy before and after the Second World War. The section below situates Taiwan's economic development in the political economy that involves multiple nation-states in disparate space and time. I first discuss Japanese colonial occupation in Taiwan beginning in the late nineteenth century, the subsequent KMT regime and United States foreign aid that aimed to contain communist China and the former Union of Soviet Socialist Republic (USSR). Then I look at the timely world economic restructuring that gave Taiwan the opportunity to grow rapidly.

Taiwan's colonial experience started with the world system in East Asia of the nineteenth century. After the Meiji restoration, westernization made Japan a military core in the region although it stood only as the semi-periphery to the larger world system centered in the West. Requested by Korea, China sent its troops in 1894 to help suppress Korea's domestic problem: the Tonghak Rebellion that had developed within the country. Japan came uninvited. When the rebellion was suppressed, China evacuated its troops but Japan remained. Again at Korea's request, China once again sent its troops to drive out Japan, and the two countries started the Sino-Japanese War on Korean soil. When Japan defeated China, it ceded Taiwan by the Treaty of Shimonoseki in 1895 and Taiwan became a colony of Japan.[2] Taiwan first served as the periphery for the core of Japan. Later Taiwan became the military base for Japan's Southern Invasion to the periphery in Southeast Asia and South China, to form Japan's ambitious East Asia Greater Co-Prosperity Sphere that would become a world system in the region, and part of the global world system as a whole.

During its colonial occupation, Japan instigated land reform, updated Taiwan's infrastructure, building additional railroads and harbors, hydro-electric power, transportation, and sanitation systems. It began six years of public education, and Taiwanese elites were able to attend universities in Japan (Lamley 1999). After the First World War, heavy industries such as chemicals, textiles, and machinery began to grow in Taiwan. It later supplied Japan its war machines during the Second World War. By the 1930s, Taiwan was producing far more rice and sugar than it needed, and nearly two-thirds of its crops went to Japan (Copper 1996: 30–31). Under a police state, Taiwanese became mostly an obedient colonial population. Japan conscripted Taiwanese in Japan's confrontation with the Western Allies during the Second World War. Japan lost the War and surrendered Taiwan in 1945.

However, the disciplined labor force, increased human capital, improved physical infrastructure, and ties with Japan accumulated during the colonial era constituted the early contributions to Taiwan's later economic ascendance in the world economy of the twentieth century.

The KMT headed by Chiang Kai-shek evacuated to Taiwan in the name of the Republic of China, when it lost the civil war to Mao Zedong's Communist Party that established the People's Republic of China in 1949. Shortly after the takeover of Taiwan, the KMT regime declared martial law on the island that, among others, prohibited labor unionization and public demonstration resulting in a disciplined labor force. It implanted another land reform: "37.5 percent reduction in farm land rents, the release of public land for farming, and the transfer of farm land ownership to the tiller" (Chiu 1992: 155). The KMT elevated the quality of human resources. It expanded public education from six to nine years. Institutions of higher learning increased from four in 1952 to fifteen in 1960 (Wang 1999: 329). Chiang Kai-shek's totalitarian state suppressed labor activism, and the labor force was both literate and disciplined. These policies all helped account for Taiwan's eventual economic success, despite the oppression that the same state instilled.

More important, Taiwan's economic ascent was a development in a time and space made possible by global political economy: the geopolitics of that historical juncture and the increasing globalization of economic activities in the past few decades. The end of the Second World War ushered in the beginning of the Cold War. Mainland China sided with the USSR with its eastern bloc versus the Allies of the West. To maintain its military hegemony and to "contain communism," the United States provided financial and military aids to Taiwan, just as it did to South Korea, South Vietnam, parts of Latin America and the Middle East. The United States continued to pour technical and financial assistance on the island where the KMT kept its rhetoric of reclaiming China from Mao's Communist regime. According to CIA figures, between 1945 and 1978 Taiwan received $5.6 billion, or $425 per capita in military and economic aid including loans and grants (Aseniero 1994: 289). The Taiwan Strait that separates island Taiwan from Mainland China is the equivalent of the thirty-eighth parallel that demarcates communist North Korea and South Korea of the first world. Taiwan acted as a buffer for the United States in its combat against communism. American economic aid to Taiwan ceased in 1964, but the Vietnam Conflict erupted in Southeast Asia, involving the United States. Taiwan financially benefited from American bases in Taiwan and spending in the region.

"The state has, whether explicitly or implicitly, played an extremely importantly role in the process of industrialization in all countries" (Dicken 1992: 148). With American financial and technical aid, in the 1950s Taiwan's central government installed an import-substitution program to produce for its own consumption, particularly textiles for daily necessities and fertilizers for its agricultural sector, complemented by some products that had export potentials (Wang 1999: 329). Import-substitution reduces capital outflow to pay for imported goods, and residents consume local products to protect the nation's industries in the initial stage so that the industrial structure can develop. It also reduces dependence on foreign technology and capital (Dicken 1992: 177).

Later in the 1960s Taiwan went full-force into an export-oriented economy (Chiu 1992: 155), made possible in the context of a globalizing economy. First, labor cost had risen in industrialized nations making Taiwan's lower wage attractive, and the Taiwan state encouraged labor-intensive industries. Second, industrialized nations such as the United States and Japan headed toward production in advance technology, leaving room for Taiwan's manufacturing industries like shoes, clothing, electronics, foodstuff, and the like. The Taiwan government established export-processing zones and other tax incentives that attracted foreign industrial investments, and excised no tariffs on import materials for the manufacturing of export goods. That lowered the costs of production for goods. Further, the government liberalized foreign exchange control, reactivated banks to finance domestic enterprises, and to facilitate international trade as well as foreign exchanges (Wang 1999: 332). These measures eased the movement of money for business transactions and capital investments in both the local and foreign spheres.

Another government policy was the use of foreign direct investments (FDI) in the form of transnational corporations (TNCs), the major venue of FDI (Dicken 1992: 47). TNCs are aspects of economic globalization, facilitated by the advances in transportation and communication technology. These inventions shortened the time and geographical distance required to conduct business, management, coordination, production, transaction, and delivery of goods among territorial locations far from one another (Dicken 1992: 192). Examples of technological innovations included the fax machines, emails, the internet, and electronic transfers that provide almost instantaneous transmittals of funds, documents, and messages that all lead to time and space compression.

Japan and United States were the two nation-states most involved with investments in Taiwan. They were also two of the leading nations in FDI by 1985 (Dicken 1992: 52–53). In order to counter the inexpensive imports from Japan, especially electronics, firms in the United States relocated manufacturing operations to Taiwan (and Mexico) in the periphery where wages were low. American manufacturers such as Admiral, Maganox, RCA, GTE, and Zenith built subsidiaries or bought existing plants in Taiwan (Turner 1982: 56 as cited in Dicken 1992: 339). Following the same strategy, Japanese firms also moved certain facilities to Taiwan to take advantage of its cheap labor (Aseniero 1994: 291).

This is a classic example for the Marxian theory of surplus value from the exploitation of labor, practiced in a global economy with international division of labor (Sassen 1988), where nation-states from the core in the world system exploit labor of nation-states in the periphery or semi-periphery for profit maximization. Japanese and American large enterprises invested in Taiwan independently or in joint ventures with Taiwanese partnership. Within Asia, Japan's electronic component and consumer electronic assembly plants were mostly concentrated in Taiwan by 1990 (Dicken 1992: 333, 339), partly due to their former colonial relationship. While large American firms also set up plants or companies in Taiwan, local Taiwanese small enterprises co-existed with these large industrial structures from the cores.

Another development that contributed to Taiwan's miracle is international subcontracting indicative of a global economy. International subcontracting is characterized by fragmentation. Instead of the Fordist assembly line mode of production where all parts of a product are manufactured and assembled in the same locale, international subcontracting is a flexible and fragmented production process. Discrete parts and components of a single product are subcontracted out to other manufacturers in different geographic locations before the final assemblage of the finished product. International subcontracting allowed the processing in less developed areas in the semi-periphery or periphery, where cost of production is cheaper, of parts used for advance technology in industrialized countries of the core. Taiwan captured its niche in this process. The advent in technology and the post-Fordist production system made room for Taiwan's flexible small to medium-size enterprises in international subcontracting. The many skilled professionals trained in the United States and Taiwan provided leadership. In addition to the above, the presence of what Deo (1989) calls the subordinated workers beneath the miracle, many of them young women (Gates 1987: 71–72), gave Taiwan a competitive edge in the global economy. It became one of the major players in international subcontracting, particularly in the computer industries. Since most of the manufacturers were small to medium enterprises, the state supported the research and development as well as innovation effort in the private sectors. It also established the Hsin Chu Science Park that houses the computer industry's research and development facilities.

Even Taiwan's electronic industry grew out of the world system relationship between the United States and Taiwan. Liu (1987, Tables 24 and 25, cited in Park 1992: 89) shows that more than twenty percent of executives in large Taiwanese firms had studied abroad largely in Japan and the United States. Many had worked in American firms before returning to Taiwan. In particular, they made significant contribution to Taiwan's competitiveness in the semiconductor industry. Taiwan's former Premier Y. S. Sun was once trained at the Tennessee Valley Authority in the United States from 1943 to 1945. He recruited several engineers in the United States, who were formerly from Taiwan, to help launch the semiconductor industry in the 1970s. The state government held bi-annual seminars that provided the main communication link between Taiwan and American engineers formerly of Taiwan (Meaney 1994: 174).

Morris Chang was another prominent figure in this industry hired back to Taiwan from the United States. Chang was a former group head at Texas Instrument and then chief executive officer at General Instruments. After his return to Taiwan, Chang recruited his former American associates to Taiwan (ibid.: 183). Between 1983 and 1989, the two Taiwan government technical review boards consisted mostly of U.S. residents formerly from Taiwan. Acer, the leading computer manufacturer in Taiwan, hired many professionals from IBM also formerly of Taiwan (ibid.: 187). Taiwan's former students to the United States contributed significantly to the increasingly interwoven texture of economic ties between these two countries, between Taiwan and the rest of the world.

Those who returned to Taiwan tended to perpetuate the educational domination of the core country. Many local institutions in Taiwan were heavily influenced by American curricula and management systems. Returnees were American trained and brought back American educational ideas, texts used, connections, and scientific methods of inquiry. They applied methods and evaluation standards learnt from the United States (Cheng and Yang 1998: 633; Liu and Cheng 1994). American educational influence was evident among high-ranking governmental officials in Taiwan. Former President Lee Teng-hui received his doctoral degree from Cornell University. In 1997, twenty-three out of the president's thirty-eight cabinet members held educational degrees from foreign universities, and seventeen of these twenty-three had studied in the United States, followed by three in Japan, two in Europe, and one in Canada (McBeath 1998: 93). In 1996, seventy-two of the 164 legislators had studied abroad. Fifty-one were educated in the United States, only eleven in Japan, six in Europe, and four in other countries (ibid.: 99). While the statistics reflect a highly educated governing body, they also bespeak the strong hierarchical relationship between the United States and Taiwan, the core and the periphery in a world system of education.[3]

While returnees to Taiwan injected human capital on the supply side, American professionals formerly of Taiwan further strengthened the close business relationship between Taiwan and the United States. Several high tech firms in the Silicon Valley of California were owned and operated by entrepreneurs originated from Taiwan, as were many computer business owners in southern California. Their personal and professional ties that transcended the territorial boundaries of both the United States and Taiwan gave them networks that facilitated the economic development of Taiwan. For example, members of the Southern California Computer Business Association went back and forth to Taiwan to place orders and participate in trade shows, as Taiwan turned into a manufacturing center in the semiconductor industry. The linkages between the two countries in the Pacific Rim were dense and frequent. One of the men I interviewed was a businessman. He commented on the situation to me thus, "Taiwan is the fifty-first state of the United States."

Taiwan became the fastest growing economy in the world in the 1960s. Export growth rose "from US$174 million in 1960 to US$1.56 billion in 1970—eightfold growth" (Wang 1999: 333). The gross national product per capita in 1981 constant prices grew from 5.1 percent in 1980 to 10.7 percent in 1987. In new Taiwan dollars it escalated from NT$94,580 in 1980 to NT$146,111 in 1987. The overall monthly earning growth rate was 81.7 percent in 1987 (Fields 1992: 397–402). When labor-intensive industry declined in the late 1980s and 1990s, information technology industry became the leading manufacturing sector. Assisted by government programs, Taiwan supplied almost fifty percent of the world's computer hardware and peripherals by 1996. Taiwan's trade surplus totaled US$18.7 billion by 1987. By 1996 its cumulative trade surplus exceeded US$100 billion, second only to Japan (McBeath 1998: 121–25).

This robust economic performance in Taiwan brought living standard up, and the surplus savings of its citizens enabled some breadwinners to support split households: one with a spouse and children living in the United States, and the other with a spouse working in Taiwan to support those in the United States, forming the Taiwanese American transnational families. Some husbands, and occasionally wives, continued to run their businesses in Taiwan. Professionals remained in or returned to Taiwan for better opportunity due to certain disadvantages encountered in the United States, including non-transferability of skill and licenses as discussed below.

DISADVANTAGES EXPERIENCED IN THE AMERICAN WORKPLACE

Transferability of skills has long been identified as one of the determinants of economic progress for immigrants. As Chiswick has observed, "Immigrants from countries with a language, culture, technology, and economic and legal structure similar to that in their destination would find their skills more readily transferable than those from countries with greater differences" (Chiswick 1979: 378). Like Hong Kong astronaut families, immigrants from Taiwan encountered disadvantages in the Untied States because their qualifications and work experience were not recognized, or they lacked English proficiency. One problem posed on them was the non-transferability of professional license or certificate. Chang's situation exemplified such a case. Chang and her children immigrated to the United States in 1988. She told me that her husband did not live with her and the children. Instead, he continued to work in Taiwan but flew to visit the family here from time to time. Other times Chang would fly back to visit. I asked her why the husband decided to live in Taiwan. Chang attributed the situation to her husband's profession and non-transferability of his license. She said,

> My husband is a physician. He's already a director of a hospital in Taiwan at the time. If he came here he would have to take the local board exams. Then he would have to do internship and everything from the beginning. My parents-in-law had wanted him to live here with us together, but we discussed with the children and decided that he would stay in Taiwan.[4]

The issue of licensing is not the only obstacle to overcome. Language barrier is another. In Taiwan, I met the grown son of a former transnational family that used to be split between Taiwan and California. This son was interested in my research topic because that was precisely his family situation when he was growing up, and he invited me to give a public lecture on the topic at the university where he worked. I met his parents and their family friends at a sumptuous seafood lunch hosted by his parents before their attendance at my lecture. Subsequent to this event, I was able to interview the father, Mr. Wang, but only over the telephone due to his busy schedule at the time. Mr. Wang and his family immigrated to California on the fifth preference (sponsorship by sibling) of the 1965 Immigration and

Nationality Act. Mr. Wang's brother had completed his doctoral education in the United States where he remained to work and live. This brother sponsored Mr. Wang and his family. In the early 1980s, Mr. Wang, his wife, and their daughters and sons all immigrated together to California. At the time, the age of the children ranged from nine to nineteen.

Mr. Wang reflected as follows, "I didn't produce much in the United States." He had long been a school principal in Taiwan. Although he had many years of experience in his line of profession, in the United States he could not get the kind of jobs that he was trained for. I asked him why. Instead of alluding to non-transferability of teaching licenses, he said, "It's mainly the language." Mr. Wang had completed his university education in Taiwan where the language of instruction was written Chinese and spoken Mandarin (versus Cantonese in Hong Kong). When he moved to the United States, he did not speak much English even though he was an educated person. "So what did you do?" I asked him. He answered, "I did piecemeal work. My brother had a real estate company so I helped him there. I did maintenance and repair work on houses." In other words, he worked as a handyman at first. Mr. Wang was well mannered. He spoke and acted with a natural air of authority. During the lunch that he hosted, he told us about the art film festival that he and his son both attended, because they were trying to bring in more film artists and their productions to the local people. I found it difficult to envision him as a manual laborer.

Evidently he also did not see that kind of work as a permanent solution. He and his wife soon opened a Chinese restaurant. They chose the restaurant business for a calculated reason. Mr. Wang said that a restaurant offered different kinds of job requiring low skill. Their own children could work in the same restaurant part-time while they were attending school and full time during their summer vacations. He said, "When we had the restaurant, the kids had a place to work as well. They worked on the cash register, as a bus boy, waiter, and waitress. I did maintenance work and repaired houses, and my wife took care of the restaurant business." Mrs. Wang also attended the lunch with us on the day of my public lecture. She donned a long sleeve white silk blouse and an A-skirt in pastel lilac complete with high heels. She was a gracious hostess, greeting and exchanging words with every guest in turn at the table. There was a large diamond ring mounted on platinum on her left index finger. Both husband and wife worked hard in manual labor after migration to the United States mostly due to their inadequacy in English.

Taiwanese immigrants made up a high percentage in entrepreneurship among Asian immigrants despite their high level of education in their countries of origin. Koreans immigrants as well demonstrated a concentration in grocery stores, dry-clean services, and import-export businesses. An export-oriented economy in their countries or origin (Chin, Yoon and Smith 1995), and the immigrants' business skill and resources accumulated before migration (Tseng 1995) both contributed to their high proportion in entrepreneurship. However, the language barrier indeed constituted one of the reasons that turned many new immigrants to self-employment. By comparison, Filipino Americans and South Asian Americans had encountered less difficulty of the same nature. The Philippines is a former American colony where the language of educational instruction is English. India was a colony of Britain until 1947. Educated Filipinos and South Asians generally have commanded proficiency in English in their former home countries. Many Filipinos have worked in the United States as physicians and nurses, while South Asians show a concentration in engineering as well as the medical field. Even Filipina who work as domestic helpers command English well enough. But in Taiwan, the language of educational instruction is Mandarin Chinese. In the past, English was not taught until the ninth grade although it is now incorporated in primary education curricula. Due to this language disadvantage, Mr. Wang eventually returned to Taiwan and again worked as a school principal, while the wife continued to run the restaurant and the children attended school in California. This arrangement continued until the wife returned to Taiwan in the early 1990s.

New immigrants face other disadvantages. More then one husband interviewed repeatedly voiced their unfamiliarity with local business environment. After immigrating to the United States, one husband was not sure if he should start his own business or work for someone else in California, so he first worked as an employee to learn about local conditions. Although he made about US$4,000 per month managing a warehouse, he was the one person responsible for all the work involved: office duties, locking up, janitorial service, and any necessary manual labor. Although he did not mind this kind of work, his wife disapproved of his "downward displacement." She said, "In Taiwan he was the boss. He dressed up in suits and his subordinates respected him. Here he works like a laborer." After about two years in southern California, the husband was contacted by a former employer in Taiwan to assume an executive position in the office in Taiwan. The wife encouraged the husband to accept the offer, so he returned to Taiwan and started the transnational family arrangement.

Another husband, Mr. Lo, returned to work in Taiwan where his earning power was higher. He said that his English was considered good in Taiwan, but not in the country of destination where he could not earn as much as he could in his country of origin. In addition, he was more familiar with the investment environment in Taiwan, where he also had friends and business contacts who invested with him in business partnerships. At the time of the interview, he worked as a highly paid corporate executive, invested in the local stock market, and co-owned a few other businesses with his friends who acted as his managing partners. Mr. Lo illustrated the situation with his personal experiences. He summed up his circumstance as follows

> I stay in Taiwan for economic reasons. Here in Taiwan my English is still considered good. I have enough command for my work. Income tax rate is lower in Taiwan, about thirteen to twenty-one percent for me. I am very familiar with the investment environment in Taiwan, and I have friends and contacts here I can invest with together. I also know the local stock market here. The stock market was good for the last three or five years and I made quite a bit of money. . . . So financially, it is more money wise for me to stay in Taiwan.

Transnational husbands were disadvantaged in more ways than one in the United States.

In my sample of twelve husbands interviewed, five pointed out their lack of connection or social network as one disadvantage in their new environment after migration. One remarked, "In Taiwan I was the boss. I knew people in high places. I had connections. We socialized with educated people and the elite. In the U.S. as new immigrants we had none of that." Indeed, social capital (Bourdieu 1980, 1986; Coleman 1988) contributed to some of these people's employment success. Shi's husband needed to return to Taiwan for an extended period to accompany his mother after his father's death. He failed to find a job there on his own for six months. He then visited a former university classmate in Taiwan who had been working in the high tech industry and requested his assistance. During the same period, the husband of Shi's former classmate was visiting in the United States. Shi also told him about her husband's quest for a job. Later, Shi said, "My friend found a job for my husband, his own classmate also got a job for him. So all at one once he got two job offers."

Social capital also played a vital role in the career development of Professor Yang. Yang had come from Taiwan to pursue his doctorate in business management in the United States. His wife accompanied him and during his studies two children were born. After Yang received his doctorate he tried for six months applying for jobs in the United States, all to no avail. At that point a university in Taiwan offered him a teaching position.

He accepted the offer and returned to teach in Taiwan while his wife and children remained behind. According to him, the entire process was conducted over the telephone. The university hired him without any face-to-face interview. I asked him, "Is it common that universities in Taiwan hire professors over the telephone?" He answered, "I did my undergraduate in Taiwan. My former mentor was teaching at this university. This former mentor highly recommended me to the university." Yang was able to launch his professorial career partly as a consequence of his social capital accumulated in Taiwan.

Various disadvantages, in addition to the lack of necessary social capital, handicap not just new immigrants alone. As cited in Zhou and Gatewood (2000: 20), the U. S. Commission on Civil Rights points out that U.S. born Asian children and similar to other American children "suffer from persistent disadvantages merely because they look 'foreign.'" The various disadvantages affect former graduate students who have worked and lived here for a long time as well as those who are native born, despite their possession of requisite educational or professional qualifications and experiences. Being a country of immigrants, the workplace in the United States often face issues that concern workers from different ethnic and racialized backgrounds. An important issue involves the presence of glass ceiling faced by Asian American professionals. In 1991 the U.S. Department of Labor offers the following definition for glass ceiling, "The glass ceiling is most clearly defined as those artificial barriers based on attitudinal or organizational bias that prevent qualified individuals from advancing upward in their organization into management level positions" (quoted in Woo 2000: 43). One woman's husband returned to Taiwan because of the glass ceiling that he experienced in the United States. Her name was Jeanette. According to Jeanette, her husband had obtained his doctorate in biochemistry in the United States and worked in the United States in the 1980s. The wife said,

> My husband was in a high position in that firm, but there was no more room for him to advance. He had reached a bottleneck after ten years. He accepted a better job in Singapore. That company paid for our living expenses, accommodation, and the children's tuition fees in a private English school. In 1998 he accepted an even better position in Taiwan.

Although he was sought after in both Singapore and Taiwan to fill high level positions, his career was stagnated at the same level for a long time in the United States where he could not advance any further.

Chen was another former graduate student trained in the United States who also returned to Taiwan for better and higher positions. I met Chen in

Taiwan. I had run a press release in the monthly electronic newsletter of a large business organization for Americans. Mr. Chen was the only private individual who responded to my quest. He wrote that he was one candidate that I was looking for, and that he would be glad to share his experience. I was elated. I went to his office for an interview. At the main entrance of this large premise there were two security guards on the street side of the gate. I needed to check in. I told them the name of the person I was visiting, and they called him to confirm. I was then let through the gate to a kiosk within to check in again. I gave them my government photo identity card to exchange for a visitor's badge to wear on my jacket. From the kiosk I proceeded to the main building of the offices, where more security guards stood by to make sure that I had security clearance with the visitor's badge. Then I was guided to the main reception area. I gave the receptionist my name, the purpose of my visit, and the person I was visiting. She called Chen to inform that I had arrived and to confirm that indeed he was expecting me. In about ten minutes Chen appeared at the reception area. He led me to a small conference room where he shared his experience with me. Although Chen did not attribute his situation to glass ceiling, his experience pointed to this problem.

Chen received his doctorate in industrial engineering in the United States in the mid 1980s. Subsequently he accepted a position in an American computer company and he later became an American citizen. He was already married in Taiwan before he left, so his wife went with him and studied together. Their children were all born and raised in the United States. According to Chen, he and his wife decided to study in the United States because graduate schools and industries in Taiwan were not very advance in those early years. There was a limit to how much he could learn in Taiwan. By his own account, his career in the United States had been smooth, but salaries were just average. Chen offered his own explanation for his average salary. He said,

> Consider our handicap. First, there is the language barrier. English is not our first language. Then your connection with the local society and your network is just not deep or extensive. If it is only your professional skills that matter, there is no problem. But there is more than that in our industry.

Chen and his wife moved to California for another job in an aerospace corporation, but he conceded that he did not feel all that comfortable there. He commented as follows,

> The company recognized my technical talent, but I just could not advance
> to any managerial position. I had no social contact with management
> personnel outside of work. It had to do with the entire environment and
> culture. . . . In my industry back then, besides technical skill you needed
> communication skill, you needed to know how to handle things and
> people in the way it was done, the culture. . . . Operation in organiza-
> tion needs network, cultural understanding, not just technical knowl-
> edge. So I was handicapped in those ways.

In a study on workplace discrimination, fifty-seven percent of Asian
American employees feel that they have a "harder time finding a sponsor,
or mentor, than whites." Forty-two percent feel that they are "likely to be
excluded form informal networks by whites." On the other hand, of the
whites who acknowledge barriers, thirty-two percent of them agree that
minorities are "excluded from informal networks by whites" (Fernandez
and Barr 1995: 257, 260–61, cited in Woo 2000: 45). These informal
networks consist of several nexus: the cliché of old boys club, the ties
cemented by social activities such as a game of golf during the weekend,
the conversations on similar topics, a glass of martini with two olives
over lunch, or a beer on Friday happy hours after work all help to cement social relations outside of formal professional ties. There are also
the holiday parties that celebrate Christmas and New Year both at the
workplace and at superiors' homes, and the proper etiquette of what to
say and how to interact with them and their spouses. Who get invited is a
telltale of who are in the bosses' minds. It is not just what one knows but
also whom one knows.

One's own spouse also counts in these occasions. The spouse needs
to be able to fit in and socialize with proper etiquette in this circle. He or
she can add strength to one's upward mobility in the social world. Birds
of the same feather flock together; the caliber of the spouse affirms one's
own. "Taste is a match-maker. . . . Two people can give each other no better
proof of the affinity of their tastes than the taste they have for each other"
(Bourdieu 1984: 243). Further, the status of a man with wealth can be mea-
sured by his wealth. That of a man without wealth is reflected by the caliber
of his wife. Discussing the connection between family status and women,
Papanek (1979: 779) cites a Pathan proverb in Pakistan: "a man is known
from the qualities of his wife." In societies where women usually marry up,
the higher the caliber of the wife as evidenced by such attributes as her reputation, family background, education, social grace, cultural competency,
artistic talent or beauty, the higher the status bestowed upon the husband by
the beholder—the trophy wife.

Woo (2000) studies an aerospace corporation and finds that professionals with cultural backgrounds different from Anglo Americans are impeded in their career advancement. Asian Americans' mannerism and behaviors deemed appropriate in their cultural milieu are perceived to be lacking in leadership and management ability in the boardroom of corporate Anglo America. These day-to-day interactions and attitudes manifest in organizational structures and prevent the full incorporation of certain ethnic groups in the organizations. As Woo (2000: 15) points out in the following:

> The majority of glass ceiling barriers involves subtle biases, sometimes imperceptible or ineffable, quietly or unconsciously reproduced. Some are embedded into the routines or practices of institutions, others reflected in attitudinal orientation, which over time chisel racially contoured outcomes into the workplace experience, even when there is no discriminatory intent.

These biases are acted out in our daily behaviors and some become customary practices that evade our conscious vigilance.

Even Chen did not think that his inability to advance was the result of discriminatory actions. He reflected on the situation and offered the following thoughts, "I do not consider that discrimination. You were outsiders, you went to other people's country and you took their jobs." This apology amounts to blaming the victim; only that in this instance the victim blames himself. It smacks of internalized oppression and a hidden injury of "race" (Osajima 1993: 82). Chen's apology might be polite fiction. Or, to borrow a Marxist term, it might be mystification. Chen was educated in the United States. He was a legal citizen of this nation and not at all a foreigner. He was fully entitled to the rights and privileges conferred on all rightful members of this nation-state. As such he deserved to be promoted according to his human capital when the opportunity arose. However, membership in a nation is also a social construct that varies with perceptions.

Women of transnational families in my sample recounted their own feelings and experiences as Asians in the United States. Ching compared her experiences on the East and West Coasts:

> In Boston there were very few Asians, mostly whites and Mexicans. They looked at me like I was a monster. I felt very uncomfortable. I felt like a third class citizen. Here in California it is different. You see yellow faces everywhere. I feel such a sense of comfort and ease.

Sue related more overt negative treatments due to her phenotype in her daily life activity:

> I definitely feel certain discrimination or racist attitudes in public places. For example, when I go to American supermarkets, the cashiers do not greet me like they do white customers. They see that I am Asian and hardly say a word to me. Sometimes I forget to show my club card and the cashier just charges me regular price without saying a thing. I have heard him asked white customers for club cards when they forgot to show them. It gave me the feeling that I was looked down upon. I do not work so I have no opportunity to experience discrimination in the workplace, but I get it at supermarkets, even at restaurants. When I was in Taiwan I was at least upper-middle class. Why should I come here to put up with such treatment?

Ming more strongly expressed her opinion and reported second hand information on discriminatory practices in the labor market:

> I did not directly experience discrimination in the workplace because I did not work for others as an employee, but my friends told me their experience. They say when you go to look for work, they might not hire you because you are Asian. It's the same with us. We hire Taiwanese first before workers from other ethnic groups. It's not good to live in the United States. Asians live as second-class citizens. In Taiwan I could be king or queen. Why should I put up with such treatment?

These women and men's negative experience is partly a legacy of the racist policies of the United States. As discussed earlier in Chapter Four, several Euro Americans continue to perceive Asian Americans as foreigners and intruders, often with antagonism. The image of a rightful citizen of the United States of America, of an American, is informed in part by the policies of the United States as formulated by the people who held power in the state, from its formative years all the way to the present century. These policies at once reveal the contradiction and inconsistency between the American ideology of democracy and equality versus actuality and legislative practices. The very first 1790 Naturalization Law stipulated that only free white persons were eligible for citizenship. In addition, the 1870 Naturalization Law permitted persons of African descent or origin to become citizens, but Chinese were excluded from eligibility after congressional debates. Both legislations demonstrate that the United States of America was founded on unequal inclusion and exclusion based on racialized boundary.

This image of an American was consistently and legally upheld and reinforced through the centuries, contingent upon racialized categories and skin color. In the Asian American experience, two landmark legal cases attested to such experiences according to race and skin color: the 1922 Ozawa versus the United States case, and the 1923 United States versus Bhagat Singh Thind case. Ozawa was a Japanese immigrant well assimilated into American society. He graduated from high school in Berkeley, California and completed three years of education at the University of California, Berkeley. He then moved to Honolulu. His 1914 application to become an American citizen was rejected. Ozawa challenged the decision to the U.S. District Court for the Territory of Hawaii in 1916. The court denied him eligibility on the ground that he was not white. Ozawa appealed to the Supreme Court. It ruled that "Ozawa was not entitled to naturalized citizenship . . . because he was 'clearly' 'not Caucasian'" (Takaki 1998: 208). The 1923 Thind case involved a naturalized American of South Asian descent, Bhagat Singh Thind. Thind was born in Punjab and immigrated to the United States in 1913. He was drafted into the U.S. military, served for six months, and was honorably discharged. He applied for and was granted American citizenship by the district court. The Immigration and Naturalization Services (INS) appealed Thind's case to the U.S. Supreme Court. Based on the 1790 legislation, it ruled that Asian Indians were ineligible for naturalization because Asian Indians were not white even though they might be Caucasians. The court further noted the 1870 Act. The two federal legislations passed in 1790 and 1870 combined limited American citizenship to whites and blacks. As a consequence of this case, The INS annulled several naturalized citizenships already granted to South Asians (Ng 1995: 1594).

Asians were not the only group excluded. Native Americans were not allowed citizenship until 1924 although they were native to this land, and their arrivals by far predated those of the founding fathers of the United States. In recognition of China as a wartime ally, the United States granted citizenship eligibility to Chinese in 1943, and to Filipinos and Asian Indians in 1946. After Mao Zedong's Communist Party took China in 1949 followed by the outbreak of the Korean War in 1950, Japanese also became eligible for citizenship in 1952 when the United States courted Japan to ward off the spread of communism. Racialized American citizenship officially ended in 1952 when the Congress reformed naturalization statute. Arguably, Asian Americans continued to be excluded by the quota system until the 1965 Naturalization Act.

And then, even if they have become legal members of this country, Asian Americans continue to be perceived as foreigners (Tuan 1998). When Chinese American figure skater Michelle Kwan lost the gold medal to Polish American Lipinsky, the media blasted "American beats Kwan" as if Kwan was a foreigner, although she was a bona fide American born and raised in southern California. When Kwan lost in the 2002 Winter Olympic, the Seattle Times again headlined "American outshines Kwan." The paper's executive editor later apologized twice. Another example is Chinese American nuclear physicist Wen Ho Lee, the former Los Alamos scientist falsely accused by the United States government of being a spy for China, partly because of his Chinese ancestry (for Lee's account of this incident see Lee and Zia 2001).

Membership of a group that is not Euro American in the United States also places one in an internal colonial relationship vis-à-vis the dominant group (Blauner 1972). This relationship exists between the dominant and dominated groups within the same nation-state, just like the former colonial relationship between Americans or Europeans and Africans, Asians, or Latinos where the former were the colonizers of power who conquered, ruled, and subordinated the colonized subjects in Africa, Asia, and Latin America. This relationship between the colonizers and the colonized subjects among Americans within the single polity of the United States corresponds to their ancestral countries of origin in the hierarchical political world order based on military might.

Historically, European immigrants to the United States constitute the dominant group. These transplanted Europeans mostly managed to blend in to Middle America, leading to Milton Gordon's assimilation theory (1965). If an immigrant works hard, learns the language and local customs, he can move up from the bottom and achieve the American dream. He will become one of the many Americans. This indeed has worked for many Americans of European descent, including the Irish and southern and eastern Europeans despite continued anti-Semitism. But the performance of African Americans, Asian Americans, and Latin Americans appeared to pale by comparison. In large part, Euro Americans have held political, socioeconomic, and cultural powers over the minority groups of people formerly colonized by the Europeans. That includes the Asian Americans who initially entered the United States in the nineteenth century as stoop laborers in an already developed capitalistic economy dominated by Euro Americans (see, among others, Cheng and Bonacich 1984; Daniels 1988; Takaki1989; Chan 1991a).

Advances in civil rights have removed some racialized legal barriers such as segregation in housing, schools, and public places but only to certain extent. Some even argue that Asian Americans have become a model minority,[5] with high income and high student enrollment in elite universities. The model minority thesis turned out to be largely a myth (see Cheng and Yang 2000). First, the statistics accounting for their high income were gathered in urban cities where incomes were higher along with higher cost of living. In addition, their high median income per household were combined income pooled from several members of the same household, compared to the high income earned by a single member or two members of a white household (see Osajima 1988). High ratio of Asian American students at elite universities had created controversy. In the 1980s, complaints were filed against Brown University, Harvard University, Stanford University, Yale University, as well the Berkeley and Los Angeles campuses of the University of California that limited undergraduate admission of Asian Americans (for details see Au 1988 and Takagi 1990). These charges were based on statistical evidences, but the universities also interpreted the same statistics to defend its policies. One example is a practice at the University of California, Berkeley. In 1985 a Task Force charged that Berkeley implemented policy changes, unannounced, to intentionally reduce Asian American admission. As Takagi (1999: 580) points out, "For two years, the university officials denied that the SAT minimum policy had been implemented." The policy memo, written by Director of Admission Robert Bailey (1984) to Vice-Chancellor Laetsch, surfaced in 1987. After investigations and a hearing by state senator Art Torres, he scolded university officials "for their failure to recognize that Asians were disadvantaged in the admission process" (ibid.: 589). Shortly after, Berkeley Chancellor Heyman issued an apology to the Asian community for having disadvantaged Asian American applicants.

Contemporary domination within the United States is carried out by different mechanisms in society including the labor market. This market is segmented into the primary and secondary sectors. The primary and secondary markets are characterized by occupations, with white-collar jobs in the primary sector and blue-collar jobs in the secondary sector (Edwards, Reich, and Gordon 1975; Gordon, Edwards, and Reich 1982). Both the primary and secondary sectors are further divided into the first and second tiers. Within the primary sector, the first tier made up of managerial and decision-making positions are held by members of the dominant group in society, namely Euro Americans. Members of other ethnic groups and women are mostly confined to the second tier of the primary and secondary sectors, even though women, other ethnic groups, and Euro Americans may belong to the same class under capitalism (Baron 1975; Piore 1975; Stevenson 1975). Assigned to a subaltern position, Asian Americans could only advance so much in a segmented labor market that is informed by the ideological legacy of colonialism, and structured by the internal colonial relationship. The Federal Glass Ceiling Commission found the following:

Non-Hispanic White males hold 95 to 97 percent of all managerial positions in the private sector. Women hold only 3–5 percent of senior positions and Asian/Pacific Islander Americans less than one one-hundredth
of one percent of all corporate directorship (quoted in Woo 2000: 44).

To counter the disadvantages brought by this subordinated position
in a context of colonial relationship between the dominant and dominated
groups in the United States, and making it only in the second tier of the
primary sector in a segmented labor market, Chen looked for opportunities where his human, social, and cultural capitals worked most to his
advantage. He found it in his former country of Taiwan. He managed to
obtain satisfactory employment there. He said, "Our friends helped me
find jobs in Taiwan. So I came back in 1998 and first worked at a small
firm as a consultant. That job gave me a lot of exposure." When I met
Chen in the early spring of 2001, he already became a senior vice president
of an electronic company. After the scheduled one hour of our interview,
the overhead intercom system was paging him to attend the next business
meeting.

While some spouses returned to Taiwan as corporate executives, other
husbands (occasional wives) lived in Taiwan to conduct their businesses. Some
business owners expanded their manufacturing sites to Mainland China and
Southeast Asia to take advantage of cheaper wage labor and lower land cost.
Lu was one of the few women who commuted. She and her family immigrated to the United States in 1990 solely for their children's education. They
came as investment immigrants on the E1 visa by purchasing sixty percent
of an existing American business. They invested over US$1 million. Lu said,
"I fly back and forth to take care of the factories in Taiwan and Mainland."
She returned home to see her family in southern California. The husband
of another woman Kai commuted between Taiwan and Shanghai where
he also owned a business. After Kai and her son immigrated to the United
States in 1997, the husband flew between the United States, Taiwan, and
China. Some husbands were employees of firms in Taiwan that sent them to
work in China while the family lived in the United States. They commuted
between China, Taiwan, as well as the United States. A sibling sponsored
Yu and her family to immigrate to the United States, and they received their
green cards before 1994. They went back to work for a Taiwan firm that
later sent the husband to China in 1994. In 1999 Yu and her child returned
to the United States to qualify for citizenship residence requirement while
the husband worked in China, reported to Taiwan, and flew to the United
States for family reunion.

Other husbands had originated from Taiwan to pursue their doctorates in the Untied States. They were then hired by American corporations and became citizens. Beginning in the early 1980s, these American corporations started to send them to Taiwan, Korea, or China to work in the branches or subsidiaries in those countries. The career path of Dana's husband reflected the crisscrossing of global capitalism. He received his graduate training in the United States and first worked for an American company in southern California. Later an electronic firm in Taiwan hired him so he went from the United States to Taiwan. The company then sent him to Beijing, China. Later in Beijing he was hired by a German enterprise that sent him to Singapore and Malaysia. Dana and the children followed camp but returned to the United States for the children's schooling in 1997, while the husband stayed in Asia and commuted back and forth until he returned to work for an American company in southern California. On the other hand, Kate's husband worked for an American electronic company after his graduation in the United States. In the 1980s the company often sent him to Asia for training. Her traveling family life in part mapped out the traverse of the global economy. Kate relived the journeys as follows,

> In 1982 my husband joined Hewlett Packard. HP often sent him to Asia for training. Then they sent him to South Korea when HP undertook a joint venture with Samsung of South Korea. Then HP sent our whole family to Taiwan for two years, and then to Hong Kong. Four years later they sent us to Beijing and we stationed there for eight years as expatriates.

The global economy impacts on individual social relations. Kate remembered some of such effects on her husband's colleagues. She commented, "It's not uncommon that couples went away on overseas assignment and returned as divorced singles." Husbands on assignment remained preoccupied with work, and spouses were left to their own to handle family life and adjustment to an unfamiliar environment. Dana remarked,

> The whole time we stationed in Beijing my husband was always on business trips to other parts of China, to Europe, to the States. . . . He was not with us much at all. He was on the phone even if he returned home. . . . He would be home for one week then he would be gone on business trips.

Kate gave credit to a transnational corporation's concern for family integrity. She recounted the effort made by her husband's company before it transferred them to China. She said:

> Before the company even offered the opportunity to my husband, my husband's boss and his wife, this boss's big boss and his wife invited us out for dinner. The six of us were all together. At the dinner, the big boss casually asked me how I felt about living overseas if my husband was given an assignment in Asia. I answered that I would gladly live in Asia for a while since I left Taiwan long time ago. Only after that did they later promoted my husband to the overseas position. I give credit to this company. Looking back, I am sure that it would not have given the assignment had I harbored a strong feeling against it.

The above experiences reflected the increasingly globalized production relationships. These production relations are processes in globalization that interconnect various parts of the world into an integrated whole, at a historical juncture etched out by a globalized political economy. This global political economy provided the backdrop to nurture a Taiwan miracle that helped supply the economic resources for the formation of the Taiwanese American transnational families. Without this most causal financial ability, no spouse would be able to support a family in the United States with income generated in Taiwan.

SUMMARY

Due to various disadvantages faced by the Taiwanese immigrants in the United States and shifting capitalist expansion of production sites and markets, husbands and wives from Taiwan adopted the split household transnational family strategy to maximize returns on their labor. To capitalize the most of their various forms of capitals, they engaged in economic activities in Taiwan at a time when Taiwan could afford to compensate them sufficiently. Families could financially support two households, one in the United States and one in Taiwan, with income and profit generated in Taiwan for living expenses incurred in the United States where the cost of living is supposedly higher.

This is contrary to the usual pattern of migrants working in the United States to send remittances to support the family in their countries of origin where the cost of living is much lower, like the Filipino domestic and construction workers, the migrants from the South Asian subcontinent, Mexico, Puerto Rico, the Caribbean, other countries in Latin America and

Africans in Europe, and so on. This reversal is made possible by Taiwan's economic ascendance in the world economy. Taiwanese American transnational families arose from the opportunities that grew out of a global political economy. This chapter thus analyzed the macroscopic global and intermediate local backgrounds. The next chapter discusses the dynamics of Taiwanese American transnational families at the familial and individual levels.

Chapter Seven
Migration Decision and Power Relations

The last chapter situates migration and the formation of Taiwanese American transnational families in the historical context of geopolitics, global economy, and disadvantages in the society of Taiwan and the United States for the children and parents. This chapter turns to the dynamics in the decision to migrate and power relations at the family and individual levels with gender and generational perspectives.

A variety of theories exist to explain the initiation of international migration in both the macro and micro dimensions. Focusing on the micro level, neoclassical economics views the individual as the decision maker who migrates for income maximization. The new economics of migration focuses on a family or a household as the unit that uses migration to minimize income risk or to better control resources (Massey 1999; Massey, et al. 1993). For example, Harbison (1981) stresses the importance of family as the unit of analysis in the decision to migrate; Pessar (1982) advocates the primacy of the household in the study of migration decision-making. Migration decision-making is not polarized into the individual on the one hand, and the family or household on the other. It ranges from an individual's deliberation to a family project (Lauby and Stark 1988: 474), as exemplified by Taiwanese American transmigration with split household arrangement. It represents a family's strategy to counteract socioeconomic and political forces, as well as individual efforts to circumvent personal situations. In both instances, migration is a move that involves the relocation of the family and full participation, although not equal decision-making, of all family members.

In addition to the global context, migration decision-making is contingent upon the individual's particular circumstances and gender; it is also influenced by social and cultural milieu. Often these decisions are embedded in the relations of power position between genders and within the family, where family is in turn a microcosm of larger institutional and structural ideology as well as socioeconomic hierarchy. My interviews with the thirty-five women revealed that sometimes parents, parents-in-law, sisters, or brothers also played major roles in the decisions to migrate. Some women talked about migration as determined by all members or some members of the family, whether their influence was direct or indirect. While eight couples jointly decided to migrate (22.8 percent), five women made the decision independently (14.3 percent). For ethnic Chinese Singaporean professionals who migrated from Singapore to work in China, resulting in transnational families in some instances, "in many cases, the wife was presented with a *fait accompli*. This was particularly the case . . . while the wives were in lower-paid jobs" (Willis and Yeoh 2000: 258). Out of the thirty-five women in my sample from transnational families, sixteen (42.8 percent) indicated that their husbands were the sole decision makers and that they just followed the husbands' wishes, some against their own will, even if they were high-salaried career professionals. This high percentage reflects the social and cultural norms in Taiwan characterized by unequal gender power and hierarchy, as in Singapore (ibid.). Often, migration is a gendered process beginning with the decision to migrate, and including who migrates, how funds are obtained to migrate, where to settle, how jobs are obtained, how long to migrate, and the like.

This chapter examines gender and kinship in the process and mechanism of decision-making prior to migration, within the household and the cultural context of Taiwan. It looks at decisions described by participants as being done at the family level, then at those made by individuals. Conflicts over migration occurred between several of the husbands and wives. In these conflicts in the decision-making process, one can see the gendering of marital power often embedded in the institutional, structural forces of the society, as well as the sources and limits of women's influence in families and wider kin networks.

DECIDING "AS A FAMILY"

As Hondagneu-Sotelo (1994) points out, migration is not always a collective goal and strategy for all members of a family as a unified unit. Rather, it often involves generational conflicts and gender politics. While husbands or wives in some Taiwanese American transnational families jointly or severally made decision to migrate to the United States, other women reported migration as a result of "family consensus" after what they considered to be "democratic" processes. The section below discusses two examples where the entire family participated in decision-making process that reflected more egalitarian relationships across gender and generation.

In Faye's case, she, her husband, and their two children all took active roles to settle on the international move. Faye recounted the process,

> Our older child was thirteen years old in the eighth grade, the second one was nine years old in the third grade. Our questions were: should we come here for the children, and should my husband come to work here in the U.S. or stay in Taiwan and work to support us.

Her husband's brother had applied to sponsor them to come to the United States under the family reunification provision. When the family was notified that they were approved, an extensive set of discussions ensued. They could not come to a consensus. Then they all decided to vote on the issue. As it turned out, Faye was the only one who voted against migration. Respecting the wishes of the majority, Faye joined the rest of her family to come to southern California together in 1997.

Yen and her family also immigrated after several family discussions. Her younger son was in senior high school and the older one had just started college. Her husband's sister, who had come to the United States in the 1970s, sponsored them to immigrate to the United States under the 1965 family reunification provisions. When Yen's family finally received approval to immigrate, the husband, the wife, and both children discussed the issue for a long time before they came to an agreement. Yet even such "consensus" was not reached at once. Although both parents had wanted to migrate for a better educational opportunity for the younger son, who excelled in art but not in academic subjects, the older son named Albert disliked the idea of emigrating. He had just started his freshman year at a prestigious university in Taiwan; he was popular and doing well at the university. He was also reluctant to part with his friends. Eventually his own friends persuaded him to leave. These friends envied his opportunity to study in the United States and convinced Albert of the value in an American education. The chance to study in the United States presented a highly seductive imaginary for those who lacked such opportunity. Albert's friends convinced him that he would not waste any time even if he had to repeat a few years. Had he stayed in Taiwan, they argued, he would have to spend two years in military service at any rate.

The above two cases exemplify fairly democratic processes, an effort to make migration a collective decision as a family unit. In other situations, the husband or the wife initiated the long-distance move. In some cases, the spouses disagreed about migration. The process and outcomes of these conflicts revealed the gender politics of migration decision-making.

DECIDING AS INDIVIDUALS
AND GENDERED POWER RELATIONS

In a well-known classic sociological study of marital power, Blood and Wolfe (1960) pioneer the tradition of using decision-making as a major indicator for marital power, and conclude that spousal contribution of resources constitutes conjugal power positions. Despite criticisms (see, e.g., Gillespie 1971; Sifilios-Rothschild 1970), the outcome of decision-making continues to be the main indicator (McDonald 1970). Studies on the division of labor in Taiwan demonstrate that despite women's labor participation and income contribution, power is still very much in the hands of husbands. Women's roles and positions in the family do not change much with her entry into the labor market, due to state and community support of patriarchy. Husbands are the main decision-makers in most families. As Lu has observed, "Sex role segregation of traditional patriarchal society has a strong effect and accounts for much more of the variance in family power structure and role-playing than does women's employment" (Lu 1983: 143). Even in family enterprises, women's responsibilities and roles are extensions of their roles and responsibilities in the family (Lu 1996).

According to Weber (1947: 152), power is "the probability that one actor within a social relationship will be in a position to carry out his own will despite resistance." In most of the above situations, husbands carried out their will to migrate without significant or effective objection from their wives. On the other hand, while husbands dominated within the family, some women influenced husband's decision-making by persuasion. May, for example, initiated her family's migration through persuading her husband. Between husband and wife, power can also be "the potential ability of one partner to influence the other's behavior. Power is manifested in the ability to make decisions affecting the life of the family" (Blood and Wolfe 1960: 11). May worked as a bookkeeper prior to migration, but her husband was the main breadwinner in the family. She was unable to effect the migration alone, requiring her husband's agreement and financial support. According to May, she had to persuade her husband. May kept telling her husband about the advantages of such a major move. She reasoned with him that the price of housing was very reasonable in southern California compared to that in Taiwan. If they sold the house in Taiwan, she explained, they could afford to buy a very presentable and spacious two-story new house in a suburb with a large backyard and two-car garage. Possession of such a house could be used to boost family standing among friends and relatives. May further suggested that education was too competitive in Taiwan, and that schooling in the United States was much better for their children. The children could even attend public school in the United States free of charge.

However, the above reasons only partly explained May's desire to depart. She also had a hidden agenda. She said, "I wanted to get away from the obligation to my parents-in-law. I figured I'd done my share, so let the other daughters-in-law take care of them."

Although her hidden agenda was to evade an onerous set of obligations towards her husband's parents, May could not effect her family's international migration at will. Instead, she actively negotiated the move to southern California with reasons that emphasized long-term familial benefit. May maneuvered her husband's desire to better the children's education and the social standing of the family, until she achieved her goal to migrate that furthered her personal interests. In this case, May could not bring about changes that she desired without her husband's support. If power is one partner's potential to influence the other to make decision that affect the entire family, then May exercised power by her strategy of persuasion. Women are not always passive in their home environment. Within the constraints of following the husband, some wives exercise power in designing their futures to serve their own interests. As Kranichfeld opines: "if power is defined as the ability to change the behavior of others intentionally, then power is at the core of much of what women do" (1987: 48). However, this power is qualified. The husband retained structural power while the wife had to anticipate his desires and construct a scenario that would help him achieve his ambition. The power of patriarchy rests with the fact that women need to maneuver and persuade.

Instead of attempting to persuade her husband, Kai made a unilateral decision to migrate all on her own. More than twenty years ago her sister had come to the United States for graduate studies. This sister subsequently became a citizen in the 1980s, qualifying her to sponsor siblings under the family reunification provision of the 1965 Immigration and Nationality Act. At that time Kai discussed with her husband the advantages of migrating to the United States. Her husband was a successful business owner in Taiwan. He felt no need to leave home. Since so many people wanted to come to the United States yet could not, Kai thought, she did not want to lose the opportunity. She told the sister to sponsor her, her daughter, and her son, without her husband. When the approval finally came in the 1997, her sister told her to visit first before the move. Kai said, "I told her that's not necessary. I had been here before and I liked it." She moved with her son to southern California while her older daughter attended university in Taiwan, and her husband remained in Taiwan to manage his business. The daughter came home to the United States during school vacation, and her husband visited for family reunion every few months.

Traeger (1984: 1274) and Young (1985: 167) see little impact of wives on migration decision-making in a patriarchal setting. Kai's experience contradicts their claim. In addition, Kai's authority to make an important family decision such as international migration that relocated household residence and mobilized all the family members including the husband, stands in contrast to other research that stresses Blood and Wolfe's resource theory (1960), where the wife gains power in marital relation through her contribution to family income. Kai had resigned from her paid employment, and had stayed home to tend to her family since the birth of her first child. Kai's authority evidently did not derive from her contribution to family income. Pyke (1994) argues that a wife's employment does not necessarily bring her power. A wife would derive less power from paid work if the husband considers her income a threat or a burden rather than a contribution. Alternatively, the husband views her employment as his granting her a favor to allow participation in the labor force, and therefore sees himself as exercising patriarchal authority or even as entitled to greater power. He may assert his dominance in the marital relationship as a compensation for the cost of her contributing income. Further, a wife may garner more power from domestic work if her husband appreciates and values such contribution rather than paid work. In her study on Dominican immigrants, Pessar (1995) finds that some wives stay home instead of work to elevate family social status. In these cases, the husband might value his wife's contribution to domestic work in lieu of income. In a patriarchal context, participants sometimes reported that the "separate spheres" of market work and domestic work also define areas of distinct authority (Kaufman 1991). Hence a woman's choice to remain at home may be indicative of her sphere of influence.

Kai remained at home without participation in the labor market, that is, without contributing directly to the family income. Resource arguments surrounding employment, therefore, cannot explain Kai's power in her marital relationship. In accordance with Pyke's argument above, Kai's power might well have come from her husband's appreciation of her family work. However, both the resource theory and "economy of gratitude" (Hochschild 1989a) focus on the sources of power internal to the couple's relation dynamics and individual effort. In my opinion, Kai's power in this important decision arose not from the economy of gratitude alone, although it appeared to have played a role. In Kai's case, one needs to consider exogenous forces that arose from beyond the dyadic dynamics between husband and wife. Lukes (1974) identifies three dimensions of power: overt power, covert power, and latent power. Applied to a marital relation, a spouse's final say in important decision reflects overt power. A spouse's avoidance of expressing a different opinion to evade conflict exemplifies the other spouse's covert power. Latent power is the ideological forces that shape a person's thoughts and wishes, as in Gramsci's concept of hegemony where the ruling class rules with consent of those being ruled. As Pyke (1996: 528) states, "it is necessary to examine dominant cultural ideologies to understand interpersonal power dynamics." For example, pro-familial orthodox Judaism confirms and values woman converts' roles as mother and wife. It empowers married women to promote their status and interest, and to legitimately make demands on men in their roles as husband and father (Kaufman 1991). However, cultural ideologies do not account fully for Kai's effective agency. I propose that Kai's authority was primarily due to her natal family's elite socioeconomic and political status. In other words, studies of marital power need to account, even in patriarchal settings, for the influence of social class or relative wealth and societal power.

An university graduate, Kai came from a prominent family in her hometown in Taiwan. Her grandfather was a city official and her father attended university in Japan, reflecting their family's elite status. Kai was married to her husband by the careful arrangement of both families with similar background and standing. Her natal family's prestigious position in society bolstered her own status and power in her nuclear family. Kai said, "We have comparable family background. It's very important. In Chinese it is called 'matching doors and households.'" Kai exuded an air of confidence and authority. She said, "My husband might have biological needs or might even have started a secondary little family, but I know he won't abandon this family that I lead. Home is where I live. . . . I have faith in his family." In addition, Kai also maintained control of her family budget in the United States where she kept portions of family assets. In Kai's case, decision-making power derived from her natal family's standing comparable to that of her husband, the reluctance of her husband and his family to displease her natal family (as well as herself), and from her retaining control of marital family resources and assets.

Further, Kai's power relation vis-à-vis her husband also exemplifies one pattern deriving from gendered spheres of influence in patriarchal societies that can be found throughout East Asia. The ideology of public versus private as gendered spheres (Rosaldo 1974; Lamphere 1993) dictates that a man manages the outside world, while a woman the domestic sphere. Although this dichotomy is found to be problematic in some parts of the world, portion of it is applicable in others. In Japan (as well as northern Italy), typically a man hands his monthly income to his wife to manage, and out of his income the wife gives him monthly allowance to spend on himself. Wives decide on domestic expenditures, husbands make decisions regarding business and matters outside of the domestic realm. Kai's comments reflected this traditional gendered ideology, "My husband makes his business decision and I never interfere with the way he runs our family business." Likewise, Kai made all decisions regarding family affairs. She continued, "He manages the outside, I manage the inside. I buy anything for the family or myself, he never interferes." Based on the 1994–1995 Taiwan Social Change Survey, Xu and Lai's findings

> suggests that Taiwanese husbands are more willing to share their power with their wives if the decisions are traditionally made by women (such as household economy), and they are less inclined to do so if the decisions are customarily dominated by men (such as career choices), even if these husbands are well educated . . . the process of decision making is still largely . . . gender polarized (2002: 241).

We need to remember, however, that wives who exercise direct authority over migration is unusual in the sample. The separate spheres argument provides this as only one possible pattern consistent with reproducing patriarchy. Another, and more common pattern, is wives having to convince, persuade, or otherwise maneuver husbands into a decision to migrate or not. Both of these come out of patriarchy and separate spheres—because migration does involve career issues.

The above cases exemplify women's maneuvering or explicit authority. The following section discusses other processes and mechanisms that reveal overt and covert gendered politics in the decision to migrate, as well as persistent structural hierarchy between husband and wife that in some cases resulted in coercion of wives by husbands.

COVERT CONFLICT AND STRUCTURAL POWER

In stark contrast to Kai's ability to make an unilateral decision that affected her entire family, Shi represented a case of covert conflict between husband and wife and her husband's structural power. After graduating from university in Taiwan, Shi came to southern California to assist her relative in a business. Shi's husband was graduated from the most prestigious university in Taiwan and came to the United States for his doctorate in the 1970s. After graduate studies, he obtained employment in southern California and subsequently became an American citizen. They met in California and were married in the early 1980s. Shi worked until the birth of their first child. All their children were American born. When the husband was laid off in the early 1990s, Shi re-entered the labor market to support the family. Although her husband soon obtained employment again, Shi worked until they moved back to Taiwan. The move was not Shi's choice.

They moved to Taiwan because her husband's brother was killed in an accident, and her husband's mother needed considerable emotional support. Her mother-in-law indicated that there were ample high tech jobs available in Taiwan. Shi's husband wanted the whole family to return with him to be close to his parents. Shi and the children were all unwilling to move to Taiwan. When the children first moved there they wanted to know how long it would last. Shi's husband replied that it depended on their grandmother's health. According to Shi, her son got excited when the grandmother passed away. He exclaimed, "Great! Now we can return to the States." But they continued to live in Taiwan to keep the grandfather company. After more than four years, the children failed to adjust well to the educational system in Taiwan. Her daughter was losing confidence in herself at school, and her son experienced problems in his relation with classmates. They teased and bullied him, and one day even pushed him into the swimming pool at school. Finally, Shi told her husband about everything that was happening with the children, and they discussed the situation. Shi said, "In my heart I wanted to return to the United States," but she did not say a word. It was her husband who finally gave the green light. He said, "Why don't you all return to the States!" Shi took her children back to the California, while her husband remained to work in Taiwan. By the time I interviewed Shi, they had been maintaining their transnational family for almost two years.

Discussing the processes of conflict between husbands and wives, Waller and Hill distinguish overt and covert conflicts. "Overt conflict is open and obvious. In covert conflict, one person takes upon himself [sic], in the interest of the relationship, the burden of suppressing some of his [sic] tendencies to act" (1951: 297). Shi's situation exemplified covert conflict. Although no open confrontation surfaced between Shi and her husband, Shi's reluctance underlay the first move to Taiwan. Shi remained silent about her opposition, however, and went along. This silence, of course, does not mean consensus. Shi considered her own silence as a suppression of her wishes and an effort to avoid arguing. It also might have indicated a sense that resistance would not have been effective. This silence indicates what Foucault (1972) considers to be domination by "prohibition of discourse." At this particular given time and circumstance, Shi censored herself as to what to say or not say about the move. Discourse defines who may speak and when to say what, and restricts what is possible to say. Shi's silence demonstrates the husband's domination over the wife, a relation of unequal power.

Shi's situation might also be viewed as what Luke terms "latent conflict." Luke considers both overt and covert conflicts to be observable behaviors. He proposes the notion called latent conflict "which consists in a contradiction between the interests of those exercising power and the real interests of those they exclude" (Luke 1974: 24–25). Komter further explains Luke's latent conflict as "a hidden discrepancy of interests of those exercising power and those subject to this power. The conflict is latent in the sense that it would arise if subordinates would express their wants and desires" (Komter 1989:189). Although Shi did not object openly to the return to Taiwan, she would have chosen to stay in the United States. Shi said,

> When he received the job offers he was very glad but I wasn't. I thought, isn't it better that the kids go to school here? I also preferred the living environment here [in California]. . . . I did not have a good relationship with my mother-in-law.

Shi expressed a counterfactual in her own words above. According to Komter, a counterfactual is "what B would have done (or failed to do) in the absence of A's power" (ibid.). In the absence of her husband's exercise of power, Shi would have stayed in the United States.

The absence of open conflict does not imply contentment or equality. In Shi's case, latent conflict characterized their move to Taiwan, and her subordination pervaded their decision-making processes in both the first move to Taiwan and the subsequent return back to the United States that resulted in their transnational family formation. Komter (1989: 196) refers to the kind of power exercised by Shi's husband as invisible power. Perhaps it is better understood as structural power, since it derived from his position as husband and his wife's subordination as both wife and daughter-in-law in a patriarchal setting where traditionally daughters-in-law subordinate to the husband's parents. Further, Shi's lack of power, hence the source of her husband's power, stemmed from her supposed lower status and position vis-à-vis her husband and his family as perceived by her mother-in-law, and legitimated by what Margery Wolf (1972) has termed "uterine family."

In traditional Taiwan, married couples take up patrilocal residence where the young wife lives as an outsider among her husband's extended family, often dominated by her mother-in-law who claims loyalty and obedience from her children. To combat that estranged position, the young wife, now a mother, actively cultivates close emotional bonds with her children, especially her sons, to build her own "uterine family" within her husband's larger extended family. Her children's strong emotional ties to her turn to loyalty that eventually strengthens the mother's position and power in the husband's extended family. Today, patrilocal residence is still quite prevalent even in the professional strata in Taiwan, and the Confucian notion of a son's filial obligation persists. Shi's mother-in-law lived permanently in Taiwan, and only visited the son's family in the United States from time to time. Yet even in the absence of cohabitation with the mother-in-law, her influence was palpable in Shi's marital relation. Shi said,

> When we decided to get married we telephoned long distance to our families in Taiwan. His mother went to my family, not to talk about the wedding but to check out my family's background. After she checked it out, she told my family that her son had a Ph. D. but I had only a bachelor degree so I was not good enough for him. She said that whenever he returned to Taiwan many rich families introduced their daughters to him. I didn't know she had done that. There were other things. She did not like me much. She was always in the way, and my husband listened to her a lot.

Relationships with mothers-in-law have long posted challenge on social relations. British anthropologist Radcliffe-Brown (1987: 55–56) points out the custom of "mother-in-law avoidance" by men in many parts of the world. Some societies also practice the avoidance between son- and father-in-law. Parents-in-law might not always be troublemakers. However, based on a rural Euro American sample, Bryant, Conger and Meehan (2001) provides empirical evidence that even married couples of more than twenty years express lower perception of marital success as a result of negative relationship with parents-in-law. Tension with parents-in-law transcends cultures and socio-economic class barriers. Problems with parents-in-law have been reported by members of the middle-class as well as working-class (Apter 1986: 20), in geographical areas spreading from the United States to Europe and Asia.

Duvall (1964) finds that the most trying in-law relationship is that between the wife and mother-in-law. Studies have shown that mothers-in-law appear to be particularly threatening and powerful in a spousal relationship (Rich 1976). Her reputation appears to have withstood the test of time:

The Oxford English Dictionary quotes a sixteenth-century remark that 'mothers in lawes bearc [sic] a stepmothers [sic] hate unto their daughters in lawes [sic]; in the seventeenth century, the reference is to the 'everlasting Din of Mothers-in-law'; and the eighteenth-century novelist Fielding acknowledges that 'the word mother-in-law has a terrible sound,' while in the nineteenth century there appeared a comment in the *Daily Telegraph* that 'The drink of this name mother-in-law is composed of equal proportions of "old" and "bitter" (Apter 1986: 19).

The notorious mother-in-law is also immortalized in poetry from the Tang dynasty of imperial China, circa 300—700 A.D. Forced by his mother and normative filial piety, the poet Lu Yu reluctantly forsook his beloved wife for another. Years later after a chance encounter with his first wife, Lu Yu composed a long poem to lament the loss of his heart desired. One of the verses says: "Vicious east wind thinned spring love." Hence in Chinese language, east wind becomes the metaphor for the reputedly obnoxious mother-in-law.

I do not remember why Lu Yu's mother forced his abandonment of the wife. In Shi's case, a woman's conscious cultivation to empower herself, the mother-in-law, results in the subordination of another woman, the daughter-in-law. Instead of female solidarity, power consolidation is predicated upon consanguine kinship that cuts across gender line and generation difference, that is, the mother and son. Domination is then enforced onto another female who is an affine, the daughter-in-law, along gender line but one generation down made possible via the linkage of the male kin, the son; as well as across gender line of the same generation, from the husband to the wife. Hence, domination and struggle also hinge on age (generation), not gender alone, and is embedded in kinship regardless of gender. Furthermore, the site of struggle spans within the nuclear household between husband and wife, and across households from the one of the son and daughter-in-law to that of the mother-in-law in separate residences. In this particular case, the locus of contention across households extends to the transnational space that transcends two countries and is facilitated by uterine kinship bond.

Despite the fact that Shi worked as a bookkeeper to support the family during her husband's brief period of unemployment, her subordinated position in her marital relation in part reflected her less affluent family background compared to her husband, and her mother-in-law's judgment of her educational attainment. Again, woman's symbolic capital that she brings to a marriage derives from the status and wealth of her natal family as in Shi's case, from her education, and from perceived endowments or skills such as artistic talent or beauty. Shi's lack of adequate capital in certain categories as specified by her mother-in-law in conjunction with the husband's structural power in a patriarchal society pre-determined her less powerful status. Her position was fixed from the beginning of her marriage and enacted throughout. For example, the mother-in-law disallowed Shi to wear her white wedding dress and consented to only a very simple wedding. She also criticized Shi for buying this or that piece of furniture for the new household. The husband's loyalty to his mother buttressed the mother-in-law's "uterine power." That filial piety evinced by the husband's sense of obligation to his mother additionally bolstered his position in the marriage; and his position was consistent with societal views of appropriate behavior.

The kind of dilemma encountered by Shi demonstrates the weakness in the income contribution theory in the discussion of marital power. Working with American couples, Blood and Wolfe (1960) find that middle-class husbands with higher income, more occupational prestige, and better education enjoy greater marital power. Kranichfeld (1987: 452) states that "the more education the husband has, the greater his power." Gillespie (1971: 456–57) concludes that in a capitalist economy based on commodity production where the value of women's work is low, women's social worth depends on external sources such as occupation, education, and participation in organization. The extent to which education, income, and occupation decide power position between husband and wife varies across cultures (Rodman 1967, 1992). In the cultural context of Taiwan's society, education acts as a significant determinant in socioeconomic status and occupation attainment. It also affects marital power.

Information from the 1994–1995 Taiwan Social Change Survey appears to support that. The survey is "an inland-wide probability sample, representing the non-institutionalized adult population of Taiwan between the ages of 20 and 75" (Xu and Lai 2002: 230). Based on that survey, and "final data consisted of 1,142 married males and females as the reporting spouses," Xu and Lai find that "the greater the educational differences between husbands and wives, the less likely it is for couples to make egalitarian decisions" (Xu and Lai 2002:239–40). Yi and Chang (1996) also report that wives with higher professional occupations tend to have more influence in family decision-making especially in family finance. It also depends on rural or urban locations. Yi and Tsai (1989) demonstrate that husband and wife joint-decision is more prevalent in Taipei metropolitan area. On the other hand, mostly the husband and his parents decide on family finance and purchases when the couple practices co-residence with husband's parents (Yi and Yang 1995). Such co-residence living arrangement "remains to be the most dominant type among all" (ibid.: 147), reducing a wife's decision-making power within the family. As I have demonstrated, this power differential is further reinforced and legitimated by the mother-in-law's uterine power, and Confucian ideology regarding both the son's filial responsibilities and daughter-in-law's marital obligation. As Yi and Yang points out (ibid.) "Taiwan is still under heavy patriarchal influence."

Shi's continued acquiescence helped to reproduce the gendered power of the relationship under that patriarchal influence. In a feedback loop, her subordination fed her husband's authority that determined two major migrations. The absence of open resistance not only attested to her husband's "invisible" power, or more correctly, structural power, but also helped to reproduce it. Women are not passive in the process of domination. By acquiescence as in Shi's case, she became an active agent in the mutually constitutive phenomenon of domination and subjugation. Her agency expressed in acquiescence in turn reinforces and legitimates her husband's power derived from society. As conceptualized by Anthony Giddens (1984), the relationship between agency and structure is interactive, "agency produces structure produces agency produces structure in a never-ending recursive process" (Thrift 1985: 612).

This does not equate to blaming the victim, as Shi's absence of resistance is not necessarily a lack of action on her part. She has experienced the futility of argument. When opposition reaches the point of diminishing return, further action begins to cause frustration and disharmony that such action becomes negatively cost effective. Sometimes, unintentional acquiescence under a condition of habitual domination only bespeaks the intensity of such domination, and the acute symptom of subjugation. Fortunately in Shi's situation, the transnational family arrangement turned into an intervention. Their physical distance in the transnational space acted as a measure to interrupt the vicious circle of recursive process to reconstitute the gender relationship between husband and wife, between agency and structure, between women and patriarchy.

OVERT CONFLICT, COERCION, AND PATRIARCHY

Some husband and wife engaged in overt conflict over migration. Henry was a husband who coerced his wife into migrating to southern California. He was in his late 40s and he appeared to be very open about his experience during the interview. He worked as an executive for an American corporation in Taiwan in the 1980s and 1990s. In the 1980s be became involved with a woman in an extra-marital affair. According to Henry, his relationship with his wife was not close and they did not communicate much. "We did not have the meeting of the minds," he said. "She was a home person and very pragmatic. That also meant that she was not interesting." That is, she was being a "good wife" in patriarchal terms. Henry said that businessmen in Taiwan entertained a great deal after work, and that they did not bring along their wives to these occasions. According to Henry, his wife also disliked attending such events. He said, "You would not bring a wife to those occasions because no one else did. It would look odd if you did." Instead, the common practice was to hire female escorts. These female escorts were part of a legitimate escort service, and were not necessarily available for sex. "My colleagues would get these women from all sources, all for a fee, including starlets and models." Henry continued,

> Often the more mature women worked in this business out of financial need to support their families. The younger ones ranged from late teen to early twenties. Many really young ones did it for a good time. They could drink and eat for free, could have fun and make money at the same time. It's not necessary sex, they just keep you company to drink. Sex or not depends on other things, there's no guarantee.

Henry met a woman at one of these occasions. He said that she was a very sensitive woman who knew "how to move his heart." There was more. Henry said,

> It's strange. Somehow, there was a meeting of the minds. There was a lot of mutual understanding. We looked at many things eye to eye. Sometimes we even thought of the same thing and said it out loud at the same time. Not just once, but often. This never happened with my wife. If I said this, my wife would say that. We had a great distance in between.

"So how did the woman move your heart?" I pressed Henry. According to Henry, she was a tender, romantic, and attractive woman with a nice figure. When they were living together, she would greet him home with comfort and care. From time to time she would run a bubble bath complete with aroma. Henry said, "just like in the movie. Not only that, she would also serve you in the bath! You know what I mean." Henry also thought that she acted "wilder in bed." For example, his wife insisted on turning the light off during sexual intercourse, but he wanted the light on. "So it made you feel, why this, why so boring, so monotonous? What a big difference!" Henry explained. The woman also assisted him in the public. She knew how to interact with his colleagues when they attended social events together. She was very much at ease with them. She also arranged interesting things to do during the weekends when Henry got off from work. She seemed to fit a man's ideal of a woman. Henry provided additional information as follows:

> She gave me what I didn't receive from my wife in public and in private. For a successful man, for someone with a very boring life at home, this life was—WOW! It was like, one was black and white and the other was color!

I asked Henry, "Why was there no divorce at the time?" Henry replied,

> Actually I wanted a divorce very much at the time, but there was just too much pressure. My mother insisted that I must not divorce because she was a Christian. She said I could not have a divorce. Secondly, I considered my kids. I thought I would wait till they went off to college then the harm on them would be minimized. I was sitting on the fence, jumping back and forth.

Against his heart, Henry remained in his marriage out of compliance with his mother's wishes and consideration for his children. Then he came up with a solution. He had long wanted the children to study in the United States, and he had already owned a house in southern California since the1980s. In the early 1990s, after his yearlong training in the United States, he bought his wife a Lexus in California, told her not to worry about money, but just do her best to take care of the children in the United States. Henry reflected,

> At the time I thought that was an excellent arrangement: a woman and a kid in Taiwan, a wife and kids in the States. Supporting a wife in the States is called *nei tsai mei* [inside person in America, i.e. the wife living in the States], it was a status symbol for a man in Taiwan. It told the world that you were financially successful.[1]

But Henry's wife refused to accept this arrangement. She wanted to return to Taiwan with him. Henry continued,

> I told her if she insisted on returning to Taiwan, then we would have a divorce. I gave my wife two choices: stay here with the kids, or we divorce if she insists on going back. Actually I gave her no choice.

At the end, Henry's wife and children stayed in the United States, while Henry lived in Taiwan with the other woman and their child. I had wanted to talk to Henry's wife to learn of her feelings and experience. I asked Henry for the opportunity to talk to her, but he never replied to my request. I felt that I ought not press the issue, lest my intrusion created any repercussion in their relationship.

In her study of marital power, Pykes (1994) concludes that women reluctant to enter a marriage appear to hold greater power in the marital relation. Based on the principle of least interest, Waller and Hill (1951: 191) posit that "that person who is able to dictate the conditions of association whose interest in the continuation of the affair is least." In Henry's example, he held explicit power over the overt conflict of interest between husband and wife. His power lay in his willingness to discontinue the marriage in order to achieve his goal. His ultimatum of a divorce corresponded to a form of power exercised as coercion. Kranichfeld (1987: 43) distinguishes coercion as follows: "The most important distinction between coercion and power is that coercion is the act of forcing another to do something against their will and requires a conflict of interest." However, coercion in and of itself does not necessarily contain sufficient force to effect the desired result. I argue, instead, that the potency of Henry's ultimatum arose from social forces of the Taiwan society.

I propose that ideology and divorce law in Taiwan compelled Henry's wife into migration despite her objection. Henry's ultimatum of a divorce was a powerful one. In the past, Taiwan's legal codes on divorce were detrimental to women. Prior to the 1996 divorce law amendment, legal code number 1051 stipulated that even in the event of an uncontested divorce, the father automatically retained custody of any children from the marriage unless mutual agreement existed. In addition, legal code number 1060 stated that minor children must take the father's residence as their residence. Therefore, if the father refused the mother's request for visitation, the mother would have little legal recourse. Of course, after a divorce, a woman was also subjected to financial insecurity particularly when she had always been a housewife. The power of the state, in this case divorce law, gave ammunition to Henry's threat. It drew strength from a highly gendered and patriarchal state, with laws detrimental to the welfare of women in the case of divorce. In addition, social milieu and cultural ideology regarding divorce added more weight to Henry's cause.

Divorce has been on the rise in Taiwan for those aged forty-five and under (Thornton and Lin 1994: 245–63). According to Taiwan's official statistics released in December 2003, over fifty-six thousand couples filed for divorce during the period January to November 2003, an increase of 5.9 percent over the same period the year before. 2.5 percent of them had been married less than three years, and sixty-one percent less than ten years (Chinese

World Journal, December 13, 2003). On average, these couples remained under forty years of age. When I stayed in Taiwan from 2000 to 2001, more than one person in the early forties, both male and female, told me that divorce was getting more acceptable for younger people; but for those who were older and those concerned with reputation, divorce remained a strong stigma. One afternoon I joined a group of people for refreshments, and the conversation shifted to the divorced status of a young scholar in his early thirties. A social scientist in his early fifties who had appeared to be progressive-minded commented, "Nien qing ren [young people]!" According to a woman professor at the National Taiwan University, there is considerable social cost for a divorce. Friends, relatives, and colleagues who disapprove of the divorce condemn and isolate the partner who instigates it. Sometimes this partner would even encounter difficulty in obtaining employment (personal communication, N. Chang, April 2001). This is also the case in Japan, where one "loses face" in society due to a divorce, and "traditionally, many companies were reluctant to promote employees who had divorced or who had major problems at home" (Kristoff 2002/03: 122).

Apart from Henry, how did men view divorce? One of the husbands I interviewed in Taiwan elaborated on the forces of collective sentiment. He was a sixty-year old bank executive who had been a transnational husband for eight years when I met him. He told me the following:

> Why don't people divorce? You're under social pressure, pressure from family, relatives, and your community. Divorce is a shame and a major problem. You don't want to be criticized and ostracized so you just live and let live. You want to uphold your social reputation as a moral, responsible person. You let the status quo stand and keep a marriage in name even when it is just an institution without substance.

To Henry's generation, it was shameful to be divorced. It was a shame especially for women and the stigma associated with divorce was gendered. As in Japan and South Korea (see Gelb and Palley 1999; Uno 1999), in Taiwan often a woman's honor and accomplishment stemmed from her role as a wife and mother, especially for women who stayed home as a homemaker. A woman's social status derived from her husband's success. A divorce stripped a woman of her respectable married woman's title; it separated her from her husband's status and success. Hence a divorced woman was dishonored. A divorce deprived a woman of her wifely and motherly role. It took away the possibility of honor and accomplishment from her. A professional woman told me that, in that generation "often a divorced woman is regarded lower than a prostitute." In a very practical sense, it was also more difficult for women with children to find another partner, particularly for women who were already middle-aged.

I interviewed a woman who was a university graduate and recently retired from teaching in Taiwan. I asked her about her generation's view on divorce. She said that recently divorce was getting increasingly common and accepted among the younger generation, particularly those in the twenties. However, in the past and still now for those in her generation, a divorce would raise eyebrows. She further stated that an established person with a position in society would be concerned with his reputation. Divorcing one's wife for another woman would cause a scandal. Divorced from a husband, a woman lost her social worth. She related the real life experience of a woman friend named Mrs. Ho. Mrs. Ho married a lawyer from a well-to-do family, both for the first time. Mrs. Ho prided herself for marrying so well. Although her parents-in-law had been good to her, in time the husband started to get involved with other women and ignored his wife. He also began to treat Mrs. Ho with verbal and then physical abuses. This situation continued for several years. Why did Mrs. Ho tolerate the indignation and abuse? The retired teacher answered as follows,

> Mrs. Ho does not want to lose her social status as the wife of a successful lawyer. It would be a great loss of face in front of her friends. Besides, Mrs. Ho said she did not want to make things so easy for him and the woman. If she presses for divorce, she loses the social status and financial security. She would also make it easy for the husband and the other woman to get married. After all, what would she get after a divorce? In Taiwan, even older men would only marry young women. Once a woman reaches the thirties, her chance of getting married becomes slim. So you have a lot of single older women in Taiwan. At least now Mrs. Ho is entitled to all the financial support, privileges, and the title of Mrs. Ho.

Not being divorced does not prevent men from having extra-marital affairs or mistresses. Yet, sexuality outside marriage is acceptable for men but condemned for women. Men openly appear in the public with a mistress. Multi-millionaire industrialist Wang Yung-ching of Taiwan is known to have three wives. Even under normal circumstances, husband and wife often lead somewhat separate lives. I met a professional woman separated from her husband for several years. Her husband had maintained a paramour, but the woman remained celibate. She was very close to another professional man who had been unhappily married as well for several years. However, these two people remained platonic friends despite emotional closeness. This woman told me,

We have to maintain our moral persona in the public. We're both professionals in the same field and people know us. We have to keep up our
reputation as moral people. There are many unhappy couples in Taiwan
who stay in their marriages for things like that.

Even in the United States, many couples remain in their unhappy marriages. Many couples stay on for the sake of the children. Indeed children
are the innocent ones, yet they suffer the most from adults' folly. Children
who grow up in homes without love's life force also experience confusion
and loss. A lawyer friend recently told me that he just concluded a client's
divorce after fifty years of marriage, which should have ended twenty-five
years ago. Life is so short, twenty-five years of lost youth is such a long time.
When wife and husbands are not meant to be, the heart becomes a lonely
hunter. The lack of intimacy and tenderness withers one's soul. I have known
men whose eyes betray their lack of affection and therefore their yearning
for the same. They look dried out in spirit. They exude a forlorn air in their
eyes, their faces, their speech, their entire being. I have also seen men married for the second or third time and finally found their niches. They seemed
rejuvenated, happy, and full of energy. Even their faces shone. The nourish-
ing bliss from the compatible union of the yin and yang and the power of
loving intimacy is overwhelming.[2]

Not every couple is meant to be husband and wife. When they don't
mesh as a unit, it takes courage, strength, and wisdom to end misery so
that each may find happiness with another. When there is no more joy
but constant bickering and no longer loving care but apathy, to remain
in the marriage is to be masochistic to oneself and sadistic to the partner.
There is a Chinese expression: "same bed but different dreams." It depicts
the distanced hearts of husband and wife that no longer belongs to each
other.

But in Taiwan, society imposes restraint on the individual, and women
seem to lose out more than men. One of the women I interviewed named
Ting remarked as follows,

If men have their needs, so do women, just that women in Taiwan don't
talk about their needs. It's a big unforgivable crime if women have extra-
marital affairs, yet it's acceptable if men do. Women have biological
needs too!

This double standard bespeaks the inequality in ideology and structural
forces that impact members of society along gendered line. Ting said that
she and her husband had a good talk before they adopted the transnational

family strategy. She told him to make sure his conscience was clear with his actions, and whether he wanted his family and children or not. Ting said,

> So you're lonely? So am I. You're an adult. You must discipline and control yourself. If anything should happen, I will not accept any excuses, nor will I forgive. This is the way I am.

I asked her, "Does it mean a divorce then?" She answered affirmatively, "Yes." Ting was forty years old, the youngest one in my sample. As of the time of my interview, the husband continued to work in Taiwan and financially supported the wife and children in southern California.

SUMMARY

Migration decision-making is dependent on an individual's particular circumstance and gender, it is also informed by social milieu and structural power. Reflecting male domination in patriarchal society, most of the participants in this study reported migration decision-making by the husbands, with the wives as followers. A few families practiced what they considered "democratic procedure" in which all family members, adults and children included, participated in the decision-making process by direct voting or full discussion. Some decision process reflected power relations in a married couple. While some women effected migration by persistently persuading the husband, other women made unilateral decisions to migrate on behalf of the family.

Contrary to theory that stresses resource contribution and dynamics between husband and wife, such authority derived from the strong socioeconomic position of a woman's natal family, a factor external to the dyadic relationship. On the other hand, women who lacked such support remained subordinated to husbands bolstered by structural power in a patriarchal society. Still other decisions revealed overt conflict and coercion, with the husband wielding power over the wife due to gendered social as well as legal forces in Taiwan that proved partial to male domination. Intentionally or unintentionally, men draw upon the structures of patriarchy to constitute migration.

Migration is gendered. Migration decision-making is complex, often involving generational and gender conflicts even if a family migrates together as a collective unit. The next chapter looks at the impact of migration on women as workers, mothers, and individuals.

Chapter Eight
Impact on Women as Workers, Mothers, and Individuals

In the foregoing chapter, I maintained that migration involved power relations. It concerned decision-making within a nuclear family as well as extended kinship, and particularly gender politics between husband and wife reinforced by societal forces and uterine power. After migration, gender differences continued to shape transnational families split in the United States and China in the past, as well as between the United States and Taiwan in the present. One aspect was the gendered notion of the putative private sphere characterized by domesticity and public domain associated with paid work.

Michelle Z. Rosaldo (1974) proposes this private and public dichotomy between women's association and orientation within the home, versus the ties and opportunities available to men in the public. This oppositional paradigm has been shown to be problematic (Lamphere 1993). Management of production occurs at home in some societies (Leacock 1978: 253). In the Middle East, some women actively participate in political affairs in men's world. They also affect decisions of political or social alliances by approval or sanction. Rosaldo (1980) re-considers her thesis and concedes that male domination is not universal, and that in some society women indeed assert influence in the public world of politics and social organization (Nelson 1974).

Bose (1987) points out that even in the early part of American history, husband and wife worked together on their farms in a use-value economy. Except perhaps urban white middle-class wives, women in the industrial American economy have worked both in domestic services as well as in public places including factories and offices. Hence, the boundary of the dual spheres is blurred, and women's domestic cult within the home is also class-based (Lamphere1993). Often, it is also contingent upon "race." Scholars argue that racialized minority American women of color have always needed to work for a living (Dill 1988, 1944; Glenn 1985, 1986, 1992; Almquist 1995). However even among women of color, it is also their respective socioeconomic class positions in society that characterize their participation in the labor force or housework. Within Asian America, the notion of public versus private polarity is largely class specific.

In the nineteenth century and early twentieth century, most wives of Chinese merchants in urban United States were confined to their living quarters at home (Ling 1999). This was practiced partly to protect these women from possible abduction for prostitution, from over-exposure to male strangers as mandated by propriety, and partly due to these wealthy women's relative immobility caused by their bound feet. In addition, Chinese traditional ideology dictates that men manage external and women take charge of domestic affairs. This dichotomy is even reflected in genteel language: the husband is referred to as one's "external person" and the wife is termed "internal person." This is not to say that all women of means remained indoor. H. Ling recounts the story of an energetic and capable successful Chinese business woman born in late 19th century San Francisco. She co-owned a business with her Chinese husband, managed the general merchandize store, and took in money while the husband kept the book:

> Gee Guok Shee was also responsible for the monetary transaction of the firm. She went to the San Mateo Bank regularly to deposit or withdraw money for the firm, though always accompanied by one of the male members of the company" (Ling 1998: 69).

However, out of necessity, women in working-class and in rural areas always worked for a living.

In urban areas, working-class Chinese immigrant women labored in the laundry, restaurant, grocery and the garment business. H. Ling (ibid.: 70) commented that Chinese farm wives on the mainland United States followed the traditional division of labor and performed housework. However, their "housework" extends to the use-value economy of farm livelihood. Polly Bemis is a famous early pioneer Chinese woman in the United States. Sold into slavery in China by her father in the mid 19th century, and then resold in the United States, Polly eventually married Charlie Bemis of Idaho who "bought her freedom in a poker game" (ibid.: 80). After marriage, the couple lived on a farm. Polly grew fruits and vegetables, raised poultry and livestock. She also ran a boarding house.

On plantations in rural Hawaii, Chinese women were also paid, albeit less than men, to work shoulder to shoulder with men who might be their husbands. In Hawaii, pictures brides[1] from Korea, Okinawa, and Japan worked on the plantations for wages, took in boarders for fees, cooked meals or laundered for bachelor workers to supplement income (Kawakami 1986). Women were subjected to debt bondage in the sex trade (see Ichioka 1977 for Japanese prostitutes and Cheng 1984 for Chinese prostitutes). Farm wives worked side by side with husbands to till the land (see, e.g., Kikumura 1981), and many Japanese immigrant women labored as domestic servants (Glenn 1986). In contemporary Asian America, Filipinas are employed in homes as domestic helpers and in the health care industry (Parreñas 2000). Chinese and Southeast Asian immigrants toil in sewing factories (Steir 1991) and some Vietnamese immigrant women tend their customers in nail salons that are organized along ethnic lines. Korean immigrant women run dry clean services, liquor stores, or grocery stores as unpaid workers in family businesses. These are working class women whose necessity to earn an income fuses the private and public domains.[2]

Yanagisako points out that the concept of private and public domain entails both a spatial and a functional metaphor (1987:111). In the study of a village in southern France, Reiter [Rapp] delineates the separation of the public and private domains by gender. She states, "One of the earliest patterns of sexual division of domains that I encountered in Colpied was geographic" (1975: 254). She found that in the village men worked in the fields or fraternized at cafés and other public places. Women preoccupied themselves with kinship network and housework inside their homes. Women's presence also dominated the church and food stores. However, even geographically the public and private domains are often juxtaposed and stratified. For example, when paid domestic workers take care of household and/or children for professional couples who participate in formal labor market, the public domain of work for the domestic helper is the private home of the employers (see Wrigley 1995; Hondagneu-Sotelo 2001). Thus the two spheres intersect and conjoin yet are distinguishable by class.

As a spatial metaphor, Taiwanese American transnational families split across more than one nation maximize this separation between husbands at work and wives at home across national political boundary, and international migration affect wives of these families as paid workers in the public and as mothers at home. At the same time, living out a transnational family life challenges the dichotomy when women act as de facto heads of the household and single parents in the absence of their husbands.

This chapter diagnoses the impact of migration on the women as paid professional in the labor market and as full-time homemakers, as well as their experience in the transnational space where functions were fused and the public-private boundary dissolved as a consequence of the split-household strategy across territorial, political borders.

IMPACT ON WOMEN AS PAID WORKERS IN THE LABOR FORCE

Several of the women in my sample had completed university education in Taiwan. Besides their high level of education, those who participated in the labor market in Taiwan had engaged in professional or non-manual occupations, with the exception of one woman who worked as a nurse's aide. Before the start of their transnational family arrangement or before their departure for the United States, eighteen women stayed at home as full-time homemakers and seventeen were labor market participants. Table 8.1 shows a break down of these women's occupations prior to migration.

In most Taiwanese American transnational families, the world of work associated with men who remained in Taiwan, while the women took care of children in the United States, although some eventually returned to the work force. The geographic separation of paid work and mother work in the transnational space is complicated by the long distance international migration. This complication in turn subverted the roles of women as paid workers and mothers, with profound implications on the gendered nature of migration.

Before their journey to the United States, the women who worked as paid professionals in Taiwan were able to manage both their domestic responsibilities as mothers to care for children, and as workers for productive

Table 8.1 Occupation

Business Co-Owners (with husband)	5
Accounting	1
Civil Servant	2
Manager	2
Teacher or Professor	2
Human Resource Specialist	1
Commission Sales	1
Nurse	1
Nurse Aide	1
Total	17

labor. For these women, the boundary of the public and private was porous. They merged the two spheres within the territorial confine of Taiwan.
However, long distance international migration across national demarcations disrupted this fluidity between the two domains. In order to immigrate to the United States, some women discontinued their careers already
established in Taiwan.

When the families of these women became transnational, the distinct
geographical location of the private and public separation emerged in the
transnational field, with the wife and children living in the United States but
financially supported by husbands working in Taiwan. At the same time,
in the absence of their husbands at work in Taiwan, these mothers became
head of their households at home in the United States with increased autonomy, authority, and responsibilities for their homes and interactions with
the public. Hence, international migration disrupts professional women's
career paths in Taiwan, to fulfill their role as mothers in the United States. In
the prolonged absence of their husbands, women take up the responsibility
of double parenting. As de facto heads of household, they assume authority and autonomy although they depend on their husbands for financial
support. Women interact with their communities, traversing the public and
private domains. The public-private separation dissolves for my sample, just
like these transmigrants' working class counterparts from Latin America
and the Caribbean. Scholars argue that the boundary of the dual spheres is
blurred for working-class American women including racialized minority
women (e.g. Almquist 1995, Dill 1994, Glenn 1992). In the transnational
space, the juxtaposition of the private and public spheres transcends socioeconomic class demarcations.

For most Taiwanese American transnational families, the quintessential reason of migration was to ensure the social reproduction, if not
the upward mobility, of the class position for their children. This pattern
stands to contrast the many women from Latin America, the Caribbean (see,
inter alia, Grasmuck and Pessar 1991; Hondagneu-Sotelo 1994) and the
Philippines (Parrañas 2000, 2001), mostly from working class background
who migrate to engage in paid productive wage labor in the United States
out of everyday economic necessity. It is the class difference of the women
originated from Taiwan, who largely came from non-working-class background with adequate financial means that induced the geographic reversal.
This reversal also subverted the women, at least initially, from their role as
active participants in the labor market to one dictated by traditional ideology as mothers primarily responsible for childcare. At the same time, in the
absence of their husbands at work in Taiwan, these mothers became head

of the household at home in the United States with increased autonomy, authority, and responsibilities for their homes and interactions with the public, much like the women left behind in Mexico by husbands in the United States as working-class laborers (Hondagneu-Sotelo 1994). However, migration and transnational family arrangement affected individual woman in disparate ways. The following section discusses their different experiences as well as the personal cost and benefits that came with the goal of class reproduction and/or upward mobility for the next generation.

Lin had been a business executive for many years. At work she often had to travel out of the country on business. Her son and daughter envied her opportunities to travel abroad. One time Lin took them to visit her parents who had immigrated to Hawaii. The children liked the life style there and did not want to return to Taiwan, and they asked Lin if they could also live in Hawaii. Eventually, Lin's parents agreed to sponsor their immigration. Lin quit her job to migrate with the children to Hawaii. Her husband stayed with them for the first few weeks, but subsequently returned to Taiwan to continue the management of his family business. He sent money to support his wife and children now living in Hawaii. Later Lin and the children moved to California for their schooling. In order to be together as a family, the husband flew to California about once a year, and stayed with his wife and children for a week each time. They lived in two separate households on either side of the Pacific Ocean for seven years before the family reunited again. During the seven years of transnational family arrangement, Lin stayed home as a full-time mother and homemaker. Lin enjoyed her time and opportunity to stay home. According to her, "Some women have to work. They have no choice. I have a choice. I don't have to work if I don't want to. I enjoy staying home as it is now." In Lin's case, her migration disrupted her career, and the transnational family arrangement made her a homemaker in the Untied States; but Lin welcomed the change. Not every woman considers a life at home as oppression.

Like Lin, some wives of professional expatriates in Singapore are found to enjoy their leisure, and paid work was not an economic need. A Japanese wife in the mid-30s says,

> Many Japanese ladies in Singapore do not work ... we need not work. ... Here we can live in a large house ... we can employ a part-time maid, and everything is so cheap when compared to Japanese price. ... So we can play golf, tennis. ... Why work? Why not enjoy our comfortable life? (Yeoh and Khoo 1998: 168).

An American woman in the early forties comments as follows,

> I had no problems giving up my job. . . . it [the move] was like a pleas-
> ant extended vacation, and I would have been silly to fret over it!. . . .
> I was looking forward to the time I would have to catch up on things I
> wanted to do (ibid.).

This appreciation of the opportunity to not work transcends class distinction. In Hondagneu-Sotelo's study (1994: 127) of Mexican immigrants in
the United States, two working-class husbands forbid their wives to work as
manual laborers. Both women welcomed the privilege. They have worked all
their life, now they find gratification as mothers and wives who stay home to
care for their children. Some women choose to stay home for instrumental
reasons. Dominican immigrant women in New York (Pessar 1995), and
middle-class women in Haiti (Fouron and Schiller 2001: 555) voluntarily
elect to stay home instead of work outside of home for money, in order to
elevate the prestige and social status of their families and husbands, even
though their participation in paid work outside of home would contribute
to increased family income that could very well be used. Loss of income indeed created concern for some women in Taiwanese American transnational
families, but such loss was secondary to what some women considered to
be far more important.

Yen was a nurse in Taiwan who also taught nursing part-time. In the
United States, Yen's employment prospect looked very different. Her nursing
license was not valid in California,[3] and her proficiency in English was less
than adequate at first. Consequently, she became a homemaker after migration. Giving up her career to be a full-time housewife also meant the loss of
her income. This loss reduced her discretionary spending. I asked her if she
considered this financial inconvenience a sacrifice, she answered, "N-o-o!
As parents, we want to give the best to our children, to the best of our ability." By traditional values in Taiwan, as in Japan and South Korea (see Gelb
and Palley 1994; Uno 1999), women derive their higher accomplishment
primarily from their roles as mother and wife. A woman is considered self-
ish and at great fault if she neglects her expected responsibility of these roles
in order to advance her own development or career (Wu 1992). Women in
Taiwan have managed both work and children in various way in recent time.
However, studies have shown that women value their family's needs above
their own: generally women wish to curb their own labor participation to
facilitate family needs. They take precedence and priority in the event of
conflicting demands (Lu 1982; Chien and Hsueh 1996).

The professional women in my sample also voiced the conflicts and
struggles over their migration which affected their career paths. In Taiwan,
more educated women appear to have a greater commitment to career,

compared with women who have completed only a high school education. These educated women are unwilling to renounce their professional work. They tend to insist on maintaining the dual roles of mother and professional worker. Their ideals and goals are to simultaneously maintain both family and career (Lu 1982: 147). However, another study finds that "in the case of family care-giving, wives from higher income families are more likely to quit jobs or change employment patterns to adapt to the role of care-giving, with a higher value on family time rather than market time" (Lu 1997: 3). Lily received her bachelor's degree in Taiwan. She eventually became a top executive in a large private corporation. Her husband was an executive in a large corporation and taught part-time as a university professor. The salary of husband and wife were comparable. In Taiwan they lived in one of the best areas in the style of elites served by a chauffeur and maids. They also rubbed shoulders with influential people in town. Lily's profession prior to migration provided a great sense of accomplishment for her: her boss appreciated her and her subordinates respected her. She knew in advance that as new immigrants in the United States they would lose their socioeconomic standing, and that she would stay at home as a housewife, at least in the beginning. Family needs to migrate conflicted with Lily's individual career path. The struggle thus created is well expressed in her own words: "I wanted to migrate rationally, but at heart I resisted it."

Another highly educated woman named Wah gave up her profession before retirement age for the sake of her child. Her son had trailed behind in school and requested to go to study in the United States, but her husband had a well-paid, highranking position in Taiwan. In order to grant her son's wish and to give him a better chance in education, Wah took early retirement from her professional job in order to accompany him in the United States while the husband continued to work in Taiwan. The family bought a house near her relatives in the United States, and the son went to school in the neighborhood. Wah gave up her successful career to get the best of both worlds for her son without compromising her husband's career. Wah spent four months in the States to be with her son and flew back to visit her husband, and the husband traveled to the States to spend time with the wife and son twice a year for about ten days each time. Wah and her son also returned to Taiwan during his summer vacation. Wah suffered conflicting feelings with this arrangement. While she was glad that she was able to take early retirement to be with her child in the States, she also experienced difficulty within herself regarding her career. She was a very successful professional, heading many well-funded projects at the institution where she worked. She said,

I did have a conflict. I was well-known and respected. I was efficient, hardworking, and energetic. I retired early. I gave up my career. I felt empty. I felt that I had nothing left. All of a sudden I was good for nothing. I felt contradictions and struggles. I was a successful professional, well respected, a modern woman. But when it comes to my family, I am expected to do all the domestic chores.

In a study on professional expatriates in Singapore by Yeoh and Khoo (1998), a German wife in the early thirties laments the loss of employment, not out of economic hardship but the social and psychological amenities that paid work provides, "Working keeps me occupied . . . it makes me feel good about myself . . . besides, it allows me to meet more people and get involved in the local way of life" (ibid: 170). For Wah the professional woman, the social and psychological loss affected her sense of self worth and created internal turmoil. After struggling for two months in the new situation, Wah designed a research project to engage herself.

In the past two decades, married women's participation in Taiwan's labor market has climbed from 31.9 percent in 1979 to 45.1 percent in 1994 (Chien and Hsueh 1996:113). However, society continues to look upon the husband as the main, or even sole, breadwinner, while women's income is considered as secondary. Often women exit from the labor market due to marriage or childbirth, although they may rejoin the work force later in their life cycle. In Taiwan, the mother shoulders the primary responsibility for children's school performance, instead of the father whose main duty is to provide financial support for the family. Mothers take charge of supervising and educating children (Lin 1999). In addition, the career development of wives is subject to that of husbands, even though husbands often support wives' participation in the labor market out of economic needs (Wu 1992: 83). Regardless of labor force participation, society continues to expect women to fulfill their traditional female roles and responsibilities, such as mothers and wives; and working women are still charged with the bulk of household chores (Lu and Yi 1999).

In my sample, struggle around gender roles and responsibility was not confined to individual internal conflicts. At times husbands and wives argued over migration, especially when the wife was committed to her professional development. One woman's career was disrupted twice. Yang was a university graduate in Taiwan who worked as an officer in an American corporation. After the husband and wife received their U.S. green card as permanent residents, they returned to work in Taiwan. When her husband was transferred from Taiwan to China in the early 1990s, she gave up her job to follow him, subordinating her own career to her husband's. It was her effort to keep family together despite the cost to her career. After they moved to China, Yang found a job at the local operation of the same American corporation. When the politics between China and Taiwan became tense, the husband urged Yang and their child to leave for the United States to fulfill their residency requirement for citizenship. Yang confided as follows, "He and I argued about this all the time. He wanted us to come in the mid-1990s. We argued because I didn't want to come. When we were in China, I had a good job. He wanted us to come so I got angry and frustrated. In 1999 he insisted and I compromised." Yang had stayed home as a full time mother since her arrival. The husband utilized migration as a strategy to counteract potential political danger, but it was enacted at the cost of the wife's career path against her will.

Kay's situation presented another such a case. Kay had been working as a department manager in a foreign financial institution in Taiwan. She enjoyed her work and made good money. All her natal family members and most of her close friends lived in Taiwan. In sum, she was well positioned in both her professional and personal life. She had no intention to migrate but followed her husband and family to southern California despite her adamant objection. She said,

> Look at me now! I gave up my profession, the whole past, and the life style, friends, family, everything, to come to a different environment and culture. It is as if everything you did in the past became nothing. So you worked for nothing and you have to start from ground zero here. It is hard establishing yourself. . . . I felt empty.

Why did Kay consent to migrate? I later learnt that the husband was very adamant about the move, and that they had argued over the issue heatedly and repeatedly. In the end he gave her an ultimatum: divorce if she insisted on staying in Taiwan. Having given in because of her husband's threat, Kay compromised her professional career to stay at home as wife and mother after they came to the United States. Arguably, Kay might have compromised out of her love for her husband and children; she could also have acted to avoid a divorce that largely worked to a woman's disadvantage in legal as well as practical measures. As discussed in Chapter Three concerning migration decision-making and gendered power relations, in the patriarchal society of Taiwan, the prevailing divorce law as well as social milieu and cultural ideology incriminate women far more than men in a divorce. In Kay's case, migration was again a gendered process. It served to prioritize and legitimize women's role as wife and mother, while it marginalized women as active and contributing participant in the labor market. In contrast, men retained the provider role. He continued to work and support the wives and children living in the United States. Migration was gendered, and the structure of patriarchy became the cause as well as the result of a gendered migration.

To borrow Hartmann's term (1981), the transnational family was "the locus of gender struggle," but one must also extend this locus to include the larger institutional structure of a patriarchal society. At the familial level, mutual dependence between husband and wife in the interest of social reproduction of their class position had not precluded the use of coercion. This coercion in turn derived its potency from a society pervaded with expectations, legalities, and values that subject a woman to serve the interest of her children and husband. The Taiwanese American transnational family was an agent of change to counteract certain undesired forces and to achieve certain goals, but this family was not always a unified interest group. Further, class reproduction came at a cost borne by women. International migration disrupted these women's career growth and development. Transnational family life made it difficult for most of the women to combine their established professional path and domestic responsibility like they could in their country of origin. While their husbands continued their careers to support their transnational families, the impact of migration as well as the conflicting demands and conditions of class reproduction in the transnational space re-domesticized these women at the cost of their careers, although they were one of the most prepared to transform gender roles. The cost of this class reproduction and of migration is gendered. The value of such cost is also not included in the gross domestic product. Hence, the cost borne by women in this situation is both unrecognized and hidden, although the cost involved directly contributed to the husband's ability to produce in the national and international economy.

The cessation of work also created monetary problems for some women. Kay reflected on this concern,

> Maybe because I was used to working, when I had no income, I felt no security. It affected my spending as a consumer. I was a new immigrant unfamiliar with the local system and society. Although we had savings we couldn't just bleed our savings. There was no sense of security.

When Kay first immigrated she was not at all happy with her situation. After about two yeas in California, she located an entry-level position at a foreign bank from Taiwan. Yen also mentioned this concern. Yen's non-transferable nursing license led to her becoming a full-time mother at home in the United States while her husband continued in the work place in Taiwan. She said,

> We used to have two incomes and my husband paid for all household expenses. I never had to think twice if I wanted to buy something. I have not been working since I came here, and now we have to carry two mortgages, one in the United States and one in Taiwan. The cost of living here is also higher and we have to prepare for the children's university education. Now I have to be thrifty.

Four years after Yen's arrival in southern California, and one year after my initial interview with her, she began as a clerical worker at a travel agency owned by a Taiwanese immigrant. Because of their perceived money pinch after migration, both Kay and Yen accepted employment below their qualifications.

International migration made jockeying the women's established career paths with their responsibilities as mothers impossible. In some cases, migration was the husband's strategy and decision despite the wife's resistance. For several of these managerial class families, migration was a measure employed to maximize their children's educational and future employment prospects. At first sight, women who sacrifice their own career in the interest of their children might appear altruistic. However, their action could also be interpreted as self-serving, as in the long run, they also negotiated a potentially better status position for the family in the future. To achieve these family-oriented goals, some mothers in my sample gave up their professional lives when they made the transition to full-time homemaking. Husbands, on the other hand, continued to pursue their careers uninterrupted and financially supported their families. Some women thrived with these new changes; others grappled with the conflicting desire to continue their profession, while they acknowledged the pressure to conform to traditional Taiwanese patriarchal definitions of woman as wife and mother. In most cases, women's personal ambivalence and conflict between husband and wife were suppressed in the interest of future prospects for the family as a unit. Both the strategy and the inherent compromise or capitulation was gendered.

While some women gave up their careers to migrate, four of the women continued their careers in Taiwan and commuted between Taiwan and the United States. The geographic separation of the two households in the transnational field presented additional challenges to these women, who juggled to fulfill their responsibilities at both homes and in the workplace. The physical demands were the most taxing. One woman who co-owned a family business with her husband had first suggested to her husband that he open a branch factory in California. Her husband stayed with the children in the United States and she flew back and forth. She said, "I would come back at least once a month, three to five days each time. At times I came twice a month. It was very tiring." Non-stop plane flight one way from Taiwan to Los Angeles takes at least twelve hours. As an entrepreneur with a more flexible schedule, she was able to return to the home in the United States frequently. Another woman named Lily who worked as a corporate executive had to arrange her returns using holiday leaves and vacation time earned.

Lily's husband made the decision to migrate to the Untied States for the children's education. As mentioned above, Lily was reluctant to forfeit her high position at work. It would also be financially unsound to do so. After migration, her older child got admitted to a private university on the East Coast. "It cost $30,000 a year for tuition fees alone, not including room and board," she recalled. "We started this transnational family strategy to maximize our income. It was a necessity." Her husband who was a former graduate student in the United States found work locally as an engineer. Lily flew back and forth between her work in Taiwan and her home in California for five to six years until both of her children graduated from university. In the interim, her husband would go to Taiwan for vacation, and she would fly here two or three times a year to be with the family. Lily had worked for a long time at her company so she was entitled to thirty vacation days each year. She extended these vacation days with public holidays, weekends, and sick leave. Her taxing schedule is best expressed in her own words:

> I usually took the first flight out to come here. I would leave Taiwan Friday evening right after work, and arrived here Friday night due to the international dateline. Before I left home in California I cooked lots of food to be stored in the fridge and cleaned up the whole house, then I took the latest possible flight to arrive Taiwan Tuesday about six in the morning. I rushed home to wash up and then went straight to work. Tuesday was usually the busiest day so I would not fall asleep at work. Tuesday night I would be so tired that I fell asleep without problem and that would adjust the time zone difference.

The demands on her role as wife, mother, and worker in the transnational field exerted a physical toll on her health. She described it as follows:

> One time it was tough. I went straight to work on Tuesday but for some reason I could not sleep that night. I worked straight through Wednesday and I could not sleep that night. The third day I worked straight through and after work I fainted on the street! Another time I came here shortly after a back surgery. I had to wear a steel back support during the long flight, the whole time sitting upright stiff on the plane. Imagine! That's how it was. Good thing I was healthy and chubby!

The long distance separation of her transnational family exerted additional physical demand on Lily. She attempted to fulfill her responsibilities at work in Taiwan, and in her home in the United States that included cooking, cleaning, and other chores. Hartmann's study argues that

> Women who have no paid employment outside the home work over fifty hours per week on household chores: preparing and cleaning up after meals, doing laundry, cleaning the house, taking care of children and other family members, and shopping and keeping records. . . . Their husbands, as reported by their wives, spent about eleven hours a week on housework" (1981: 378).

Despite women's entry into the labor market, men have not contributed much more to share the burden of housework (Huber and Spitze 1983; Berk 1985; Pleck 1985). In addition,

> Women who worked for wages thirty or more hours per week had total work weeks of seventy-six hours on average, including an average of thirty-three hours per week spent on housework time. Yet men whose wives had the longest work weeks had the shortest work weeks themselves (Hartmann 1981.: 379).

To find out how housework was shared by men and women in recent years, a study by the Institute of Social Research at the University of Michigan, Ann Arbor found that "women still do much more than men. . . . Nowadays women are averaging 27 hours [a week], men, closing the gap, average 16" (Newsweek 2002: 41). Regardless of their managerial class background, women remained servants of their transnational families along gendered line in the absence of hired help. Household labor demands on women transcended class difference (Hartmann 1981: 386). Women in the work force struggle with the demands between paid work outside of home and household chores generated by family members. Hochschild (1989b) terms this phenomenon the "second shift," other common expressions are "the double day" or the "double shift" (Steil 1995). Despite their transnational arrangement, there is little to indicate that these Taiwanese American families differ from the general pattern.

One of the chores that Lily continued to perform was her maintenance of what di Leonardo defines as kin work:

> The conception, maintenance, and ritual celebration of cross household kin ties, including visits, letters, telephone calls, presents, and cards to kin; the organization of holiday gatherings; the creation and maintenance

of quasi kin relations; decisions to neglect or to intensify particular ties; the mental work of reflection about all these activities; and the creation and communication of altering images of family and kin vis-à-vis the images of others, both folk and mass media (1987: 442).

Speaking of upper middle income Italian American women in her study, di Leonardo posits that kin work is part of household labor. She points out (ibid.: 443) "it is kinship contact across households, as much as women's work within them, that fulfills our cultural expectation of satisfying family life." It is largely women, not men, who labor on kin work. Further, women poor and rich perform kin work to both kin and public quasi-kin, hence di Leonardo opines that kin work is "gendered rather than class based" (ibid.: 449). However, her discussion neglects the significance of kin work that takes on different meanings and objectives for households with different class backgrounds. She concedes that "households, as labor- and income-pooling units, whatever their relative wealth, are somewhat porous in relation to others with whose members they share kin or quasi-kin. We do not really know how class differences operate in this realm" (ibid.: 448).

I propose that the meaning, significance, and objective of kin work vary with class differences. As alluded to by di Leonardo, "kin work is not just a matter of power among women but also of the mediation of power represented by household units" (ibid.: 445). Poorer folks participate in kin work for mutual emotional and material support (ibid.: 448). For the non-working class, especially the middle-class where social mobility could be relatively more porous, work with public kin contributes to family status production (Papanek 1979). When it is performed for status production,

it is an option, not a necessity for survival, that is undertaken only at certain levels of class or income when these imply sufficient control over scarce resources to assure family survival. The choice of status-production option once this point is reached is determined by interacting social, economic, political, and cultural factors (ibid: 776).

Kin work assumes vital significance for these non-working class Taiwanese American transnational families intent on reproducing their socioeconomic position in the next generation. Entertainment of colleagues and friends, in addition to relatives, reinforces and maintains the family's standing and ties within these social networks. This managerial class of people worked to bolster ties with kin that extended to the public to potentially increase the family's social capital that is convertible to economic capital in the future. Proper kin work in the present ultimately also works to enhance future network and assistance for their children. Thus, the nature and significance of kin work is class specific, while the performance of kin work is gendered as women shoulder the labor.

A suitable wife capable of kin work, to both relations and public kin, directly adds to a husband's asset. She turns increasing essential as the husband moves up the socioeconomic ladder and political arena. Corporate America is replete with examples of the corporate wife. In such a wife's public role, she had to "look and dress the part. . . . She was expected to entertain—sometimes extravagantly, sometimes informally, at the drop of a hat" (Fortune 1998: 71). One corporate wife reports her husband's recognition that since they "have been entertaining as a team, his business has grown appreciably" (ibid.). At the University of California, Riverside it is well known that former Chancellor Raymond Orbach administered the University in his office, while Mrs. Orbach supervised a full schedule daily to run social functions at the Chancellor's residence.

A consultant to chief executive officers comments that "wives are significant and very important—however they are disposed" (ibid.: 72). In politics, Jacqueline Kennedy utilized her linguistic skill in Spanish to campaign for John F. Kennedy's presidency. Her charm and grace added legend to Camelot. More than once Madame Chiang Kai-shek spoke in front of the American public, in her fluent English with an American southern accent, to rally ideological, financial, and military support for her husband against Mao Zedong.

Family status production is women's work (Papanek 1979). Likewise, kin work is mostly women's work, dependent on an adult woman in the household. By extension, kin work includes the cultivation and maintenance of social network with friends as fictive kin in addition to relatives. "When couples divorced or mothers died, the work of kinship was left undone" (di Leonardo1987: 443). Taiwanese American transnational families parallel this division of labor. Lily juggled with household labor including kin work in United States and paid labor in Taiwan as she flew back and forth. According to Lily, her husband was an introvert. Whenever she went to work in Taiwan, her husband had no social life. He did not know how to entertain or initiate socializing with friends. He and the daughter just lived with each other and the whole house turned quiet. Lily commented, "whenever I came I invited our friends to get together. After I left, the friends left too. . . . It's important for a man to have his wife with him for social life."

Indeed, Lily was the wife who cultivated kinship and business socialization for her husband. When I arrived Lily's house for the interview in July 2000, a lively game of mahjong already started well on its way. In that summer afternoon, friends of Lily and her husband congregated in their living room. Another couple was visiting California from Canada, and they dropped by to see Lily and her husband. Two men and two women were sitting around a bridge table intent on playing their game, with a women on the side watching them play. Lily had put dishes of candies, nuts, cut oranges, grapes, and cups of tea on a side table for the players to consume through the game. Lily served me tea and candies in the family room, and then excused herself from the mahjong game in the living room to join me. She said that those people were all old friends going back a long time when they were still in Taiwan. They had all immigrated here, and renewed their friendship circle in southern California.

In the transnational space, some women continued to assume most of the household chores and kin work, extending the "double shift" across political borders. Class reproduction came at the cost of women's physical exhaustion as they managed work and home over long distance. Lily played a vital role in maintaining the network of social relations for her husband and family. While women assume the work, it is the family as a unit that benefits from their labor. However, women may also benefit from her present paid work, housework, and kin work when her children succeed in the future. Women as mothers can take pride in her children's success in the world, when they add weight to family status, and/or when they provide some sort of support in the parents' old age. Lily remarked as follows:

> Children are parents' hope. They're their life extension, their reputation, their glory. Their responsibility is to bring honor and glory to the family, the clan, and the ancestors. . . . The kid's accomplishment is parents' accomplishment. This is traditional mentality.

While Lily conformed to traditional mentality as she stated, some of the women interviewed are caught between modernity and tradition, between personal aspirations and the interest of the family as a unit. Taiwan's modernization educates and prepares these women to be contributing workers; tradition dictates that women remain as primary care givers for their children. These modern, educated women were successful professionals in the work force, yet they were constrained by the traditional roles and expectations of mothers and wives. They were held responsible for childcare and housework. The sacrifice is made for the continuation of the family as a unit in face of socioeconomic and political adversities. More often it is made for the sake of children, in an attempt to give the children an academic education that would enhance their future career prospects. This move is seen as necessary to improve or to reproduce the parents' current socioeconomic class position for the children.

Like women in historical Chinese American transnational families who shouldered work in and outside of home in the absence of the husbands, Taiwanese American transnational families challenged and dissolved the separation of the public and private spheres, as both functional and geographic metaphors. Working women shuttled across time and space between two countries to actively perform reproductive labor, paid productive labor, household work, and kin work. Even women who did not participate in paid labor market became head of household in the prolonged absence of their husbands. Women represented their families to deal with the public in their communities, all necessary interactions for the maintenance of their households that they now headed. The public and the private domains merge in the transnational space that transcends geographical, territorial, and political borders.

Some Korean immigrants in New York also maintain transnational families between the United States and Korea (Min 1998). Although their arrangement and situation are somewhat different, it might be helpful to look at them for the purpose of comparison. In two cases, the husbands first came to the United States for graduate studies, subsequently got married, and then established themselves in the United States. In one case, the husband arrived with his wife and two young children to work in an American company. After living in the United States as a family together for several years, these husbands returned to Korea while the wife and children remained in the United States. "In Korean transnational families, the wives participate in paid work while taking care of the children by themselves" (ibid.: 112). In all three cases, the husband underwent the process of migration and personal relocation. They interrupted their career paths and uprooted themselves for their return to Korea, instead of the wives. In addition, the wives had already established their families and careers in the United States before the husbands departed for their country of origin. Given the circumstances, these Korean women could combine their roles of mother and worker better and more successfully in comparison to their Taiwanese counterparts in California.

Split family in the transnational field also generated gendered problems for mothers who coped with children alone. The following section illuminates these non-working class women's challenges as mothers in transnational families.

IMPACT ON WOMEN AS MOTHERS

Several women lamented the difficulties of dealing with children in the prolonged absence of the husbands. These difficulties include physical and mental stress as well as discipline issues. Physical stress was acute for the few women such as Martha and Diane who also worked in the United States. Martha had come to the United States for her undergraduate education. After graduation she married her husband who was a former graduate student from Taiwan. In the 1980s they moved to California for his job and then the company sent him to Asia. Martha's siblings all lived out of state and her parents remained in Taiwan. Before Martha joined her husband again she was a de facto single mother who also worked until her daughter was two years old. In order to arrive at work on time she often had to rush in the morning. She said,

> I spoon fed her breakfast in such a rush that sometimes she took in everything too fast and could not swallow. Then she just threw up and spit everything out from her mouth. That's when I really wished someone could be there to lend me a hand. It was also hard when I got sick.

Mothers with extended family nearby coped with different problems. Diane's husband had been flying back and forth since 1992, often gone for four or five months each time. In Diane's words,

> He came back here like back to a motel. The children grew up without their father and any social life. I came home from work exhausted so I just wanted to rest. When I had to take them out I did not enjoy it. The children had no social skill. They became loners, and I became a loner too.

When I visited Diane at her home in the summer of 2001, her three children were aged between seventeen and eleven, and the oldest child needed special care. The children had coped with the father's absence since a very young age.

When Diane's husband started in 1992 to leave on business for months on end, her parents-in-law came to live with her and assisted with childcare. This arrangement turn out to be problematic due to different parenting styles. In Diane's opinion, her parents-in-law helped with the physical care of young children but not their emotional needs. Further, the grandparents' favoritism toward the youngest child fostered resentment in the middle one. Several counselors had told Diane about the middle child's lack of concentration in class. The transnational family situation also affected her relationship with her three young children. According to Diane, the children might have needs sometimes but they chose not to bother her since she was so busy. Instead they took care of themselves as much as they could.

As a consequence, the children grew up to be independent, but in her view they were not sufficiently attached to her. Further, while they took care of themselves physically, emotionally they were still children with children's needs but they could not express themselves. According to Diane, they accepted their father's absence but deep down they wished he were around. The children's homeroom teachers told Diane that they could always tell from her children when their father went away again.

While working mothers tried to cope with physical demands as de facto single mothers, other women experienced added mental stress. Problems arose even for women who did not work. When Wen's husband left for Taiwan, she was bitter. She reflected,

> It was his choice, not mine. It turned the whole house and family upside down. When the kids wanted to learn to drive, when they needed to prepare for SAT, when the girls wanted to go out with guys, it was all me to deal with these difficult things that went with their growing up.

As the only parent around, Yang considered it her responsibility to educate her son to the best of her ability. She felt compelled to show her husband the best in her son, so every time he came home to the United States she sensed pressure. On the other hand, Lai considered that she and her husband made the move and endured separation partly for the children's education. To make such efforts worthwhile she constantly pressed her son and daughter in high school to study harder. The urging often ended in arguments, because the children had their own pressures at school as they attempted to adjust to a new educational system, a foreign language of instruction, and a different environment. When arguments erupted, the tension remained after the arguments ended when there was no other adult at home to mediate or defuse it.

The absence of a father's input was most keenly felt when a mother needed to play the role of a father for a teenage son. One mother said,

> I have only this one son. How do I use a male's approach to teach him? For example, how do I talk to my son about sex education? I need my husband to teach him about this. It's hard for me to cover this topic. My son also doesn't feel comfortable discussing this subject with me. I have to be his father, too, but I don't know how to fulfill this role.

A mother cited gendered activities as her problem. In her opinion, families with fathers could experience outdoor lives and sport activities, she could only take them shopping at the malls. She said,

The kids lost all the fun. There was no father around for real family life with both parents. For seven years he was no father and no husband. He just sent the money. I think he felt guilty about that.

Double parenting added cost to women in the Taiwanese American trans-national families in their effort to reproduce their class positions. In the prolonged absence of their husbands, women assumed full responsibility for their children's physical and emotional health, education, growth and development. Despite the financial support from husbands, the physical and mental demands became taxing.

A father's sense of guilt also posed challenges for mothering. The challenges often concerned discipline. When some fathers returned home to the United States after a long period of absence, out of guilt they did every thing their children wanted to compensate for their time away. One father would give the older child US$1,000 for presents when he was only a teenager. The child learned that if he persisted then the father would give in, the father yielded to his children's demands every time he returned. When I interviewed the mother, she was upset because her husband had just agreed to buy a car for his son who barely reached fifteen years of age. "I am concerned for his safety. He also has no need for a car," she groaned. She and her husband argued more now than before concerning child discipline. Another father interrupted and undercut the mother when she was disciplining the children. The mother lamented, "When their father comes back, he plays the good guy. I am strict but ineffective. They are too used to me."

In the fathers' absence, some mothers marshaled older children to help handle the younger ones. In one woman's account, she was close to her three teenage daughters, and the three teenagers were close with one another, but the youngest one had a mind of her own. The mother found that this daughter was hard to discipline. Whenever major problem arose and the mother failed to work things out with her, the mother recruited her oldest daughter to communicate with the youngest one. Another mother was close to the oldest daughter but argued with the younger teenage son not to do certain things, such as spending too much time on the computer. The mother asked the older daughter to play a role to defuse the tension yet the daughter declined, saying that it would jeopardize her relationship with her brother if she appeared to side with the mother in the arguments. In circumstances such as these, the mothers remarked, the transnational family arrangement placed a lot of pressure on the mothers and children.

Different infrastructures in the country of destination also reconfig-ured a woman's relationship with her children. In densely populated Taiwan, public transit is necessary to transport the masses from one place to another. A modern subway system, frequent bus services, a well built rail network, and the many available taxis all contribute to transportation convenience. Such convenience also makes adults and children very mobile. Students, including those in grade schools, swamp the buses and subways every week- day morning and afternoon to commute between schools and homes. The buses come frequently during peak traffic hours—a service every five min- utes or so, and the subway trains run just as often. Passengers line up in files to get on board the trains that extend to the four directions. The buses and subways serve till past midnight, the taxis run 24 hours a day.

I was a little nervous the first time I went out alone in Taipei shortly past ten o'clock at night. It normally took forty-five minutes on the subway to get back to the Nangang suburb where I lived. I feared that I would be attacked or robbed walking alone on the street that late at night, like I probably would be in Los Angeles. To my astonishment, when I arrived at the subway station, more people stood in line to wait for the trains than I had ever seen on any streets in the suburb of Los Angeles at that time of the night. I soon found that in Taipei, stores along the streets opened till late into the night. I learnt to meet friends at the cafes and teahouses that remained in operation past midnight. We also ate and shopped at the night markets that began to get busy only after dark. In Taipei, there was much life after school and work. A lively night life, combined with convenient public transporta- tion, kept even children away from mothers. A mother complained about such distance from her two adolescent sons,

> In Taiwan we never spent much time together. The children had to go to school, after that they went straight to cram schools. They did not appear before me until after ten o'clock. Then they went out with their own friends for sports or movies on weekends. There's lots of entertain- ment and public transportation was convenient even for kids. I needed to make appointments with them in order to have dinner with them together!

In the suburbs of southern California, where automobiles are a neces- sity rather than luxury, minors depend on adults to transport them. Now her children came home after school, and stayed home more frequently than when they lived in Taiwan. The mother noticed the difference. She said, "I spend time with the children as a family. We have more time together. It's a quality life." In Taiwan, her children attended many more social events and extra curricular activities independent of their mother. She exclaimed, "It seems like one is always busy there!"

Despite the many cost borne by women, they also reaped as they sowed. One benefit that a woman received in return was the formation of her "uterine family" as discussed in Chapter Seven. Mothers who had weathered their husbands' absence among their children offered some words of comfort. One woman looked back at all the hard work in the past and marveled at the harvest that followed, "My friends told me that I had to chauffeur the kids when they were small, but when they grew up they would chauffeur me. It's true! Now they drive me wherever I want to go!" Another mother told her children to care for the family together as a unit because there were only the few of them around since the father was not. She taught them that they must be close to one another, discuss and share things together. The children and mother grew to be very close. Now that the youngsters had grown up, parents and grown children still telephoned at least once a week. She said, "When one thing happens, the whole family knows about it." The mother continued to keep the whole family together by keeping them involved. For example, before she had the family house painted she asked for everyone's opinion on the choice of color. She described her family relationship as follows, "My son's cat recently died and he felt sad. Everyone in the family felt sad for him. We have concern for one another. We are scattered in places but we live like we are under the same roof."

On the other hand, the few women who commuted across the Pacific Ocean juggled with the strain on motherhood in the transnational space. Liu naturalized childcare as mothers' work. In her opinion, it was less satisfactory when fathers stayed in the United States to care for the children. "Maybe some men are good with caring for kids, but not my husband." She lamented. She considered her husband to be less attentive, taking care of only the physical needs but not emotional needs or the health of their children while she was gone. She also commented that her husband did not monitor the children's studies close enough, leading to their less satisfactory results. She remarked, "If I had stayed with them I would have disciplined them more with their home work." Liu also dealt with any money problem by herself out of her concern for the children. To supply sufficient stock for the family company in the United States, she purchased merchandise for her husband to sell in the United States. She also needed to cover the operating expense for their factory in Taiwan. She said,

> I didn't dare to ask my husband to send me money because I was afraid that if he didn't have enough money then the kids would not have enough to eat and use. I just tried to manage and borrow money here. I was under constant pressure.

The transnational family arrangement became particularly taxing for women who were emotionally close to both husband and children who now lived separately under different roofs across the vast Pacific Ocean. In such a circumstance, their role as caregiver to both husband and children also pulled some women in opposite directions. Janet's two sons attended school in southern California and her husband worked in Taiwan. They had maintained a transnational family for ten years when I interviewed her. Her parents and siblings all lived nearby. She would fly back to be with her husband two or three times a year while her relatives watched her teenager sons. Her husband visited them in the States once or twice a year. Janet reported acute mental anguish in the first few years of the split household arrangement. She said,

> When I was here to take care of the children, I worried that no one cared for my husband in Taiwan. When I was in Taiwan with my husband, I knew I was taking care of my husband but then I worried that no one was here in the States to care for the children.

To fulfill their role of caregivers to both husband and children now apart in the transnational space, some women shuttled between husbands at work and the children at home. These women mediated the transnational separation of the two domains by traveling frequently between the United States and Taiwan to perform their roles as caregivers to both husbands and children. One woman named Lan had been flying back and forth since 1996. Her husband lived in Taiwan and her two youngest daughters (now university students) lived in southern California. The father came once a year for about a month each time, and the mother spent half her time here and the other half in Taiwan. Since her older daughters and their spouses lived near Lan's home in Taiwan, they could take care of the father when Lan came to stay with the two daughters in the States. She said, "The family is split in two places far apart. I miss the children. It's hard. I cry every time I have to leave for Taiwan. It's not that I worry. It's just hard to be apart from them, not to be together."

One woman handled a particularly hectic schedule as she tried to take care of both her husband and son on each side of the Pacific Ocean. The following itinerary in one year was representative of her effort:

- To the U.S. in August, to Taiwan the following January
- To the U.S. in March, back to Taiwan in the same month
- To the U.S. in April, back to Taiwan in May

- To the U.S. in June, back to Taiwan in September
- To the U.S. in October, back to Taiwan in November

She commented that her husband was not good with household bills and daily routines. She said, "I went back and forth to take care of my child in the States and my husband in Taiwan. One year our airplane tickets cost over US$10,000."

Transnational mothering became more complex when young children in the same family were split in two countries. To care for youngsters in both households in the United States and Taiwan, a woman resorted to "kinscription, which is the process of assigning kin-work to family members" who are primarily female (Stack and Burton 1998). Influenced by her sister's suggestion and urging, in the mid-1990s Ling came to United Sates with her first child who was thirteen years old to start his ninth grade in southern California. Her second son was still young and remained in Taiwan. Her husband was often away on duty in the military. In order to take care of both sons and households now in two different countries, Ling recruited her mother to assist in her transnational mothering. In the initial period of the transnational arrangement, Ling came and stayed for six months with the older son in the States, while her mother looked after the younger son in the home in Taiwan. Ling then returned to Taiwan to be with the younger son, and her mother came to the States to care for the older one. After two months, her mother returned to care for the younger child in Taiwan and Ling came to live with the older son in southern California. After about a year and a half of such arrangement, the older son grew more accustomed to the new environment and Ling started to live in Taiwan for three months with the younger child, and two months in the States with the older one. Her mother continued to switch places with Ling in order to care for both youngsters. While Ling stayed in Taiwan she frequently telephoned her mother and older child in the United States to keep in touch. Ling's transnational mothering would not have been possible without the assistance of her mother. In the transnational space, childcare turned into a kin-centered collective endeavor that is gendered work within the extended family.

The mode of transnational mothering also varies with class. It concerns, first, the class membership of the individual involved; and second, the class standing of the home country in the world economic order. With relative affluence, the non-working class mother in the above example flew back and forth between Taiwan and the United States, in order to be with her children who resided separately in the two countries for the express purpose of caring for them personally. In stark contrast, many transnational mothers from Latin America, the Caribbean, and the Philippines (Alicea 1997: 620; Hondagneu-Sotelo and Avila 1997; Parreñas 2000) perform wage labor in more economically advanced countries such as the United States, and send remittances to support their own children and kin back home. "Transnational households are in fact the dominant strategy of household maintenance for migrant Filipina domestic workers" (Parreñas 2000: 337).

These economically dominated women work as housekeepers or nannies to care for children of professional or wealthy couples. The domestic workers with children of their own subordinate their personal reproductive work and interest, to that of their professional and wealthy employers for a wage. Unable to fly back and forth at will due to employment and cost or legal barriers, Latina and Filipina transnational mothers maintain connection with their children by post, telephone calls, photographs, and gifts. While these women from less developed countries earn their wages as domestic workers, they in turn entrust their own children to kin or even hired hands in the home countries, paid with wages earned from childcare and housework for others (Hondagneu-Sotelo 2001; Parreñas 2000). Transnational mothering for these women means earning a wage by manual labor in the country of destination, in order to reproduce the next generation separated from them in space and time in the hands of someone else in the country of origin. It illustrates the stratified mode of reproduction due to an individual's class membership.

Differences in transnational mothering also reflect on the relative economic, or class, standing of their home countries in the world economy. Mothers who earned a wage in developed core countries in the world system, as in the United States, can provide more financial support for their children being raised in the less developed periphery countries of origin, such as the Philippines or in Latin America, where the cost of living is much lower. "Gladys, who had four of her five children in El Salvador, acknowledged that her U.S. dollars went further in El Salvador" (Hondagneu-Sotelo and Avila 1997: 563). The relative economic standing of Taiwan and the Philippines in the world economy is shown by the example of a transnational Filipina mother working in Taiwan, who earned far more as a housekeeper, factory worker, or a janitor than she did as a public school teacher in the Philippines (Parreñas 2000: 344). Reproduction is stratified according to individual class membership as well as the class standing of one's country of origin in the world society. Hence, transnational mothering is affected by class privilege, or the lack thereof, at the individual as well as state level.

In mothering, migration also induced some role reversals between Taiwanese American mothers and children. In some immigrant families this role reversal involve what is called "language brokering" served by the children (see, e.g., Chao 2002). One of the challenges faced by some immigrants in the United States is the problem of language barrier. Children in these immigrant families may command better English than their parents after some years of education in American schools. They often act as interpreters or translators for their parents, and as intermediary between their parents and the larger community. This reliance on children for "language brokering" may reverse or compromise the parent-child authority relationship. Although some of the women I interviewed indicated language problem, particularly those with only a high school education, most of them have relied on friends and the dictionary. Further, language barriers appeared to be less a problem for the interviewees who lived near "ethnoburbs" that are complete with Chinese-owned supermarkets, restaurants, banks, and various services needed for daily living. Speaking only the Chinese language, whether Cantonese or Mandarin, one can function very well in the Chinese ethnoburbs.

However, lack of proficient English at times diminished the mother as the authority figure at home. Children witnessed mother's weakness in English, and some interpreted that weakness as a shortcoming. The mother was not the "supermom" who could do it all. One mother admitted that because of her limited English, she did not understand much about the local school situations. Often her two teenage children had to make their own decisions regarding school-related matters. Once another mother requested her teenage son to call a home repair insurance company to explain some problems in English, he refused her request claiming that when problem arose he had to help himself so she should handle problems by herself. In one case, role reversal for one mother involved gendered dimension. Since the father lived away from home most of the time, her teenage sons assumed the role of guardian watching over the mother's activity. They became protective of the mother, and checked on her social life to see if she was going out with a male or female.

While less educated mothers encountered language problems, highly educated women with English proficiency assisted their children with school matters that contributed to a closer mother-child relationship. One woman spent all of her time in the United States with her son during his senior year in high school. She considered the time well spent as she kept him company through his SAT testing, assisted him with applications to several universities and subsequent interviews with different schools. She handled most of the paperwork for him so he could concentrate on schoolwork. "He had only one eighteen-year-old," she said, "I am glad I was there for him to give him moral support and encouragement, otherwise I would feel guilty." According to this mother, the children were much closer to her than to their father.

IMPACT ON WOMEN AS INDIVIDUALS

In these Taiwanese American transnational families, wives at home in the United States lived physically apart from their working husbands in Taiwan for extended period of time. This experience affected women as individuals in gendered fashion. They resembled the ways that impacted Mexican women in transnational families where the working-class husbands live in the United States. Hence, these gendered ways traverse class backgrounds. Like the Mexican wives, several women in my sample reported independence and freedom, particularly relief from housework and care work associated with husbands as well as respites from their domination. Despite the added burden of childcare and responsibility around the house, most women appeared to cherish more relaxed time away from their husbands after the initial loneliness subsided.

Studies on housework time of single parents in the United States demonstrate that "single women spend considerably less time on housework than wives, for the same size family" (Hartmann 1981: 383). From data on the minimum time necessary for house care, Hartmann estimates that "the wife spends perhaps eight hours per week in additional housework on account of the husband" (ibid.: 385). Similarly, husbands' presence appeared to create extra household for the wives in my sample. Several of them reported less household chores and cooking in the husband's absence, giving them a sense of freedom and relaxation. One woman named Ying felt much freer and somewhat relieved whenever the husband left for Taiwan. Despite more responsibility for the children, she no longer had to cook his breakfast and dinner every day and take care of him.

Kate also reported extra work "on account of the husband." She said,

> I'm a very tidy person but he's not. He throws things around the house so I must tolerate that. I pick up after him. It's better now than before when we're together everyday.

Kate appreciated the respite from caring for her husband. She commented,

> I have more freedom when he's not around. I come and go as I please. When he's here I can't go anywhere if he doesn't want to go some place. Even if I get to go, I have to first prepare his lunch or food for him.

Yeh also described her freedom, "There is no one to stop me from doing what I wanted to do. I attend school and my kids go to school. Everything is well arranged." Chu mentioned that when her husband came back, he made the whole family follow his wishes. Everyone had to go with him where he wanted and did whatever he desired. She said, "The good thing about the transnational arrangement is freedom. It's more relaxing with just about everything. Even the children can feel the difference." Likewise, Faye expressed similar sentiments, "Sometime it's kind of nice when he's not around. When he's around I have to do things the way he likes. I pay him extra attention and care, and cook some of his favorite dishes. It involves more work."

Further, women experienced independence and growth in their husbands' prolonged absence. While most husbands used to make decisions in Taiwan before migration, wives in the United States now had opportunities to make judgment and decide on their own since the husbands worked in Taiwan. In the past, some wives must discuss everything with their husbands before any decision, leading to arguments and frustration in some cases. Now they could act unilaterally. The ability to make certain decisions alone provided a sense of relief for some women. Ying related her experience as follows:

> When we were together, I had to discuss with him and we often had difference of opinions. Take my son's education for example. In the past he wanted my son to attend a local public school. I wanted him to go to the private international school. We argued. Now that he's not around, he doesn't know the situation here so I can make decision on my own quickly.

One woman, Shi, in particular cherished the transnational arrangement. Her case involved money issues. Women in my sample reported various ways to control money between husband and wife. One wife who worked for pay and another who did not work both reported egalitarian access to a pooled joint account with direct deposit from employers. Both the wives in the United States and the husbands in Taiwan could access their account information and management by on-line banking. Yet another wife involved in her family business knew how much asset she and her husband co-owned. Some husbands turned over their monthly income to the wife who in turn gave the husband a monthly allowance. Others sent monthly remittance to the wives in the United States for household expenses. Studies on money control in the household often focus on issues of power (see, e.g.,

Volger 1998), but Shi's experience illustrates the access to money as a mea-
surement of individual esteem.

When Shi and her husband lived together in Taiwan, the husband was
the sole breadwinner who controlled money distribution for household expenses. Shi said,

> One time we argued a lot just over a sofa. I didn't dare to make decision,
> afraid that I would make the wrong one. If I bought some thing he could
> criticize that I paid too much. He would return or exchange the item.
> That's what he did with one of the kid's bed.

He also made all decisions regarding purchases for the family including
household appliances, sofas, and beds. She only bought groceries. Instead
of a monthly fixed amount of money in a lump sum, the husband gave
Shi little by little for grocery expenditure. "It was painful when it came to
money," Shi continued, "every time when money ran out I had to ask him
for money with my palms wide open." Shi gave me the example of getting
NT$5,000 (US$150 approximately) to feed a family of five—husband and
wife with three growing children. When she had expended all the money on
food she asked her husband for more and he said: "Why did you spend it
all so quickly?" Shi told me, "You know how little NT$5,000 can buy." I
knew. I lived within walking distance to a traditional open market during
my year in Taiwan. During my first month of residence I visited the market
every morning. To feed a family of five in Taiwan, food expenditure became
a challenge even for a careful money manager like Shi.

Now that Shi's husband worked in Taiwan, he wired remittance to Shi
every month. Shi no longer had to ask him for food money with her "palms
wide open" like she did before, unless she used up the remittance before the
next wiring. "I only spend on what's necessary. I'm not a spendthrift." Shi
remarked. Now that Shi took care of everything in the husband's absence,
he also trusted her more. The monthly remittance from Taiwan liberated Shi
from former subordination to her husband. She was able to decide on how
to spend money. In Shi's opinion, the husband did not respect her much in
the past. Her marriage had subjugated Shi to her husband. The current split
household arrangement freed Shi from his domination. The transnational
space provided her some room and opportunity to establish herself as an
individual. The individual is gendered. In Shi's case, family life in the transnational field acted as mediation to negotiate a less asymmetrical position
for a woman in a hierarchical relationship with her husband. Shi felt more
like an individual, not an appendage. The transnational split household

arrangement provides the wife an opportunity for liberation from subordination. In transnational families, women experience autonomy, authority, and freedom despite their continued economic dependence on the husbands for financial support.

As individuals, these women also interacted with others across households and with the community. Except for one woman who arrived southern California in the mid-1970s, and another woman in the 1990s to open local branch offices, the rest all reported the presence of kin and/or friends in the area. These social relations provided support system and assistance when necessary. Some women's entire natal family lived in the region. They simply transplanted their kinship network from Taiwan to southern California. Janet's situation reflected this. She was a housewife in Taiwan, and continued to stay home after her arrival in southern California in 1990. When she first arrived, she spent her time visiting relatives and friends and shopping. She had studied floral arrangements in Taiwan. Via a friend's connection, she later worked part-time as a floral designer at a flower shop. She led a busy life. She said, "My own family all lived nearby in the same neighborhood so we get together on weekends or special holidays, such as Mother's Day and the Spring Festival." Other times she met friends for lunch. She continued, "My time is all booked up. I am very busy now." Some women also took their children for long trips with relatives to Hawaii or national parks.

Many women spent time with other women in transnational families to commiserate, much like women in historical Chinese transnational families. The women in contemporary Taiwanese American transnational families visited women with husbands and children here, but during the day when they were away in schools or at work. Women met for lunch, practiced yoga together, or went to the gym for exercises. They baked at home and brought these home made pastry to visit their neighbors. Many women also went to public adult schools to study English as a second language (ESL). In the summer of 2000 I went to one school in a neighborhood with a high percentage of residents from Taiwan and sat in the classes. The ESL classes were divided into beginning, intermediate, and advance level. Some classes were further divided into A and B for each level. Classes started at eight o'clock in the morning until twelve-thirty in the afternoon with recess breaks in between, everyday from Monday to Friday. On Saturday mornings the school offered computer classes such as Microsoft Word. Elderly as well as younger men and women of all adult ages listened attentively to the teachers, but there were many more females than males. The males were presumably at work. When the recess bell rang all the adults came out to the schoolyard. Every one was chatting away in Mandarin or Minnan Hua. A woman told me that she met many friends at the school.

Those women with fewer relatives around reached out to religious organizations for social network. Approximately half of the women in my sample joined Christian churches that conducted services in Mandarin or Minnan Hua; a few attended the Hsi Lai Buddhist Temple. Not all of them were religious. Some sent their children to participate in youth activities organized by these churches, or they joined their women's group for social purposes. Churches provided several activities that kept the entire family busy. When children joined Youth Group on Friday evening, women met other women at Mother's Meeting. One woman remarked,

> Church is good for us because it gives us a lot of support. I also learn from other women's experience. It is good for the kids too because their classmates are not close friends. They find close friends in the youth fellowship group and they do things together so church life is very important to them.

For women in transnational families with few local adult family members, religious organizations appear to provide a vital outlet for social interactions and support. Kate attended her church's activities that included Friday Fellowship and Bible Study on Saturday. She worshipped at her church on Sundays. "I'm so tired after work, besides church activities I just live a simple life," she commented. Women who did not work gathered in the middle of the week for special purpose activities.

Religious organizations played the role of a big family that provided certain support system for members such as individuals in transnational families. However, church services did not always meet a member's every need. Diane was a mother of three and one of them had special need. In Diane's opinion, her church friends did not help in a way she needed, such as a male role model in her husband's prolonged absence. In addition, she said,

> I wish they would offer to take my children out to sport events or to participate in a sport game. When mothers take their daughters to a hair cut, they could call to see if they could take my daughters along for a hair cut too. Very few offer that kind of help. I need help with the day-to-day activities, not theory.

Women close to their family members who remained in Taiwan continued their ties by frequent telephone contacts or personal visits. Liu came to southern California with her husband to open a branch company and her relatives all lived in Taiwan. She called her sister regularly. Yen arrived in the mid-1990s primarily for her children's education. The family immigrated on kin sponsorship by her husband's sister under the family reunification provision. Her sister-in-law's family lived nearby in the same neighborhood, and Yen maintained regular contact with her natal family. Yen came from a very close family and she had always been close to her parents, her brother and his wife. Every year Yen went to Taiwan to spend Chinese New Year with them. Her gratification from her visits recharged her gendered role as a mother and caregiver. She said,

> Here I'm a mother, I give love and affection to my children. When I go to Taiwan, I receive love and affection from my own parents. I need that. Here I must depend on myself, there they give me support and help me.

Migration entailed an emotional toll on women in transnational families, particularly those uprooted from their kinship network and social relations. Away from marital partners, they took on responsibility as de facto single parents to shepherd their children. As individuals they needed support and affection from friends and family. For those who lacked such nurturance in the immediate environment, they sought them from sources still left in Taiwan. These are ties that bind an individual to a larger whole, even in transnational space.

Although little has been done to study what women do in their husbands' prolonged absence, women in my sample related rather ordinary daily activities of household chores, childcare, work, and the usual interactions with relatives and friends. There is a lot of living to do, wherever the husbands may be. It bespeaks women's intense involvement in housework and childcare that consume so much time and energy. In fact, as remarked by the women, there appeared to be even more work and less freedom when the husbands returned. Despite the emotional ties with husbands, their presence also became more a physical burden than relief. In a transnational family, a wife enjoys more freedom, independence, authority, and autonomy in the absence of the husband; although she continues to depend on him for financial support.

SUMMARY

The transnational family split in the United States and Taiwan is a gendered formation with both cost and benefit to women as workers, mothers, and individuals. While professional women in Taiwan were able to combine their roles as mother and worker, the long distance involved in international migration disrupted professional women's career path in Taiwan in order to care for their children in the United States. Although some women welcomed the opportunity not to work, others gave up their successful careers only after personal internal conflict. A few professional women capitulated to migration under duress. While migration was a strategy to benefit the family as a unit, it was professional women who bore the cost in order to fulfill their role as mothers. Despite the benefits of a closer relationship with children, mothers as de facto single parents shouldered full responsibility for parenting. The difficulties involved physical and mental stresses, as well as disciplinary issues with children. Migration and the transnational arrangement made some wives more dependent on husbands for economic support, but it also provided opportunity for women to become the head of the household to exercise autonomy and authority. Wives also enjoyed some relief from extra work caused by their husbands' presence.

The next chapter attends to the impact of transnational family arrangement on marital relations.

Chapter Nine
Impact on Marital Relations

Beside those from Taiwan and United States or Canada, transnational families are also widespread between Hong Kong (a former British colony) and Australia, Canada, or New Zealand.[1] These families adopt this transnational practice primarily for political reasons. By the mutual agreement of 1984, Britain retroceded Hong Kong to China in July 1997. Prior to this date, many Hong Kongers emigrated in order to establish a safe haven in other countries with a democratic government to avoid communist rule (see, e.g., Skeldon 1994, 1995; Ong 1993, 1999). Some of them, predominantly non-working class, subsequently formed transnational families. Several studies investigate these families split in Hong Kong and Australia or Canada. In the literature, they are referred to as "astronaut families." Within a smaller regional context and to a lesser extent, transnational families have also emerged recently when Singaporean corporate husbands relocate to China while their wives and children remain in the home country (Yeon and Khoo 1998; Willis and Yeoh 2000), and when Chinese-Malaysian professionals work in Singapore with their spouses and children residing in the home country of Malaysia (Lam, Yeoh, and Law 2002).

Out of the above, far more work has been done on those families originated from Hong Kong that migrated to Australia, Canada, and New Zealand (see, e.g., Ho 2002; Ho, Ip, and Bedford 2001; Pe-Pua, et al.1996). Pe-Pua, et al. (1996) discuss those families' adjustment difficulties in Australia. Hui (1993), Lam (1994), and Man (1993, 1996a, 1996b) report contradictory effects of the transnational family arrangement on marital relations in Canada: 1) positive and improved spousal relationship such as renewed love, increased appreciation, stronger and closer emotional ties; but also 2) loneliness, increased conflict and arguments, discontent and divorce; and 3) continuity where there is little change before and after migration. However, the above studies offer little in-depth explanation for the various consequences. With such disparate conclusions, there is need for further research to explain the discrepancies.

This chapter looks at the effect of transnational split-household formation on marital relations, and examines the range of conditions that affect different marriages in various fashions within Taiwanese American transnational families.

COMMUTER VERSUS TRANSNATIONAL MARRIAGES

In what the participants viewed as traditional marriage in this study, husband and wife routinely live under the same roof in a shared residence. The salient feature of transnational family is the split household arrangement where married couples regularly live apart in separate countries. Dual residence marriages, where partners live away from each other, are not unique to transnational families. In the United States many married couples also maintain separate households within the same country (see Farris 1978; Kirschner and Wallum 1978; Gross 1980; Gerstel and Gross 1984,1987; Johnson 1987; Winfield 1985; Anderson and Spruill 1993; Hendershott 1995). Referred to as "commuter marriages," they are relationships in which "employed spouses who spend at least three nights per week in separate residence and yet are still married and intend to remain so" (Gerstel and Gross 1984: 13). Often husbands and wives live and work apart in two different geographical locations during the week and reunite on the weekend. Some couples live apart for longer periods—one or more month at a time. Commuter couples are largely non-working class professionals. This class background is similar to that of the Taiwanese American transnational families: professionals, business executives, and a high proportion of academics (Anderson and Spruill 1993: 133)

Gerstel and Gross (1987: 423) distinguish three types of commuter couples: the "adjusting couples" who are younger and earlier in their careers and most likely to be without child; the "balancing couples" who are older, more advanced in their careers, and have children at home; and the "established" couples whose children are grown and no longer at home. The transnational families in my sample all had children at home during the period when they maintained separate residences across national boundaries. Hence, they were most comparable to the balancing couples. In the sections below, American commuter marriages will be discussed as commuter marriages, and Taiwanese American transnational marriages will be referred to simply as transnational marriages.

Fundamental disparities exist between transnational and commuter marriages despite parallels. Commuter marriages are often formed to accommodate the career or occupation continuity of both spouses. Sometimes one spouse is relocated out of town where the other is unable to obtain satisfactory position, or when the spouse is unwilling to relocate and discontinue the current employment. Commuter couples voluntarily choose to establish separate household in different geographical locations so they both can pursue their careers to which they are committed (Gerstel and Gross 1987: 7). Often commuter couples adopt separate residences in order to advance the wife's employment interest. It is the wife who benefits from this arrangement.

Wives in Taiwanese American transnational families were seldom the focus of concern. Instead, considerations centered on the husband's career or business, on children's education opportunities, or on the family's future survival as a collective unit. More often than not, a woman severed her career path in Taiwan to migrate to the United States in order to care for the children. Contrary to the recognition of wife as career woman in commuter marriages, in transnational families a woman's professional interest remained secondary. Commuter spouses are motivated by beliefs that each partner's professional advance has priority over shared residence. Given the high cost of commuting and maintaining two households, it is rarely practiced for monetary gain. In contrast, transnational families adopted the dual household strategy for economic reasons: the husband returned to or remained in Taiwan to maximize family income. With husband and wife living in different countries, how did they keep up their marital relations and communication? The following section attempts to answer this question.

MAINTAINING TRANSNATIONAL MARRIAGES

One common characteristic between commuter and transnational marriages is the long distance marital relationship split in discrete geographical locations. While commuter wives live apart from their husbands within the United States, the territorial distance between transnational couples extends across the vast Pacific Ocean and transcends national political borders. Far apart from their spouses, both types of marriages rely on communication technology to maintain day-to-day interactions in their relations. Most of the women in my sample cited the regular use of telephone to maintain contacts with their husbands and family members. Some couples arranged a set time to talk to each other once a day, once a week, or twice a week, but placed additional telephone call whenever it became necessary. Others called any time spontaneously. While the expense of long distance telephone inhibit some American commuter couples (Gerstel and Gross 1984: 57), Taiwanese American transnational women cherished the low rate of trans-Pacific telephone calls. One woman exclaimed,

> Now you can use those prepaid phone cards to call Taiwan. It's so cheap. We called when it cost forty cents a minute. Then it went down to twenty cents. Now it's only about eight cents a minute. I owe it to myself to call!

Most women spent about two to three hundred U.S. dollars a month on long distance calls to husbands (not counting the amount paid by their husbands in Taiwan). They also kept up social relations with friends and family members in Taiwan via telephone.

Such long distance maintenance came at a cost. Yen and her two sons scored the record high expense in maintaining social relations by long distance telephone. During one of the early months after their arrival in southern California, the telephone company cut their access to international dialing even before the bill was due. Yen said,

> I guess the phone company was afraid that we could not pay the bill. It was $2,900! My children and I had a family meeting two months ago. We resolved to limit our long distance bill to $500 a month, so it's been $300 to $500 lately.

Yen's husband also called the family here from Taiwan. According to Yen, he called them every day when he returned from business trips. She said, "Sometimes he calls so often that our sons feel harassed!"

Some commuter couples in the United States consider telephone contact less than satisfactory. They miss the touching, hugging, and kissing that are not possible given their physical separation (Gerstel and Gross 1984: 56–66; Kirschner and Wallum 1978: 517). None of the transnational women and men interviewed expressed similar regret about the lack of physical affection. Typically East Asian couples now in their middle age rarely display physical affection such as kissing and hugging in the public or in front of third persons, including their children. American commuters also complain about the insistency of telephones. Whenever one spouse calls and the telephone rings, the other has to answer the phone. It interrupts their work in progress, they claim. Transnational couples seldom reported such problem. They made phone calls at mutually agreed set time each day or each week, and called whenever there was matter to be discussed. Faye did mention that she was very dependent on her husband and called whenever she needed help from him regardless of time. Sometimes, she said, it could be very disruptive for her husband especially when he was busy at work. For commuter couples, communication over the telephone at times contribute to frustration and anger due to the lack of face-to-face communication (Gerstel and Gross 1984: 60). However, in Kay's opinion, communication by phone actually improved her marital relation. This might point to the tension in this couple's daily interaction when they lived in shared residence. It could also reflect their lack of recognition for each other's contribution in the past that only began to be noticed. This new-found appreciation for one's spouse is also reported in studies on astronaut families in Hong Kong and Canada (see, e.g., Man 1993).

Two transnational husbands interviewed in Taiwan reported the use of computer electronic communications; both men had completed their doctorates in the United States. Chen was a professor in information management systems. In the 1980s he and his wife went to the Unite States for his advanced education. Their two children, now aged eleven and twelve, were born and raised in the United States. The couple had been married for seven years when he returned to Taiwan in the early 1900s for a professorship. Being an academic, Chen had a flexible schedule that enabled him to visit and spend time with his family in the United States. He would go to the States for almost two months in the winter during the Spring Festival break in Taiwan, two to three weeks during spring break, and about two and one half month in the summer. His wife stayed in the States on a visitor's visa and returned to Taiwan every six months.

When apart in different countries, Chen and his wife utilized the computer and telephone to keep in touch. Chen said, "We talk on the phone once a week, for about sixty to ninety minutes each time. But we mostly do chat room. My computer is always on, so whenever my wife writes, it pops up!" "Chat room" is a feature that allows spontaneous written communication over geographical distance. When both partners are on-line, rapid message transmittal permits immediate responses, exchange of thoughts, and relatively spontaneous expressions that can be put to words. The Internet contributes to maintaining social relations stretched over geographical distance, allowing speedy and regular contact. According to a year 2000 report by the U.S. Department of Commerce, "among home Internet users, 96.6 percent of women and 93.6 percent of men reported using the Internet to communicate with friend and family (Hughes, Jr. and Hans 2001: 783).

The second husband named Liang graduated in the United States in the mid-1980s. After facing glass ceiling in corporate America, he returned to Taiwan in 1999 to work as an executive officer in the computer industry. His wife received a master's degree in computer science, and she stayed in the United States with their three children ranging from seven to fifteen years of age. In addition to family time together, Liang communicated with his wife via email and the telephone. While Chen used the chat room to cut cost, Liang preferred the telephone. Husband and wife talked every day on the phone to keep in touch, to talk about their daily life and work. Liang said, "Email is one dimensional like a letter. You get personal feelings over the phone. You can detect emotions. It has a personal touch. You hear the voice, you feel closer to each other."

In addition, Taiwan's prominent role in the computer industry, its active participation in a global economy, and the existence of transnational corporations (TNCs) further facilitated Liang's communication with his wife and the maintenance of a family across vast transnational space. His computer firm operated factories in Houston, Texas and the Silicon Valley in California. As an executive officer, Liang returned to the States on business every other month. In the year 2000 he came back seven times. The business trips provided extra opportunity for him to reunite with his family in California. Liang said, "I would combine the first weekend, then the week, plus the last weekend. I spend the weekend with the family. During the week when the kids all go to school I go to the factories out of town, then come back for the weekend again before I leave for Taiwan." Two other husbands interviewed enjoyed similar advantage. They worked as executive officers in American TNCs in Taiwan, and made frequent business trips back to the States. Whenever they came on business, they combined business with family time as added bonus. They were the transnational corporate managers with the work place headquartered in Taiwan and the home place stationed in the United States. Their high economic power, life in the semi-periphery of the world with easy access to telephones and computers, and their incorporation into a global economy via their TNC employers all eased their maintenance of transnational marriages over long distance across national political boundaries.

They stood in stark contrast to the working class husbands in the United States and wives left behind in the periphery such as El Salvador, struggling to communicate across borders to maintain their transnational marriages. In some areas in El Salvador, wives lined up to borrow the local convent's only telephone line in the community. The long distance calls also cost far more than what they can afford (Mahler 2001). The vast difference between the ways these two classes of people maintained their transnational marriages reflects on their distinct socioeconomic class backgrounds at the individual levels, and the asymmetrical position of their home countries in the world system. Easy access to advance communication technology and frequent reunion despite the longer territorial distance characterize the professional class Taiwanese American families split across the immense Pacific Ocean. Inequality among the nation-states in terms of economic and technological development affects personal lives of their citizenry, including transnational marital relations.

As Gerstel and Gross (1984: 54–55) points out, it is not just communication involving "apathetic, sensitive, and revealing talk" that helps cement a marriage. Trivial talks, such as "what did you have for lunch today," involve a couple in each other's life. In transnational wife Wu's opinion, a relationship and emotional tie needed nurturance. Involvement in each other's life nurtured marital relation. She said,

> You can't say that since I live here in the States. then I live my life and you live your life. I let him know what goes on here and he lets me know what goes on there. We make sure there's communication.

Wu and her husband regularly shared their thoughts in person as well as over the telephone. They expressed their appreciation for each other. The husband appreciated her taking care of the children all by herself in the States; she taught the children to be thankful to the father working hard alone in Taiwan.

Besides good communication, transnational wives emphasized the importance of respect, mutual appreciation, and shared interest in their stable relations. Dana and her husband both received their education in the United States where they met and married. Dana remarked, "We respect each other very much. We never utter a harsh word to hurt each other. We think highly of each other. That's more important than love." Wu expressed similar viewpoints. She had been married for thirty years to her physician husband. They had lived apart in Taiwan and the United States for the past twelve years, when she took the children to California because of their chronic severe allergic reactions in Taiwan. The husband flew to California three or four times a year and stayed for one week to a month. Wu went to Taiwan three to five times a year and stayed with the husband from one to three months each time. At the time of my interview, their children were already attending college and could take care of themselves in her absence. They resembled the established couples in commuter marriages.

Although the frequent reunion likely helped maintain their marital equilibrium, Wu felt that mutual appreciation, good communication, and shared interest characterized her close relation with her husband. While they were still living in Taiwan, her husband always reserved Sundays for the family despite his busy schedule as a physician. He took the wife and children to the beach and the park, and both parents paid a lot of attention to the children. Husband and wife often felt thankful to each other. In addition, Wu considered their common training in medicine also brought them closer. The fathers of both Wu and her husband were physicians. Wu herself was also trained in medicine. Although she never practiced after she got married, she shared an interest in her husband's profession. She said,

> When he came home he would talk to me about his work and we could share a lot intellectually. He introduced me to his associates and we had many common things to talk about. We often spent time with his colleagues together.

Meeting of the minds, mutual respect and appreciation, compatibility, time for family life, and common interest in their children cemented the above women's relations with their husbands. Their frequent reunion and established stage in life and family further stabilized their marriage.

TIME/SPACE PARADOX

Long distance separate residences affect commuter couples in varied degrees. Despite the one advantage of extra time available for work reported by the spouse not responsible for childcare, commuter couples do not celebrate the extra time at their disposal. They simply cope with the separate residence arrangement with its many concomitant disadvantages to their marital relations. By comparison, six out of the thirty-five women in my sample mentioned that the transnational family situation definitely and positively improved their marital relations, but under special circumstances. At the time of my interviews, their length of marriage ranged from fourteen to thirty years. When they started to form transnational families, they had been married from twelve to twenty-two years. They could be considered the balancing or established couples by Gerstel and Gross's criteria above. In some transnational couples of my sample, physical separation combined with the convenience in communication technology also led to almost immediate positive improvement of their marital relations. After separation, husband and wife argued less than before when they shared residence in the same country. However, these couples all had one common characteristic: they learned to appreciate their spouses far more than before, and they looked forward to the day when they no longer had to live apart any longer. The following cases demonstrate the context of such dynamics.

Co-residence of husband and wife under the same roof assumes physical proximity for better emotional support. Commuter couples lament the loss of ability to provide such support due to geographical distance in commuting (Gerstel & Gross 1984: 53–55). This assumption fails to consider the larger environment in which couples sustain their marriages. The different ways of life in Taiwan and the United States in fact reverses the logic of physical proximity and close spousal relationship. In Taiwan, co-residence under the same roof in fact dispersed husbands and wives to different spatial locations, keeping them away from a close, meaningful marital partnership. Life in the transnational space, where husband and wife lived physically apart from each other, allowed couples to spend more time together in a way that appeared to be more meaningful and fulfilling to them. Like the Hong Kong astronaut families, some husbands and wives in Taiwanese American transnational families also experienced increased appreciation and improved marital relationships.

For Susan, the transnational dual household arrangement proved to be more satisfying than her married life in shared residence in Taiwan before migration. Susan had been married twenty-two years when husband, wife, and their teenage children immigrated to southern California. They came on kin sponsorship by the husband's brother. Her husband operated a very successful business in Taiwan, and he had been flying between the United States and Taiwan for three years at the time of my interview. The husband came to join the family about five times a year, and stayed between one to two months each time. When he returned to Taiwan, husband and wife called each other at least once every day at the beginning. Now they talked on the phone once every two to three days. Their transnational marriage differed vastly than their married life in Taiwan. Before the family's migration, Susan's husband spent a lot of time on social obligations. He was seldom home.

Like Japanese salary men who often go drinking with colleagues after work, during the week Susan's husband went out to socialize with business associates at karaoke bars and restaurants. He often came home late at night after the wife and children had already fallen sleep. The next morning he would sleep late while Susan got up early to take the children to school and went about her daily chores. When Susan and the children returned home, he would be gone again until late. Weekends turned for the worse. The husband stayed out late socializing and drinking until two or three o'clock in the morning. He came home when the rest of the family already fell asleep, then he slept until the afternoon on the following day. Even if he had plans to go out with the children, he slept too late to keep his promises. Children became disappointed with the father, and Susan kept arguing with the husband demanding that he came home early. One night Susan locked the house door from the inside so the husband could not get in when he came home very late. In retrospect, Susan said,

> We were married for twenty-five years and our married life had always been like this in Taiwan. There was this drinking culture for business people, your friends kept asking you to go out. Even for myself, there were always places to go and things to do. I went out with friends to see operas and to visit.

Hardly spending time together yielded little communication. Husband and wife each went one's own way. Living under the same roof in Taiwan also meant separate lives. Shared residence resulted in conflicts and constant arguments. In the later 1990s the family received approval to immigrate on kin sponsorship to the United States. The husband wanted a better education for the children in the United States and he requested the wife to stay and care for their children in California. He flew between the two countries to manage his business in Taiwan and reunite with the family in the States. "The different life style here slowed both of us down," Susan commented.

Since Susan and the children no longer lived in Taiwan, her husband began to experience the loneliness of living alone. He started to appreciate his wife and children, and the warmth of having a family. In his absence, Susan started to think of the husband's virtues, not just vices. She also empathized with him living alone by himself to work and financially support the family. When the husband came home to southern California, she displayed more respect toward him in words and actions. Away from business demands and social obligations, he spent quality time with Susan and the children. He drove children to school, and spent time with Susan at home. Husband and wife found time to talk and communicate. Having lived alone in their house in Taiwan, he also learned to take care of himself. When he came home to Susan, he helped Susan with household chores and washed the floor. In their total absence, the husband began to recognize the value of his wife and children. Susan admitted that the split household arrangement had effected a positive change in their marriage. The physical separation between husband and wife provided space for both to look at their marital relation from a distance. Only in their absence did we realize the value of our dear ones. The attitudes of both husband and wife altered with dual residence in the transnational space.

Unlike balancing commuter couples whose tension arises from the burden of childcare due to separate residence, living under the same roof in Taiwan induced tension in this couple divided by the husband's social functions, factors external to the dyadic marital relationship and immediate family. The quieter life style in the States decreased their social engagement with friends and business associates after work. It gave husband and wife the time necessary for companionship and communication that were both lacking in their life in Taiwan. Like commuter couples, separate residence gave rise to an enhanced value for the couples' shared time. Knowing that their partners are not always available, time allotted for couples' togetherness is given priority to intensify and enrich intimate relationship (Kirschner and Walum 1978: 519). The transnational separation also engendered spouses' appreciation for each other. Distance in time and space provided opportunity for different perspectives. Susan said, "When you are not together a lot, you look at things differently." While commuter couples are unable to share the many planned leisure activities (Gerstel and Graoss 1984: 60), Susan and her husband shared more time together. Susan reported,

> He likes the living environment here. He feels it's better for the kids. He likes flowers, gardening, drawing, and books. There are lots of libraries here where he can borrow books to read. Our migration to the United States actually paved a road for a better marital life for us.

In a different environment, separation of the spouses provided more time and space to focus on husband and wife relationship, and mutual appreciation of each other nurtured in the transnational space brought them closer together.

The experience of Shi (discussed in Chapter Seven) also illustrates this paradoxical effect of quality time based on spatial segregation. Shi's husband continued to work in Taiwan while she and the children lived in California. They had been married for seventeen years with teenage children when the split arrangement commenced. She indicated positive effect of the transnational arrangement on her relation with her husband. As discussed before, Shi had been the subordinated wife since the beginning of her marriage. She was also a sensitive and sentimental woman married to an engineer who, in her words, tended to be a "square head." When husband and wife lived together, Shi had difficulty communicating her feelings to the husband. Whenever she verbalized her emotions to him face-to-face and he ignored or refused in any way, she felt rejected and stopped immediately. The transnational separation gave them a different mode of communication to express inner sentiments. In addition to the telephone, husband and wife also maintained contact by the fax machine. She had the opportunity now to put her feelings and emotions in words that allowed her the space and time to better express herself and views. The separation permitted delayed responses that provided the time for fuller unilateral expression not possible in spontaneous face-to-face interactions. While they lacked communication under the same roof before, now the transnational space provided the opportunity to fax what Shi called "love letters." She could better express her more intimate and sensitive feelings in writing without rejection or inhibition.

The separation also brought new perspective in their relationship. According to Shi, her marriage had always included the mother-in-law in the middle, and the mother-in-law had always been more important to her husband. She recalled as follows,

> Whenever we mentioned my mother-in-law, we would argue. He always sided with his mother. We didn't have a good marital foundation. We should be considerate of each other's feelings, not always my mother-in-law.

Although the mother-in-law had passed away, Shi had also accumulated over ten years of hurt feelings. The transnational arrangement gave them a new perspective. She commented, "In the past I felt that he didn't respect me, that he was self-centered." Being apart from the husband, Shi now saw that he worked hard for the wife and children, and that he lived all alone and took care of himself to provide for the family. She no longer took him for granted. In addition, Shi said, "Now I can better express myself when I write to him." Her husband also trusted her more now with money management and decision-making since he was not always around. For Shi and her husband, the transnational separation gave them the opportunity to learn to know each other, to respect each other as capable individuals who sustained separation to care for the family as a unit. Separation turned into a mechanism of support. The time and space apart provided a healing process to cure damages incurred in the past. Physical togetherness may not always lead to harmony and equilibrium in a marriage. In this case, the ability to live independently and the opportunity for physical distance for the time being strengthened a marriage when husband and wife were committed to each other, as they looked forward to the day they could be together again.

While social obligations with friends and business associates in Taiwan stood between a business owner and his wife, the total devotion to work of an academic left little time for his marital relation that made Chi very dissatisfied. When I met Chi in 2000, she had stayed thirty years in her marriage and ten years in a transnational family. She married into a situation common among the Minnan people who owned land. Her husband's parents built a four-story building intended for the entire extended-family. The parents lived on the ground floor. Each of the sons occupied one of the floors above with his wife and children. I had visited two of these houses and stayed in one of them during the Spring Festival of 2001. They resembled apartment buildings with a self-contained unit and separate entrance on each floor. But Chi's building differed from the two I visited. The four floors shared only one kitchen. The mother-in-law, Chi, and her sisters-in-law took turn to cook enough food for everybody. Whoever could eat together at the same time did, and then food was left in the kitchen for those who were not home so they could later eat at their own time. Each son gave money to the parents for food and housekeeping expenses. It was the parents' house, and they ran the house and made household decisions.

Living in this setting involved a web of interpersonal relationship. Partly for a respite from this situation, Chi went to pursue a master degree in the United States while the parents-in-law took care of her child. After her graduation she visited her sister and friends in southern California. They found her a job that would sponsor her for a green card (permanent residency). She called long distance to discuss the offer with her husband. They decided that she should accept the job. Her husband and parents-in-law took the child with them for a visit in California. The child stayed behind with the mother, and the husband started to fly here every six months to visit his wife and child for about ten days each time. Between visits they called each other on the phone once every week or two. The transnational arrangement altered the dynamics in their marital relation. "Our relationship became better," Chi said. "When we lived together, we argued." Her husband was a professor at an university. In Chi's opinion, he was a workaholic. He devoted all his time to work and gave little time to his wife and child. Chi demanded attention and time from her husband. He felt guilty but did little to change his pattern and priority. "All he had in mind was work. We argued on this for the first three to four years of our marriage, then I left Taiwan for my education," Chi recalled.

The work of an academic is a way of life even in the United States. I had a taste of it since I started my doctoral program. I constantly felt pressed to write papers and read. It took time to prepare conference presentations and teaching lessons, to correct student assignments and examinations. Weekends turned into catch up time. I had no time or mind to socialize. After spending a day with my relatives for a holiday gathering, I felt that I had wasted time not reading or writing. I minimized my social activity. As a result I lost touch with many friends. Only the few very close friends accepted my situation and the way I related to them. They understood my not talking to them and not doing things with them did not mean that they were not dear to me. When I was not correcting papers I had to read and write for my own researches. Such work was time-consuming. For the intellectual actually engaged in the process, work was a pleasure. Academic work is a lifestyle. The academic spouse might enjoy such life, but the non-academic partner could feel very left out and bored. Two of my friends experienced precisely this. They were a married couple without any children. The husband was a professor in theoretical research, the wife worked nine to five as a professional. She wanted to do things with the husband in the evenings and on the weekends. He needed to carry out research in the office. She demanded time from him and he reluctantly obliged only after repeated arguments. After some time she felt so lonely that she started to fantasize about romantic encounters. It is a professional hazard.

Chi was unprepared for such lifestyle in her marriage. She spoke as a non-academic spouse, "This is a very lonely life. It's very painful for the wife. It's very difficult." She wanted a little family that spent time together after work, and a husband who helped her with housework. But the husband was seldom home. According to Chi, her husband was driven by parental aspiration. They were uneducated and poor so they taught her husband since he was a child to work harder and excel more than others. "Even when his body was home, his heart was at work. I was just an ordinary woman. I demanded attention from him, demanded time from him to spend together. So we often argued." Chi's husband encouraged her to find things to do on her own. She finally decided to pursue a master's degree in the United States and left their child with him and his parents to care for.

Their marital relation took a better turn with the transnational family arrangement. Their child lived with Chi in California, and life became easier for her husband with no distraction and demand from Chi. He lived in the city where he worked. There were many convenient small eateries in addition to the campus cafeteria. He ate out and sent dirty laundry to the dry cleaners. Now that husband and wife lived apart, Chi had no expectation of her husband's companionship. She also could not make demands on his time, and he devoted full time to his work. She developed her own friendship circle for social interactions. "Did you miss him when you first lived apart?" I asked. Chi answered, "I was more often mad at him than missed him. Now I'm more positive. I begin to miss him. When he comes we talk about delightful things that make both of us happy." When the husband came he gave quality time to the family for the duration of his visit. He compartmentalized his time and life for the work domain in Taiwan and for the family in the United States. Work related lifestyle and shared residence exerted stress on some couples' marriages. Transnational family arrangement resolved the conflict related to spousal expectation and demand, and marital relation improved as a consequence. The compartmentalization of marital life and work in the transnational space put both in order and designated specific time for each. The husband could dedicate fully to work and family each in its own time slot and space.

However, the advantage of such arrangement is also gendered in Chi's case. The time apart gave him more space for his own prerogative. It also meant the loss of Chi's preferred family life. It was a gendered compromise that served the interest of the husband at the expense of the wife, who bore the opportunity cost for such life style. On the other hand, the segregated space also gave Chi some distance to look at her husband's situation. She came to accept him and understand his need for solitude. Chi commented as follows,

> He's a professor and he has a lot of graduate students around. Everyday he's in his office or lab. I can call him day or night at his office or lab and he would be there. He only goes home to sleep like a motel. He's in a very competitive field and he conducts a lot of researches. Such life is a pleasure for him.

For Chi, such was a sad life for a middle-aged man because he knew no love or family happiness. For the professor whom I interviewed in Taiwan, such life was perfect for his work.

Wang was a social scientist whose wife and child lived in the United States. He visited them twice a year, and spent a whole year with them on his sabbatical. He understood the problem with time and demand from a non-academic spouse. Wang received his doctorate in the United States. When they lived together in the States he accompanied his wife for grocery shopping and social gatherings. In Taiwan he felt obligated to go with her to relatives and friends' social events. He said,

> We used to have a lot of arguments regarding social gatherings with friends and relatives. We argued about attending or not attending those functions. She wanted to go but I'd rather spend time on my work and research.

Now that husband and wife lived apart, there was no occasion for argument. He chose to go or not go to these functions, and he made his decisions based

on the relative proximity of kinship. For example, he received an invitation
to attend a birthday banquet for his wife's uncle. Wang considered that relative a little distant so he sent a regret with a monetary gift, but he attended
the wedding of his wife's brother. He said, "He's a close relative so I must
attend." That freedom and flexibility worked better for his profession and
priority. He could plunge into his work without disruption or distraction at
home. He commented, "I can do all the work I want. I hate to say it, but in
my case this transnational family is a better arrangement!" When I asked
him about sexual needs, he replied as follows,

> I am an academic. I am busy all the time. I go out of town often for
> fieldwork and conferences. I would be gone for months in the field out
> of the country or out of town. That was the way even before the split.
> This is my life style. When I have deadlines I work day and night and
> there still isn't enough time. I teach. I research. I eat. I've no time to
> think about women.

Commuter couples also report this ability to work long hours as the
advantage of their life style. Many enjoy this compartmentalized life. They
can devote many hours to work uninterrupted (Farris 1978: 101–02; Gerstel
and Gross 1984: 13; Gross 1980: 569; Handershott 1995: 79), but they also
regret the loneliness when work halts (Handershott 1995: 92). Wang conceded that this was one disadvantage. He lived alone. When he encountered
difficulty at work, he came back to an empty house with no one to share his
frustrations. And he did not want to telephone long distance only to unload
his frustration onto his wife. The few times when he was not pressed with
work, he came home only to feel lonesome. He learned to watch the television to relax.

Another transnational academic professional reported the same advantage and disadvantage. Chang wanted very much to be with his family
in the United States where he was unable to get a teaching or research job.
He said,

> I came back to Taiwan only because of work, because of economics.
> There is only one thing good about this transnational arrangement.
> There's no interruption to my work. I just work all the time I want. I
> can concentrate for a long time on my work. I work all the time includ-
> ing weekends.

Just like the commuter spouse who lives alone, Chang spoke of loneliness
away from his wife and children despite the extra time available for work,

> Sometimes I feel lonely, especially after eleven or twelve o'clock at night when the campus is deserted. Everyone is gone and I'm still here. And there are times when I don't feel like working. My wife also gets lonely. We have no companionship.

Although most men speak of loneliness when they live alone, husbands living with children report added household chores and childcare, and decreased time for matters related to paid work, while the commuter wife who lives away from the husband and children cherishes the extra time available to work for extended length of time. Transnational wives, on the other hand, almost invariable shouldered the responsibility of childcare when their husbands worked to financially support the family.

As Gerstel and Gross (1984: 53) point out, "the constant presence of both spouses does not always lead to harmonious and relaxed interaction." Kay's marriage also exemplifies that situation. In her case, the conflict in shared residence with her husband arose from her situation as a new immigrant. Kay had not wanted to leave Taiwan. She came along only after heated argument with her husband who insisted on immigrating to the United States for the children's education. Her discontent was obvious in the early days after her migration. I met Kay and her family shortly after their arrival in California. I was invited to dine with them and their friends. While her husband talked to her and about her with warmth, she would turn away and ignored him or looked at him derisively. When they first arrived, Kay was constantly worried about the household budget. They were not poor but the husband was only making US$4,000 per month, less than his former salary in Taiwan. Kay also used to earn a good income as a professional. Since she became a full time housewife at home, she now had less discretionary fund to spend. She felt isolated both socially and culturally after migration. The many inconveniences of not knowing her way around in the new environment also frustrated her. Husband and wife often argued. She would blame the husband for the difficulties in their new situation. He countered that if he could adjust then she should too.

After one year when the rental lease ran out on the house they lived in, Kay and her family bought a house near a community with many residents from Taiwan, including some of Kay's former friends. She also ran into an old family friend who had left two teenagers to attend school alone in California. Kay found out that without parental supervision and support, those two children felt abandoned and lonely and eventually ran into troubles. One even faced police arrest and legal prosecution. Kay counted her blessings that her own children were better adjusted. While Kay initially resented the migration, now she was glad that she accompanied her children to live in the United States. When the opportunity presented itself, Kay encouraged her husband to accept a job offer in Taiwan, thus instigating the formation of their transnational family. Now that the husband worked in Taiwan most of the time, Kay also appreciated him more. I asked how and why. Kay said,

> He did a lot of things when he was around. He went to pick up the kids and fixed things around the house. When there were problems he was around to discuss with. Now that he is gone, I have to assume the work of two parents. All of a sudden I had a lot of responsibility on my shoulder. And I have nobody to discuss problems with. I realize how good it was with him. We argue less now, why waste money on the phone just to argue? Besides, if we start to argue and I don't like it I can just hang up!

According to Kay, the split-household arrangement actually improved their spousal relationship. With the prospect of return to Taiwan in sight, Kay felt much better about her stay in southern California. She commented,

> After the children grow up and leave home to attend university, I would be able to go back to join him in Taiwan and live the way of life I enjoy. There is a purpose now. I have something to look forward to. My life here in this country is not indefinite. There is hope.

In addition, the husband received a higher income in Taiwan than in the States. Kay no longer felt the financial pressure and insecurity.

Kirchner and Walum (1978: 520) posit that commuter couples view their current separate residence as temporary to sustain marital solidarity. I further suggest that the women's projection into the future also helped to ameliorate uncertainty and anxiety. It gave them a sense of security about the present. Like Kay, several women in my study talked about reuniting with their husbands after the children grew up. For example, Susan said, "When our youngest one goes off to college, either I go back to Taiwan or my husband retires to live here. I think he would probably prefer to live here." Uncertainty about the future can be unsettling. With their marital relation suspended in the transnational space, these women looked to a time in the future for spousal reunion. It mitigated fear about possible loss of one's spouse to someone else, and it gave finiteness to the liminal state in which they operated. With a definite end in sight, liminality became tolerable. The future was invoked to validate the present. This envisioning served as a powerful stabilizer. Comfort and security arose from this certainty when husband and wife rejoined together. One thing characterizes these transnational marriages: both husband and wife quickly came to appreciate each other, and both conceded that the temporary separation was less than ideal. They looked forward to a marital relation when husband and wife resided together again.

Like some Hong Kong astronaut wives, the above women experienced noticeable changes on their spousal relations, but Faye felt that some times it remained the same, other times it improved, although it definitely had not deteriorated. Several women also reported that they felt no change in the marital relations before and after migration. The following section discusses the conditions that surround their situations.

BEING TOGETHER WHILE APART

Studies on commuter couples attribute the absence of disruption on marital relations to the long and stabilized life of the couple involved. They are established in their marriage, parenting, and career with grown children already out of the home. Typically, they have been married for over twenty years. Their prior long married life together sustains them during the commuter period (Gerstel and Gross 1984; Gerstel and Gross 1987). Fifteen women in my sample considered that their marriages largely remained the same as before their transnational family formation. At the time of my interviews, they had been married from twenty to thirty-five years. Their marriage had lasted from thirteen to twenty-six years when the split household arrangement commenced with children still living at home. While some transnational wives also suggested the lack of impact on their marital relation due to their older age and length of marriage, other factors emerged to explain the stability of their marriages.

Two women in the fifties attributed their marital stability to their older age and the length of their marriage. Lan and her husband resembled the established commuter couples. They had been married for thirty years when their two youngest children came to the United States to study after high school, thus starting the transnational family arrangement. Lan said,

> We have been married for more than thirty years. Absence makes the heart grow fonder. We are happy to see each other after each separation. I feel sad about leaving him alone in Taiwan, but I am happy to see my daughters here. My older married children in Taiwan take good care of him so I don't worry about him too much.

Jan also reported no impact on her marital relationship. She said, "Our relationship is the same as before, there has been no change. We have been

married a long time, over twenty some years. Old man and old lady."
However, it appeared that lengthy married life together alone could not
account for their stability while apart. While they lived in separate space,
they seemed to be together. They talked on the telephone every day, and they
reunited often. The husband of the second woman, Jan, visited the States
every three or four months for about ten days each time. The wife flew back
to Taiwan every two or three months and stay with the husband for one to
two months. Although their daughter and son still lived at home, they were
already attending college and capable of taking care of themselves. Thus,
husband and wife were never apart for very long in between. As Jan put it,

> My husband lives alone in Taiwan but we are together a lot. I fly back
> often and he flies here. I also bring the children back during summer
> vacation. I am a regular customer of China Airline. We use their Gold
> Card.

These women also attributed their marital stability to their mature age.
Although their age and length of marriage seemed to help stabilize marital
relations after migration, these women traveled frequently to reunite with
their husbands. Pre-migration emotional ties, older age, family closeness,
and frequency of togetherness all seemed to bolster the bonds between husband and wife even when they were physically apart.

For some women, their life style before migration explained the lack
of impact on their marital relations by the transnational arrangement. Six
women reported that their marriages remained the same after they started
the transnational family, mainly because husbands and wives had lived apart
during most of their married life due to the husbands' occupations. These
were wives of corporate employees, military officers, marine personnel, and
commercial pilots. Kate's husband was a successful corporate manager. He
worked for an American corporation and he started traveling out of the
country for long business trips or training since their child was an infant.
When the whole family was posted in Asia, the husband continued his out
of town business trips regularly. In 1999 Kate returned to their home in
California for their daughter's senior high school, and the husband remained
in East Asia. He returned home for three weeks to a month every two to
three months. Kate said: "Basically, I have been a single mother. Now he
mainly stations in East Asia, he comes back to California like a guest. I'm
used to it."

Military personnel, commercial pilots, and marine employees were
also used to spousal separation, and the transnational arrangement simply
moved their home bases to California. Chu's husband served in Taiwan's

military force. She said, "There's no difference before and after. He's in the military and we were apart all the time." Ling's husband used to be a member of Taiwan's air force when he was seldom home. He became a commercial pilot after he was honorably discharged. He would fly out of town for several days each time. Ling said,

> We've been married for twenty-one years and we've always been separated like this. In the past, he just brought home the paycheck and the children stayed with me. I made all the decisions. Military spouses were all like this.

Two women were married to husbands who worked for ocean liners. One husband had to leave town for more than a year on duty before the ship returned to port. He later changed to a liner that returned every two months. This pattern lasted more than ten years, and the wife took care of the household in his absence just as she did after their migration to the United States. She said,

> I went to work, came home, took care of the kids, and took them to movies once in a while. . . . We have been married for twenty-nine years and we are more often apart than together. We've a good marital relation all these years.

Yen's husband had been a commercial pilot flying all over since they got married. During their marriage of twenty-two years, he was based in their home city in Taiwan for only five years, the only years when he lived at home all the time. Depending on the route he had to fly, he could be gone for days or weeks before he returned. Yen said,

> For example, when my husband flew the Europe route, he would be gone for fifteen days and stayed home for only a few days. When he flew the Southeast Asia route then he would leave for about five days each time.

Now that the wife and children had immigrated to southern California, it became the family home where her husband returned. He came every three months. When he flew the U.S. route, he took a few vacation days to spend time with the family without extra cost. They maintained their house in Taiwan where the husband stayed when he flew the Asia short trips. Yen and her husband remained close to each other after migration.

Apart from life style, several women talked about pre-migration closeness, compatibility, their common goal in their children, and communication that continued to characterize their stable marital relation. Their close emotional bond is perhaps best illustrated by a brief telephone exchange between Ching and her husband. She said to him, "We have been split for a decade now." The husband replied, "Yes, and there won't be many more decades!" This couple started their dual household after sixteen years of marriage. The husband decided to emigrate to avoid the unstable political situation in Taiwan when the wife's sibling sponsorship was approved ten years ago. They had been married for twenty-six years now. The husband joined the wife and children once a year for two weeks each time. They called each other on the telephone whenever they thought of each other. Ching felt that marriage was the union of a man and a woman coming into one—husband and wife should not separate. But her husband was not educated in the United States, so he stayed and worked in Taiwan for economic reasons. She said, "He feels that his home is in the States and Taiwan is just the place where he works." Yen told a similar story,

> Now our family life has gotten closer-knit here after we immigrated. We are apart longer. You don't want to waste your time together on arguments and bickering. We must depend on more tolerance, more understanding, love, and trust.

Despite the longer separations, they frequently communicated by telephone. They spent "quality time" together as Yen put it,

> Our family life is better here. It is a quieter life here. Children come home after school. When my husband comes home, every night the two kids would come and sit on our bed at night and we have heart to heart talk. He now has a better father-son relationship with the children. Our goal is to live this kind of life. When he retires he wants to live here and we can do gardening and exercises and spend our years together.

The husband also preferred this life style. When he came home, he would watch TV, handle repairs in the house, and putter around the backyard. Because her husband had always been a commercial pilot flying away from home on duty for several days, Yen was used to prolonged separations. The only difference was spatial location of the family—home was now in the United States where the wife and children lived. In addition, a preference for a quiet family life (they disliked Taiwan's busy social life), and a common goal for retirement lifestyle in the future provided a bond for husband and wife that sustained them through their time apart.

Other women considered their marriages the same as before for very different reasons. It concerned their philosophical outlook toward life, marriage, and the transnational arrangement. They lived apart from their husbands, but they made no quest or demand of the husbands' sexual fidelity. They did not ask the husbands, nor did they try to find out from other sources. Kate said that she and her husband kept a very pleasant marital relation, but she never probed about his life when they lived apart. She said,

> When my husband returns home here he needs to relax and rest, so I don't ask. I ask nothing. When he volunteers to tell me things, I just listen. I don't even ask when he might come back. So every time he comes happily and leaves happily.

Her husband turned over all his income to her and she made all the family decisions.

Another wife commented that if she were around often enough then little would happen. In her opinion, prolonged physical separation between husband and wife provided opportunity for wayward behaviors. She flew frequently to reunite with her husband in Taiwan. When she returned after her stay with her child in the United States, she did not ask her husband what he had done in her absence. She said, "Even if I ask he doesn't have to tell me the truth. If I don't know, then nothing happened." However, she warned that it was important for women to acquire financial independence. From personal experience she knew that temptation could befall both men and women. For example, one day she was jogging in the park and a man asked her out for coffee. She avoided it. A physician's wife held a similar attitude. At the beginning of the transnational arrangement she worried about his having extra-marital affairs. When she called Taiwan and he was not home, she would probe him. She reflected, "That was bad. It was useless because he didn't have to admit to anything." Later she stopped asking. "I just trust him, that's my attitude now," she confessed. She had been married for twenty-six years when I met her, and ten years into her transnational family. Her husband sent money to support her and their two children. However, she advised that a woman must be independent both financially and emotionally.

Commuter couples lament the loss of emotional support experienced in the physical proximity of co-residence. Emotional closeness, however, is not necessarily the prerequisite foundation of marriages. Instead of marrying out of romantic love, Kai's marriage was arranged by her family. After eighteen years she immigrated to the United States in the late 1990s for her child's education and for a better living environment. She had stayed home since the birth of her first child. Prior to the migration, her husband had been managing his manufacturing business in China for five to six years.

During these years he was based in China, and returned to the home in Taiwan every few weeks. After Kai migrated to the United States with her younger child for his education, the husband and older child came home to California even though they still owned a house in Taiwan. So where was home? According to Kai, home was where she lived.

Kai also considered her marital relationship to be the same as before. Her husband had been commuting between China and Taiwan to run his business for several years before she came to the United States. The place called home merely changed from Taiwan to the United States. Kai said that many woman friends had suggested that she make a surprise visit to her husband in China, to spot check if he was keeping a woman. She refused. She said, "I don't want to know, don't want to think about it. What good is it to ask? If he doesn't want to tell, he could lie anyway." I asked Kai if her husband was affectionate toward her when he returned home. She replied that her husband was not the expressive type. Yet even when he did not show affection, Kai said she could tell that his feelings were present within. In Kai's opinion, kissing and hugging were romantic notions. Affection needed not manifest in physical contact.

"Do you trust him?" I asked. Kai replied, "I have faith in his family, not in him as an individual. He comes from a big extended family that enforces filial piety." A large extended family involves complex interpersonal relationships. It also contains cohesive forces and collective sentiment that bind individuals to existing social relations. A divorce or abandonment of one's lawful spouse and children would be sanctioned. Kai expressed her viewpoints as follows,

> We have very strong and deep-rooted family concept. My husband may have needs, whether physical or emotional. Since I could not be there and if a woman could be there to take good care of him, then that would be good too. Why worry since there's nothing I can do about it. I can't leave my son here and join my husband in China. I don't want to live in China anyway.

This strong concept of family instilled in Kai and her husband gave Kai faith in her marriage. Further, Kai's strength lay in her acceptance of reality, in acquiescence, and her philosophy on love and marriage. She considered romantic love to be a fantasy. It was ephemeral. Marriage and family instead were matters of real life. Life, she felt, was the day in, day out, practical and actual living together. Husband and wife had to be compatible, had to share the same goal and value in life. Marital partners must bear their responsibility and obligation toward the marriage and children.

"Life is not fair," Kai commented. "If you don't accept things in life then you'll be unhappy." Kai accepted her arranged marriage to her husband. She accepted that their marital relation was the same before as well as after the formation of their transnational family. To her, a marriage did not necessarily mandate sexual fidelity or exclusive possession. The concept of marriage as responsibility and obligation continued to keep her marriage intact, regardless of what might happen outside of the personal marital relation. Her outlook on life and the way she coped with the situation gave her peace and harmony.

In some cases, however, the physical separation created suspicion and jealousy between spouses. Like younger, childless commuters who worry about their spouses' sexual involvement with others (Farris 1978: 103), sexual jealousy and suspicion also plagued some transnational couples with children. Unnecessary suspicion and jealousy exerted pressure on some marriages as in the case of Liu and her husband. They had been married for twenty-one years when they immigrated to the United States in the late 1980s to open a branch company for their medium-sized business in Taiwan. The husband stayed in southern California to run the new branch and to take care of the children, while Liu stayed in Taiwan to manage their factory until the husband established the company here. Liu flew back and forth between the United States and Taiwan every month to reunite with the family for three to five days each time. Meanwhile, Liu's husband grew suspicious. He was afraid that Liu would get involved with other men. His friends warned him, "Hey, are you sure you want to leave your wife in Taiwan?" I could understand why her husband became anxious. Liu was quite a beautiful woman, gentle in manner and soft-spoken. At age fifty when I met her, she looked only thirty-five. Liu was brainy and interested in politics, economics, and current affairs. She also appeared to have a pleasant personality.

In addition to the operating expense of running the factory, Liu had to purchase merchandize to supply her husband's company in California. Liu dealt with a lot of money problem alone in Taiwan, but the husband did not seem to understand her pressure. Instead, he often became suspicious of her fidelity. According to Liu, their factory in Taiwan ran three shifts for twenty-four hours. Sometimes he called her at home and she had not returned; then he called at the factory and she had just departed. When he finally caught up with her, he would demand in a cold tone, "Where have you been?" Liu felt hurt as well as frustrated. She said, "He didn't trust me even though I worked so hard." Often she broke down and cried, and he apologized after she explained the situation.

One time the husband flew to Taiwan from the United States unannounced to check on her. Another time in Taiwan, Liu drove him to the airport to catch a plane but they were caught in traffic and missed his flight. The husband told Liu to return home and he would just take the next flight out. On the way home, Liu stopped by a store to pick up her lunch. When she got home and opened the bedroom door she was shocked to see a pair of man's big feet on her bed. "A-A-A-H-H-H-H-H . . ." Liu screamed at the top of her lung. A man popped up on her bed, and this man turned out to be her husband. He had returned by taxi to spy on her. "All these sound funny now. At the time it was very annoying and frustrating!" Liu complained. After five or six years Liu finally settled in California with her husband and children and ended their transnational family arrangement. Liu's experience demonstrates that the lack of trust in marital partner and faith in one's relation proved disruptive. The physical separation might have been harmless to a marriage, but the resultant uncertainty and anxiety could complicate a situation that necessitates tolerance and understanding.

DRIFTING APART IN THE TRANSNATIONAL SPACE

Douvan and Pleck (1978) demonstrate that length of separation contributes to more stable spousal relationship in some cases. It allows the wives to develop their self and separate identity as worthy individuals. The transnational family arrangement indeed provided the space and time for Yeh to develop herself as a worthy individual. However, instead of a more stable spousal relationship, living away from her husband gave Yeh the strength and independence to terminate a dysfunctional marriage. Yeh was one of the pioneers in the transnational family arrangement. Urged by her husband, she came to California by herself in 1975 to open a branch factory for their family company headquartered in Taiwan. She did not know any one before arrival. "You were very brave." I told her. "I wasn't brave," she answered. "I was stupid." When Yeh and her husband lived in Taiwan, both husband and wife worked during the week. According to Yeh, everyday her husband came home with a long face. On the weekends, he just sat in the sofa to read newspapers. He refused to do anything with the children or wife; and he did not communicate much with them. Yeh recalled, "I was like a widow in Taiwan. We never did anything as a family. I kept dreaming that one day he would change. I was young and naïve."

Yeh considered her marriage dysfunctional. The husband was always finding faults with the wife and the children. When Yeh tried to discuss family or business problems with her husband, he reprimanded her for making mistakes. She recalled, "Over time, we learn not to tell him anything." They had been married for eleven years when her husband urged her to open a branch company in the United States. She took their two children to California while the husband remained in Taiwan to manage the parent company. He came once or twice a year for about a month each time. In between reunion they telephoned once every two or three weeks and wrote letters when necessary. Yeh said,

> We drifted further apart but I grew up and matured in those ten years. We never saw things eye to eye, and he had always been abusive. After ten years on my own, I realized that we would not get any better. There was no family love, communication, or sharing. He was always criticizing.

In the mid-1980s, the husband came to live with them permanently in the United States and things turned for the worse. Yeh looked back and said, "I knew there was no hope for our marriage and family, so I filed for a divorce." Ten years of separate life on her own allowed Yeh to look at her marriage in clearer perspective. She grew stronger and independent. Transnational family arrangements did not always cause marital rupture. Rather, the physical separation acted as a catalyst to terminate a marriage that had been deteriorating. The time and space apart allowed Yeh to develop her sense of worth and courage. Life in the transnational space enabled Yeh to gain the insight and strength necessary to break a relationship in order to end personal anguish.

Even in stable relations, physical separation of husband and wife at times brought forth "reentry" problem in commuter marriages (Gerstel and Gross 1984). Wives in transnational families mentioned similar hazard. After living apart in two countries with different cultures for a while, some husband and wife experienced readjustment difficulty with each other when they reunited. It was particularly problematic for Ching during the initial two years of separation. She recalled as follows,

> I was a little tense when he came. I looked at him and felt there was something wrong with the way he talked and acted. He looked at me and at the kids and felt there was something wrong with the way we talked and acted. And we started to argue.

Finally, Ching and her husband discussed the problem thoroughly over long distance telephone. They reminded each other about the importance of acceptance and tolerance since they each lived in a different culture and environment, and that they now lived apart more often than together so they must treasure their time shared together. They also decided that as parents they must also learn to deal with the children who were growing up rapidly in a different culture. The husband agreed that when he came for a reunion with the wife and children, he must remember not to assert his authority as the father like he could in Taiwan. The mutual effort brought both spouses together. The knowledge of their situation and their willingness to work things out became their strength. Instead of constant argument, Ching and her husband adjusted to the new life style in the transnational space. After the initial two years, they became as close and intimate as before migration, and Ching telephoned her husband whenever she missed him and thought of him.

In some cases the separation destabilized the marriage or created distance and the marriage bond was threatened, due to what participants considered as a particular stage of one's life cycle. Ming's marriage was one of them. She immigrated with her husband and children as investor immigrants after eleven years of marriage. While her husband had made the decision to migrate, Ming was one of the few women who commuted. She said,

> I explained to my husband that he was better in English than I was. He had a good sense of direction but I did not. He had been in the States before and I had not. So I said that it would make more sense that he stayed here with the children while they attended school here, and I flew back and forth.

Ming would stay for two months in Taiwan to take care of the business there, and stayed two months in the States with the family as wife and mother. Everything was fine for almost nine years. "After nine years, something happened," she said. She heard from her friends that her husband was having an affair with another woman.

"How did you find out about it?" I asked. "We had been married for twenty years, I can tell if he is lying. Besides, it takes wits to tell a good lie. What he said here and there just didn't make sense. There's no logic!" Ming exclaimed. That woman was Ming's acquaintance, a single mother with children from Taiwan. During one of Ming's returns to Taiwan, the woman called Ming's husband to help with some chore at her house. When he was finished with the chore, she stood before him naked. He started the affair with her. Then the woman started to ask Ming's husband for large sums of money. Little by little, he realized that what she wanted was his money, not him. "He realized what a fool he was," Ming said. In the end, he apologized to Ming in front of the children. "I forgave him," Ming said. In Ming's opinion, her husband's stage in his life cycle complicated their transnational spousal relationship. Ming commented on the situation as follows,

> He was at the age that he needed his masculinity reaffirmed, that he could still attract another woman. Since I was not around, and another woman offered. . . . Of course it took two to tango. But good sex is luring for men. Which man would refuse if a woman stood before him naked and wanting? You know, sex.

Although Ming's marriage remained intact, she did not recommend this transnational split family arrangement. While the balancing couples in commuter marriages are considered less prone to sexual jealousy and extramarital affairs, Ming offered a different viewpoint on transnational couples in the same age range and life cycle,

> If you immigrate, husband and wife must do it together. If you stay apart, you will feel lonely and empty. One has biological needs. You need sexual love. So when there is an opportunity for a man and woman to meet there will be sparks. Sparks start fires that will burn.

Whereas Ming's transnational marital relation was compounded by the husband's stage in his life cycle, the absence of the wife, and the presence of opportunity, the marriage of another woman was jeopardized partly due to the constraints of immigration policy.

Immigration studies had long recognized the significance of immigration legislations and policies (Zolberg 1987). Borders are not always legally permeable. Despite freedom of movement within the United States, political territorial demarcation of the nation-state still regulates the entry of human bodies. Transnational families are disciplined by the legal power of the countries in which they live. The marital relation of May (first discussed in Chapter Seven) was disrupted by the multiple factors of lengthy separation and border control of the state. Almost ten years ago, May first visited her natal relatives in California. She became very fond of the local relaxed lifestyle compared to Taiwan, the suburban living environment, large yards and spacious homes. In addition, she wanted to get away from familial obligation to take care of her parents-in-law. She migrated with their two children to California where the children went to school on student-visas while she came on a visitor's visa. When her visitor's visa expired, she stayed on to care for the children. Her husband continued to work in Taiwan, sent money to support them in the United States, and came to be reunited with them twice a year.

May's migration provided her with both liberation and constraint. Like working-class women from Latin America or the Caribbean who migrated away from the home country and achieved autonomy from patriarchy, this non-working class woman left Taiwan partly to free herself from filial obligations. She no longer needed to take care of her parents-in-law. However, her newly gained autonomy came at a price: she became constrained in multiple ways. First, despite her work experience in accounting before migration, her lack of English proficiency and her legal immigration status prevented her from getting well-paying jobs. She worked in a restaurant instead. She became financially dependent on her husband's remittance for mortgage payment, household expense, and the raising of her children, just like the women left behind in Mexico by migrant husbands who came to the United States.

In addition, May's status as an over-stayer grounded her to this country. May would not be able to re-enter the United States legally once she stepped out of the border. This restriction jeopardized her marital relationship. Since she could not legally and freely leave and re-enter the United States in order to join her husband in Taiwan, their opportunity for reunion depended totally on his work schedule and willingness to come. The husband came to visit as planned for seven years. Then one winter, May noticed some changes in her husband for the first time. He arrived again to visit after several months. As she greeted him at the airport, he looked downward or sideways to avoid eye contact with May. At the end of the day that night, he did not touch her at all. "In the past, every time he came we would have a major workout right away the first night," May put it mildly, "but not this time." Nor did he desire her for the rest of his stay. He left after one week. Then remittances began to decrease a little. May could not locate him whenever she called him in Taiwan, and he did not call as frequently any more. "Even when I faxed him letters, he would not reply," May lamented. Money still came but not as much as before. May must now budget better to stretch things further. She also worked more at the restaurant for just in case.

Circumscribed by immigration law and human capital, May's migration away from her country of origin liberated her from obligation to her in-laws, yet turned her financially dependent on her husband's remittances from the home country. Despite class difference and the fact that she was the one who migrated away, May's experience to a certain extent resembles that of her working-class counterparts left behind in Latin America by migrating husbands. In this case, migration both liberated and constrained a non-working class woman who was legally undocumented. Three years after May's first discovery, the husband was still supporting the wife and children. Commuter couples reside within the boundary of the United States. Transnational marriages result from international migration across national boundaries. As such, they are subject to the jurisdictions of two nation-states and of immigration policies. Husbands and wives are disciplined by the state in which they reside. They can be divided by conflicting legislations of the two countries involved. Contradictory jurisprudence or the absence of cooperation between two national justice systems further complicate family matters, rendering them more problematic than already exist between individuals. These are macro-structural forces that condition micro-level interactions. May's quest for autonomy at her own initiative turned into financial dependency on her husband. Long period of separation between husband and wife as defined by the territorial boundary of the state and work schedule disrupted marital relations.

Other women who initiated international migration out of their own volition also harbored resentment when husbands participated in extra-martial partnership as in the case of Wang. Wang had been married for fifteen years when she immigrated with her children to the United States on kin sponsorship, while her husband continued to run the family business in Taiwan. He visited the wife and children twice a year for about a week each time. Wang sustained breast cancer about three years before I met her. Fortunately it was diagnosed in its early stage, her oncologist prescribed neither mastectomy nor chemotherapy. "I was lucky." She counted her blessings, but she blamed the condition on her husband's infidelity,

> It was lonely living on my own with only the children. There were things that children would not understand. When he came he did not even touch me, then you knew he was 'very well fed.' That's why I got cancer—sexual hormonal imbalance. I kept everything inside and I got depressed, and my immune system went down.

Wang figured that something went wrong when she called him at home in the middle of the night and could not find him. In retrospect, Wang recognized that his involvement with the other woman actually started a year before she departed. She said,

> When I finally located him, what he told me did not make sense. One thing did not fit another. It takes wit and consistency to tell logical lies. They could not do too much when I was there. Then I left and that gave them plenty of opportunity.

Eventually, in the early 1990s the husband's business suffered a major loss of profit due to a partner's embezzlement. He dissolved the partnership, took out his share, and retired to California to live with his wife and children. Wang's resentment lingered for a long time. She brought it up all the time and the husband reacted very strongly. Overtime her anger subsided. She confessed, "I got older, wiser, and mellower. Let bygone be bygone. The children are grown. There are only two of us now."

Why did these husbands returned to their wives eventually? In Ming's opinion, her husband still wanted his children and his family. He knew that she was the wife, and the extramarital affair was just for fun. She said, "I told him that if he wanted, we could have a divorce and I would take all the money and assets, but he did not want to." Another woman offered her views as follows,

> For men, they want to check if they are still attractive, but they don't want to give up their wives and children. A family is the fruit of a man's success, a testament to his accomplishment. It is his haven. An affair is only a small dot of his life and life is long. I would say that eighty percent of the men who have affairs never marry the woman. Of course they are very selfish.

Children indeed play a significant role in bonding husband and wife together. Many couples make effort to make a marriage work in order not to give a broken home to their children. In patrilineal societies, as in Taiwan, male offspring continue the family line. The Confucian doctrine recognizes three unfilial acts; not producing descendants is the gravest. Children provide a common goal for husband and wife in their life as parents and bond them together. Lily commented, "We value children. They're parents' hopes. They're our life extension, reputation, and glory. This is traditional mentality." Children aside, there is also social sanction and stigma against divorce as discussed in Chapter Seven.

While different factors disrupted the above marital relations in the transnational space, husbands in other families continued to have extra-marital affairs that had been a pattern in their marriages. The following looks at the experience of two women who coped with such a circumstance.

"ONCE A CHEATER"

Sue lived in a rented apartment in a very affordable area, and Yee owned a house in the least affluent neighborhood in my sample. Both women had initially left Taiwan for Latin America as investor immigrants, and then immigrated to the United States in the mid-1990s on kin sponsorship as secondary migration. Sue shuttled between Latin America and the United States to purchase merchandise for the business she co-owned with her husband. They had already been married for twenty years when she started flying in the mid 1990s. She came to the United States once or twice a week for about three nights each time. Within a year Sue felt something was wrong: during one of her trips to the United States, she called him long distance all night but there was no answer. She later found out that the husband had bought a small business for another woman to run. He also supported her financially. Sue said, "The woman was a divorcee and was content with a relationship without marriage. Her former husband got involved with another woman, and she in turn got involved with my husband."

Sponsored by the husband's sister, the entire family later immigrated to California; but the husband lived in Latin America and came to the United States approximately every six months as required by immigration law in order to maintain his permanent resident status. He sent Sue approximately US$1,000 per month for household expense. She worked in sales to earn the necessary additional income to support her two teenage children. Sue said,

> We have not had sex for four years. . . . I still have feelings for him but I no longer tolerate his behavior towards me. We have no talks and no interaction when he comes to this apartment to see the kids.

Despite the situation, the husband refused to grant an uncontested divorce; legally they remained husband and wife. In retrospect, Sue recognized that his behavior pattern already emerged in the 1980s when he often raved about polygamy. Sue criticized his attitude this way, "He would not sign for a divorce. He said he wanted to give the kids a home and a family, but he goes to love another woman."

The other wife, Yee, flew between Taiwan and Central America to make supplementary income for her nuclear family. After she and her family immigrated to the United States, she flew between Taiwan and southern California, where she returned twice a year for one to two months each time to work. According to Yee, her husband already started to have extra-marital affairs when they were still in Taiwan. She discovered it for the first time when their oldest child was three years old. The second incident occurred when she was fourteen weeks into a pregnancy. The affair in Latin America that took place within one year of their arrival became the third case to her knowledge in their twenty years of married life. His extra-marital affairs after the transnational split household residence represented only part of an on-going pattern. Physical separation of the transnational family apparently contributed little to the state of their marital relation. According to Yee, "In

Taiwan, both spouses have to agree to sign a divorce." Her husband already signed a power of attorney for her to file for divorce in Taiwan where they got married legally. But she had not filed. She kept hoping that one day her husband might change.

Both husbands in the above two cases carried on extra-marital affairs when the women shuttled for work. Like balancing commuter couples with children at home, the two women started flying back and forth between two countries with teenage children at home. Both couples had been married for twenty years. The length of marriage would qualify both couples as established, but length in marriage alone could not sustain a marital relation as in the established commuter couples. Rather, attitudes toward one's marriage and personal commitment to a spouse define the contour of marital relations. In these cases, it was not the transnational arrangement or the length of physical separation causing loneliness that led to extra-marital liaisons. Instead, husbands' pre-existing behavior patterns continued to shape the marriages of the two women.

While these two women remained in a marriage that was more in name than in substance, the following section discusses a marriage that ended after a period of separation in the transnational space.

A CHANGE OF HEART

With seven years of marital history, Shang persuaded her husband to immigrate to the United States where all members of her natal family lived. Her husband was ambivalent about the international move, because his own natal family all lived in Taiwan where he also held a good job. Although the couple and their two young children immigrated to the United States together, the husband did not find a job to his satisfaction. After they received permanent resident status, he took his son back to Taiwan and his former job, while the infant daughter remained with the mother. In the first year of the transnational arrangement, he came for two weeks every six months as was required to maintain his status as a permanent resident (one with the green card). Then slowly the frequency of contact and reunion decreased. Shang could not locate him whenever she called. Shang called her mother-in-law to find her husband but the mother-in-law told her that nobody knew where he was. After one year of such arrangement, Shang sensed that something had gone wrong. She went back to Taiwan to see her husband and son. The husband acted coldly toward her, and he slept in a different bedroom during her entire visit. Shang returned to southern California to care for her daughter. One year later the husband filed for divorce in Taiwan. She said,

"I was dazed. I was so naïve. I could not believe he would do such a thing. I was in denial." A court in Taiwan finalized the divorce within three years of Shang's immigration to the United States.

Divorce law in Taiwan penalized Shang for her migration in order to be with her natal family. In the earlier cases presented above, participants pointed out that in Taiwan both spouses must sign an agreement to divorce in order for it to be effective. However, the transnational situation initiated by Shang legally jeopardized her marriage in the context of Taiwan's civil laws. These laws were based on the judicial system passed in China under Chiang Kai-shek's Nationalist Party in 1930 and enacted in 1931. Chiang's government applied the same system on Taiwan when the Nationalist Party moved to the Island. Like Europe's continental law, Taiwan's judicial system is based on legal codes. According to the original Legal Code 1001, husband and wife bore the responsibility and obligation to co-reside with each other except in cases with rightful reasons; while Legal Code 1002 specified that a wife must co-reside with her husband at his residence. This code was evidently the product of a patrilineal and patrilocal Chinese society. Legal Code 1002 was amended in 1985 to allow alternative residence per agreement by husband and wife, where the husband could live at the wife's residence. This Code was again amended in 1998, where husband and wife could decide their residence according to mutual agreement. In the absence of mutual agreement or before mutual agreement was reached, the court would decide their rightful place of residence, with due consideration of their shared household registry as husband and wife.[2]

Before the 1985 amendment, Shang's husband unilaterally filed for divorce in Taiwan on the ground of Shang's abandonment because she had been living in the United States, hence her failure to fulfill her responsibility and obligation of co-residence at the husband's abode. According to Shang, she could not appear in Taiwan on the court date which conflicted with her job requirement. Instead, she mailed to the court copies of her documents that proved her return to visit her husband. The court decided the case in her husband's favor, based on the provision of Legal Code 1002 that Shang failed to co-reside with her husband at his residence. Such legal provisions, and the court decision, reflected gender inequality in a patriarchal society. Structural legal power penetrated private marital life that extended between two nation-states, and the legally sanctioned domination of male over female asserted its sphere of influence in the transnational space.

In addition to structural forces, in what ways might the transnational arrangement have caused the divorce? I asked Shang the same question. She said,

> He had a very strong sexual appetite. Frequently he wanted sex two
> or three times a night. We were in the thirties when we were apart. He
> needed sex, needed a woman. I heard that the woman was only twenty
> years old or so and only a high school graduate office attendant who
> served tea to office visitors.

It would appear that sexual incompatibility or her husband's sexual need,
given Shang's prolonged absence, had caused the marital breakup. However,
Shang further admitted that her poor relationship with her mother-in-law
might have contributed to her husband's decision to pursue the divorce. She
said,

> I was at great odds with his mother. I disliked a lot of things that she
> did, such as smoking and playing mahjong. I was young and tactless, so
> I said it as it was. She had a lot of influence over him.

While sexual need might have caused the dissolution, interpersonal relationship with other family members, the mother-in-law in this case, seemed to
have contributed directly to the negative consequence of Shang's transnational family experience. Shang concurred. She said, "His mother has a lot
of influence over him." As discussed in Chapter Seven, a mother's power
rests in her own "uterine family" to ensure her position in the husband's
family. She actively cultivates loyalty and dedication from her children, particularly the sons. A poor relationship with the mother-in-law puts a young
wife in a very disadvantageous position in her relationship with her husband. Several women in my sample reported this mother-in-law problem. A
woman recounted the following,

> My mother-in-law hated me with her guts. Little did I know that she had
> wanted my husband to marry another girl. She had consistently tried to
> make him abandon me. She always said nasty things to me but I tried
> to tolerate them and not answer back. One time I answered back, she
> stared at my husband and he hit me right in the chest. If I answered back
> and my husband did nothing, she would say, "what's the use of having a
> son, of raising such a useless son" and on and on until he started to hit
> me. That's how it was all the time.

While a mother-in-law prevented a son's divorce in the case of Henry as
discussed in Chapter Seven, Shang's mother-in-law likely encouraged or perhaps even suggested it. Interpersonal relationship with the husband's family members particularly the mother-in-law, rather than physical separation
alone, led to martial dissolution within a short time of the transnational
family formation, such as in Shang's case.

Although all the above examples portray the man as the cause of deteriorated marital relationship, I do not mean that only men get lonely or instigate affairs. It merely reflects the bias of my sample. Both men and women interviewed were unwilling to snowball me to friends or acquaintances that had experienced unhappy marital relationship as a result of transnational family life. In a study on astronaut families where husbands work in Hong Kong and wives live in Canada with the children, Lam (1994) reports of a woman who became very alienated in her new environment. She felt devalued as an individual, rejected by her teenage children, and frustrated by her husband. She was driven to a more active social life that eventually led to involvement with a local widower. When the husband and children found out about the relationship, she asked for a divorce.

SUMMARY

The stark contrast between commuter marriages and the transnational marriages discussed above lies in the commuter wife's ability to continue in her chosen career. Commuter marriages are practiced as an alternative lifestyle to protect the interest of spouses who assume that each has a right to be committed to their own work. The Women in my sample migrated to care for their children, a reason other than for their own careers. In the transnational space, husbands and wives maintained relations by telephone, fax machines, email and air travel, all reflecting the superior economic ability of their class background. Like Hong Kong astronaut families, transnational arrangement affected marriages differently, with increased appreciation and improved relationship, little change before and after migration, or less fortunate situation where a marriage ended in a divorce. Mutual respect and appreciation, frequent reunions, common goal in the children, dedication to each other, and an established marriage prior to migration all contributed to stabilize marital relations in the transnational space. It is not physical separation alone that threatened a marriage. Rather, sexual incompatibility, relationship with other family members especially the mother-in-law, and pre-existing behavior patterns all accounted for the eventual break up. Geographical dislocation merely acted as a catalyst to speed up marital deterioration that had existed prior to migration.

Chapter Ten
Summary and Conclusion

Set in a globalized political economy, this study has considered the gendered experience of dual household transnational migration of non-working class Taiwanese American married women. Using qualitative and quantitative methods, I have examined primary data from wives and husbands interviewed in California and Taiwan. The project situated micro processes involving these people in interaction with kin, against the macro factors of socio-political economy within their countries of origin and destination, and across national boundaries. Investigating the intersection of gender, class, "race" and international migration in a global political economy, I have analyzed the causes of these people's migration and transnational split-household strategy, with attention to its impact on non-working class women as workers, mothers, and wives in transnational families split between Taiwan and the United States.

My interest in this topic stemmed from my own background from five generations of transnational tradition, a tradition that has existed in the Guangdong and Fujian provinces since at least the seventeenth century. Using examples from family history, I demonstrated that the formation of historical Chinese American transnational families resulted from the issues of "race," class, and gender, and that the impact of such transnational arrangement on women varied depending on their economic backgrounds. Women in these historical families remained in the home country whereas their husbands went away to western countries to perform stoop labor, with the expectation to send remittances home to support their families.

Contrary to this pattern, wives and children in contemporary Taiwanese American transnational families resided in the Untied States, while husbands remained in Taiwan, the country of origin, to work and financially supported the family in the United States. Unlike the historical stoop laborers, these husbands were business owners, educated as well as skilled professionals and executives. This pattern presents notable exceptions to cases more represented in the transnational migration literature that focus on working-class women, men, and families. The study of transnational migration generally has not included non-working families. Current scholarship on transnational studies concentrates on connections between the United States and Latin America or the Caribbean, on working class women left behind by husbands, and men and women who migrate to the United States for productive labor. This work has contributed to theorizing the class and gender dimensions of migration, and provided needed comparative data for the study of transnational migration with a special focus on women and families in the Pacific Rim.

Immigration from Taiwan to the United States began in the 1950s, when graduate students came for advance education mostly in technology and science. Business owners joined them later. Beginning in the 1970s, immigrants started to come on kin sponsorship as a consequence of the 1965 Immigration and Nationality Act. While the early comers went to the East coast and the Midwest, subsequent arrivals were channeled to the west coast, leading to a concentration in southern California. These Taiwanese immigrants came disproportionately from the non-working class. Some of them eventually became transnational families. In most cases, wives and children lived in the United States whereas husbands worked in Taiwan to financially support them.

According to the wives interviewed, they had departed from Taiwan for various reasons: children's education, Taiwan's national political tension, political threats from China, business or career opportunity, to join family members, deteriorating social or natural environment in Taiwan, to avoid son's compulsory military service in Taiwan, to avoid in-law problems, marital problem and self education. Children's education ranked by far the most frequently cited reason for their migration. Most of the children had fallen behind in the highly competitive and rigid educational system in Taiwan; therefore, parents migrated with them to the United States in the hope of giving their children a second chance. In most cases, the husbands returned to work in Taiwan due to various disadvantages encountered in the American workplace. In other cases, the husbands remained to work in Taiwan to benefit from the robust economic boom in Taiwan and, later, China.

In a global scale, geopolitics led American dollars to modernize and industrialize Taiwan beginning in the 1950s. Taiwanese professionals trained in the Untied States and Americans provided leadership in Taiwan's industrialization designed by heavy intervention from the state. Transnational corporations mainly from the United States and Japan entered into business partnership with Taiwan. Advances in communication technology, international subcontracting, and a dominated low cost labor force enabled Taiwan's flexible small to medium size enterprises to capture a sizable niche in the world market. Taiwan's economic ascendancy in the global economy enabled these professionals and entrepreneurs to generate sufficient income in the semi-periphery of Taiwan to support their families in the United States of the core in the world-system. A global political economy made possible the formation of Taiwanese American families that lived out their lives in the transnational space, mediating the local and the global.

Taiwanese American transnational families intentionally utilized migration for their children's education, to at least reproductive their socioeconomic position in society. They formed transnational families to maximize returns on productive and reproductive labor with differential costs absorbed by parents. They accumulated economic capital in the country of origin, to transform it into their children's cultural capital in the country of destination, in order to transform it again to children's future economic and social capital. Their effort was made possible by their ability to maintain families in a transnational space that transcended the nation-states, in a globalized political economy at a historical moment favorable for their formation. They also showed that the effects of globalization at the local level were class specific.

Family migration often involve generational and gender conflicts. I analyzed such gendered conflicts in my sample, and connected their migration decision-making to power relations. Spousal resource contribution and cultural ideologies cannot fully explain such relations. I demonstrated that class position, wealth, and societal forces all played a part. Further, the significance of these transnational wives' kin work was class specific. I contend that the purpose and significance of kin work vary with class discrepancy. While underprivileged women participate in kin work for mutual emotional and material support, women in my sample performed kin work to maintain and enhance their social capital instead, a class-based purpose.

While the purpose and process of migration differ according to class, some gendered experiences converge regardless of class distinction. International migration disrupted professional women's career paths in Taiwan, to fulfill their role as mothers in the United States. In the prolonged absence of their husbands, women took up the responsibility of double parenting. As de facto head of household, they assumed authority and autonomy although they depended on their husbands for financial support. Women interacted with their communities, merging the public and private domains. The public-private separation dissolved for my sample, just like their working class counterparts from Latin America and the Caribbean. In the transnational space, the juxtaposition of the private and public spheres transcends socioeconomic class discrepancy.

In addition, while migration and transnational family arrangement were undertaken for the benefit of the children and for the family as a unit, women bore most of the costs for such strategies. Migration away from the country of origin made some women revert to roles imposed upon them by traditional patriarchal ideology. Instead of liberation (as is the case with some working-class women studied in transnational literature), migration exerted constraints and added burdens in the country of destination for some of these non-working class women. To others, migration away also brought financial insecurity and abandonment by their spouses. Still others encountered no change, or even positive experiences in their marital relations due to their particular circumstances. Hence, the impact of migration and globalization on these women were not consistently the same. The experiences of the women as related in this research demonstrated a variety of circumstances and a range of conditions that affected them in disparate ways constituting diverse individual cases. Geographic dislocation due to migration did not always disrupt social relations for these women specific to the time and space in which they occupy. However, international migration resulted in the fragmentation of some women because of competing multiple roles demanded of them due to their gender.

In sum, children faced educational difficulties in Taiwan, parents migrated with them to the United States to overcome that disadvantage. Husbands continued to run their businesses in Taiwan, or they returned to Taiwan after their encounters with occupational obstacles in the United States, to take advantage of its economic niche in the world economy. For them, migration was a maneuver to reproduce or even improve the socioeconomic position of the next generation. Their formation of a transnational family was a strategy to maximize return on productive and reproductive labor. The maintenance of these transnational families was made possible by a global political economy in a particular historical moment that facilitated that strategy. Often, women absorbed most of the costs associated with international migration and transnational practices. This study has demonstrated the intense interaction of the local and the global, in a context characterized by temporal specificity.

Epilogue

This research was initiated to fulfill partial requirements for a doctorate. In the process, it had given me knowledge. In the end and above all, it taught me how to love deeply. I learned from the women and men interviewed, from their devotion to their beloved.

Passion excites and consumes. Love sustains and nurtures. It endures. Unlike passion, love is compassionate, harmonious, caring, affectionate, and exceedingly tender.

Epilogue

Notes

NOTES TO INTRODUCTION

1. The definition for transnational family as used in this study excludes Asian or Taiwanese children sent by parents to attend elementary or high schools in the United States, away from both parents on a long-term basis, and are not discussed in this study. These children are termed "parachute kids" in the literature. For a discussion of this phenomenon in the United States, see Los Angeles Times, June 24, 1993; Chung 1994, Khoo 1995, Min Zhou 1998, Shu-yu Kuo 1991; for those in Australia from Hong Kong see Pe-pua, Colleen Mitchell, Robyn Iredale, and Stephen Casstle 1996.

2. In this study, non-working class refers to the group of people who are business owners, and educated professionals who earn a salary by performing mental labor that requires specialized skills and knowledge.

3. Transnational families resembling those discussed in this study are also found recently between Korea and southern California where wives immigrate with children for their education and husbands work in Korea. This phenomenon appears to be on the increase, but as of this date, no known local research has been conducted or published on this population (personal communication, Edward Chang 2002).

4. For such transnational practices, see, inter alia, Tian 1953 and Skinner 1957. In addition, modern China was established by transnational effort over extended period when its founding father, Dr. Sun Yat-sen, and his supporters organized for the 1911 revolution to overthrow the Qing dynasty, outside of China in countries that included Japan, the United States, and England. Likewise, the father of modern Korea, Ahn Chang Ho, participated in transnational politics when he mobilized in the City of Riverside, California, United States in the early 1900s for Korea's independence from its colonizer, Japan, in conjunction with Korean independence activists exiled in China where they set up a provisional government in Shanghai. Chinese Americans actively joined China's war effort against Japan in the Second World War. Earlier examples of transnational politics exist, such as the Qing government's extra-territorial claim of sovereignty over all Chinese overseas regardless of legal citizenship and place of birth, by jus sanguine instead of jus solis.

5. The concept of race based on genetic physical traits has no scientific valid-
ity. The distribution of genotypes is clinal, in gradation over geographical
distance. There is more genetic variation within the same population than
between two populations. If we must divide humans into racial category
by genetic materials, we will have to make each individual a separate race.
In the 18th century Linnaeus divided humans into four taxonomic clas-
sifications. Later, German anatomist Blumenbach changed them to five.
More categories appeared in the 19th century. We continue to alter them in
contemporary time. The changing number of categories alone reflects the
arbitrary nature of classifying humans into discrete "races." However, how
we are perceived and categorized based on our phenotypes affects our lived
experience, and that gives a social reality to the concept of race.

NOTES TO CHAPTER ONE

1. Up to 1997 Hong Kong continued to be a British colony with a free market
economy. China remains a socialist state ruled by the Community Party,
and Taiwan has been a qualified democracy with a state-planned capitalist
economy.
2. These two provinces are spelled Fujian and Guangdong in the Pinyin ro-
manization system, the official system of the People's Republic of China. In
this study, Chinese historical names and terms associated with Taiwan, such
as Chiang Kai-shek and Kuomintang, are romanized in the same way more
familiar to non-Chinese readers.
3. The other ten interviews were conducted in public places that more suited
those women's schedules. For example, we met right after their English
classes or other meetings that I also attended in order to meet them.
4. I worked as an active real estate broker in southern California for almost a
decade form the mid 1980s to 1990s. The purchase of a house with all cash
was not unusual with Taiwan immigrants beginning in the late 1980s.
5. I tried to ask him questions prepared in advance in my interview schedule
during a lunch meeting. However, every time I brought up the questions he
just changed the subject. I consumed a wonderful Italian lunch complete
with fine wine and he appeared to have a wonderful time, but I never got to
probe him for personal information needed for my study.

NOTES TO CHAPTER TWO

1. The high ratio of male to female was prevalent among early Asian immigrants, particular the Chinese and Filipinos. The ratio among early Japanese
and Korean immigrants was ameliorated by the arranged marriage practice
called "picture bride." The scarcity of female directly contributed to the
formation of bachelor society among both the Chinese and Filipinos in the
United States. This bachelor society is characterized by a lack of family life
and the delay of the second generation, the development of mutual aid associations, and vice industry such as gambling and prostitution, see Chan

1991a and Takaki 1998. For a discussion of Chinese prostitution in the nineteenth century and turn of the century, see Cheng 1984.

2. Mahjong is a popular Chinese tile game played like bridge. The size of each tile is approximately one inch by one half inch. It takes four players, at least three, to play the game.

3. Additional legislations ensued to prohibit the entry of Asians, such as the 1917 and 1924 Immigration Acts. However, loopholes existed. Some Chinese arrived as imposters known as "paper sons" after the 1906 San Francisco earthquake when original birth records at the City Hall were destroyed in the fire. For paper sons see Hsu 1997; Chin and Chin 2000.

NOTES TO CHAPTER THREE

1. Chiang Kai-shek was the leader of the Kuomintang or Guomindang Party (Nationalist Party). He led the Party against Mao Zedong who headed the Communist Party in the civil war for the control of China. Madam Chiang Kai-shek, his wife, came from the wealthy Soong family. For her family background and one account of how the family amassed its fortune, see Seagrave 1985.

NOTES TO CHAPTER FOUR

1. A large number of Taiwanese also emigrated to Australia and some to New Zealand.

2. For a discussion on intra-ethnic dynamics among the Cantonese speakers and those from Taiwan, see Chee, Dymski, and Li 2004.

3. Alpha Beta closed its door in the 1980s. The Hughes Market is now the Ralph Supermarket at the exact same location.

4. Di Ho Market in Monterey Park was closed in the late 1990s.

5. The so-called "Taiwanese dialect" is a diaect of Minnan, a language different from Mandarin though closely related.

6. The Ethnic Banking of Southern California Project based at the Department of Economics, University of California, Riverside has produced several articles that discuss the relationship between the Chinese American Banking industry and the Chinese American community in southern California. See, for example, Li, Zhou, Dymski, and Chee 2001; Li, Zhou, Dymski, Chee, and Aldana 2002.

7. I am a research member of the Ethnic Banking of Southern California Project mentioned above. I had conducted the interview cited herein for the purpose of the Ethnic Banking Project in the summer of 2000.

8. For a history on the development trajectory of Chinese American banks headquartered in Los Angeles County, see Li, Chee, Zhou, and Dymski 2000; for the roles played by the Chinese American banking sector in the community development of the San Gabriel Valley area, see Li, Dymski, Yu, Chee, and Aldana 2002.

9. For the events in the public and political arena during this time see Fong 1994 and Horton 1989, 1992, 1995; see also Saito 1998.

NOTES TO CHAPTER FIVE

1. Hong Kong was ceded to Britain by China by the 1842 Treaty of Nanking (Nanjing), when China lost the Opium War in its attempt to resist British sale of opium to China. In 1984 China and Britain signed an agreement to retrocede Hong Kong to China by 1997.
2. The Manchu comprise one of the major ethnic groups of China, but the Han are by far the most numerous.
3. For first hand accounts of the 228 Incident from Taiwanese perspective, see, among others, Chen 1988; for an American's viewpoint, see Kerr 1965.
4. I visited one of these home town associations, the Zhong Shan Home Town Association, during my fieldwork in Taiwan. The Association appeared to be very well endowed. It owned an office building in an upscale commercial district in the City of Taipei. The Association occupied an entire floor as its office, and rented out the other floors as offices for income. The Association was thus more than self-sustaining even without membership dues. The Association office was very well furnished and equipped. However, the officer indicated that instead of money, the Association's problem was its inability to recruit new and young members. Since offspring of the Mainlanders were born and raised in Taiwan, they were able to form personal and professional friendship circles and social network. They felt no need to turn to hometown association affiliates for mutual aid and social outlet.
5. This intermarriage pattern is common in the earlier period of the ROC on Taiwan. Many wai sheng ren military personnel came to Taiwan with the KMT as single men, or unaccompanied by their families or wives left behind in China. Families were separated for several decades incommunicado due to the political impasse between the ROC and PRC. The acute gender imbalance within the wai sheng ren population created an insufficient number of female wai sheng ren compatriots as marriage partner. According to the 1991 Survey of Social Change in Taiwan, the proportion of intermarriage among male wai sheng ren with female ben sheng ren remained high from 1953 to 1991. Intermarriage among female wai sheng ren to ben sheng ren started to rise in 1972. By 1991, the proportion of female wai sheng ren who intermarried with local ben sheng ren outnumbered in-marriage among the respondents. For more information on intermarriage see Wang 1993; for the dynamic between intermarriage and social class see Gates 1981. In the early period of the ROC, its regime also prohibited low-ranking soldiers to marry in Taiwan. This regulation combined with financial inability partly caused several ROC soldiers to remain as bachelors into their old age, see Hu 1990 for a glimpse of these Mainlander veteran-soldiers' situations.
6. For an investigation of Taiwan's contemporary cultural nationalism, see Hsiau 1998.
7. One such prisoner was the present Vice President of Taiwan, Annette Lu.

8. Environmental problems are indeed severe, but not all of Taiwan is in such dire shape. The countryside in the central, eastern, and southern part remain scenic with much greenery, white cloud, and blue sky. National parks such as the Taroko Park in Hualien province on the east coast is tooted as a tourist attraction with natural scenery.

NOTES TO CHAPTER SIX

1. For discussion of the dependency theory, see, among others, Andre Gunder Frank 1991, Ronald H. Chilcote 1974, and Theotonio Dos Santos 1970.
2. Korea subsequently was made a dependent state of Japan in 1905, and then a colony from 1910 to 1945.
3. Recent trend has shifted somewhat. Instead of the United States, several students have chosen to pursue their tertiary education in Europe, in countries such as England, France, and Belgium.
4. The problem of skill accreditation is quite common. For more details see Iredale 1997.
5. Asian Americans were popularized as the model minority in American society by the media in the 1960s and 1980s, for an analysis of the media images see Osajima 2000. On the one hand, the model minority thesis compliments and elevates Asian Americans for their success, on the other, it acts to criticize other minorities such as African Americans and blame them for their own failure. For a discussion of the model minority, see Cheng and Yang 2000.

NOTES TO CHAPTER SEVEN

1. In Korea, the transnational family arrangement in which a husband in Korea supports his wife and children in the United Stats also stands as a status symbol of financial success for men (personal communication, Edward Chang 2002).
2. I do not mean that women are not affected in similar situations. I only write about men here because I have known these men and noticed them.

NOTES TO CHAPTER EIGHT

1. The picture bride phenomenon is an arranged marriage mainly within the Japanese and Korean American populations in the early part of the twentieth century. It is based on traditional practice in Japan. The United States and Japan signed the Gentlemen's Agreement of 1907–08 that curtailed further labor importation to California from Japan. In return, Japanese males already residing in Hawaii and continental United States, if finically qualified, were allowed to sponsor their wives to join them. Often through a paid intermediary or a relative, prospective brides in Japan and grooms in the United States exchanged photographs to initiate the process. The first

meeting between husband and wife usually took place upon the latter's arrival on American soil. Japan annexed and later colonized Korea from 1895 to 1945, making the Gentlemen's Agreement also applicable to Koreans immigrants in the United States including Hawaii.

2. An exception occurs among Korean immigrant entrepreneurship, where wives work without pay in their family-owned small businesses such as grocery stores, liquor stores, and dry clean services, see Kim and Hurh 1988.
3. The problem of skill accreditation is quite common. See Iredale (1997) for more detail.

NOTES TO CHAPTER NINE

1. In the Pacific Rim, non-working class transnational families are also emerging between Singapore and Mainland China, with corporate husbands relocated to China while their wives and children remain in Singapore, see Yeon and Khoo 1998; Willies and Yeoh 2000.
2. In Taiwan, as in China and Japan, all legal residents are accounted for by the government in the household registry. Each individual is registered at a particular legal address. Each change of address, such as with a move, must be reported to the police headquarters. Hence, each individual has a legal residence or address as recorded in the household registry.

Bibliography

Abu Lughod, Lila. 1991. Writing Against Culture. In *Recapturing Anthropology*, edited by R. G. Fox. Santa Fe: School of American Research Press.

Ahern, Emily M. 1973. *The Cult of the Dead in a Chinese Village*. Stanford: Stanford University Press.

Ahern, Susan, Dexter Bryan, and Reynaldo Baca. 1985. Migration and La Mujer Fuerte. *Migration Today* 13 (1):14–20.

Alicea, Marixsa. 1997. "A Chambered Nautilus": The Contradictory Nature of Puerto Rican Women's Role in the Social Construction of a Transnational Community. *Gender and Society* 11 (5):597–626.

Almquist, Elizabeth M. 1995. The Experiences of Minority Women in the United States: Intersections of Race, Gender, and Class. In *Women: A Feminist Perspective*, edited by J. Freeman. Mountain View, CA: Mayfield Publishing Company.

Anderson, Benedict. 1991. *Imagined Communities: Reflections on the Origin and Spread of Nationalism*. London: Verso.

Anderson, Elaine A., and Jane W. Spruill. 1993. The Dual-Career Commuter Family: A Lifestyle on the Move. *Marriage and Family Review* 19 (1–2):131–47.

Anderson, Kathryn, and Dana C. Jack. 1991. Learning to Listen: Interview Technique and Analyses. In *Women's Words: The Feminist Practice of Oral History*, edited by S. B. Gluck and D. Patai. New York: Routledge.

Appadurai, Arjun. 1991. Global Ethnoscapes: Notes and Queries for a Transnational Anthropology. In *Recapturing Anthropology*, edited by R. G. Fox. Santa Fe: School of American Research Press.

Apter, Terri. 1986. *Loose Relations: Your In-Laws and You*. London: The MacMillan Press Ltd.

Arax, Mark. 1987. Asian Influx Alters Life in Suburbia. *Los Angeles Times*, April 5, 1.

Aseniero, George. 1996. Asia in the World-System. In *The Underdevelopment of Development*, edited by S. C. Chew and R. A. Denemark. Thousand Oaks, CA: SAGE Publications.

Au, Jeffery K. D. 1988. Asian American College Admission—Legal, Empirical, and Philosophical Questions for the 1980s and Beyond. In *Reflections on Shattered Windows: Promises and Prospects for Asian American Studies*, edited by

G. Okihiro, S. Hune, A. Hanse and J. Liu. Pullman, WA: Washington State University Press.

Baron, Harold M. 1975. Racial Domination in Advanced Capitalism: A Theory of Nationalism and Divisions in the Labor Market. In *Labor Market Segmentation*, edited by R. C. Edwards, M. Reich and D. M. Gordon. Lexington, MA: D.C. Heath and Company.

Basch, Linda, Nina Glick Schiller, and Cristina Szanton Blanc. 1994. *Nations Unbound: Transnational Projects, Postcolonial Predicaments and Deterritorialized Nation-States*. Langhorne, PA: Gordon and Breach.

Bedford, Richard. 1997. Migration in Oceania: Reflections on Contemporary Theoretical Debates. *New Zealand Population Review* 23:46–64.

Berk, Sarah F. 1985. *The Gender Factory: The Apportionment of Work in American Household*. New York: Plenum Press.

Bernard, H. Russell. 1994. *Research Methods in Anthropology: Qualitative and Quantitative Approaches*. Thousand Oaks, CA: SAGE Publications.

Blauner, Robert. 1972. *Racial Oppression in America*. New York: Harper & Row.

Blood, Robert O. Jr., and Donald M. Wolfe. 1960. *Husband and Wife: The Dynamics of Married Living*. Glencoe, IL: The Free Press.

Bose, Christine E. 1987. Dual Spheres. In *Analyzing Gender: A Handbook of Social Science Research*, edited by B. B. Hess and M. M. Ferree. Newsbury Park, CA: Sage Publication.

Boswell, Terry, and Christopher Chase-Dunn. 2000. From State Socialism to Global Democracy: The Transnational Politics of the Modern World-System. In *A World System Reader: New Perspectives on Gender, Urbanism, Cultures, Indigenous Peoples, and Ecology*, edited by T. D. Hall. Lanham, MD: Rowman & Littlefield Publishers, Inc.

Bourdieu, Pierre. 1980. Le Capital Social: Notes Provisoires. *Actes de la Recherche en Sciences Sociales* 31:2–3.

———. 1984. *Distinction: A Social Critique of the Judgment of Taste*. Translated by R. Nice. Cambridge, MA: Harvard University Press.

———. 1986. The Forms of Capital. In *Handbook of Theory and Research for the Sociology of Education*, edited by J. G. Richardson. New York: Greenwood Press, Inc.

Boyd, Monica. 1989. Family and Personal Networks in International Migration: Recent Developments and New Agendas. *International Migration Review* 23 (3):638–70.

Braudel, Fernand. 1975. *Capitalism and Material Life, 1400–1800*. New York: Harper and Row.

———. 1980. History and the Social Science: The Longue Duree. In *On History*. Chicago: University of Chicago Press.

———. 1984. *The Perspective of the World*. Vol. 3, *Civilization and Capitalism*. Berkeley: University of California Press.

Buijs, Gina. 1994. Introduction. In *Migrant Women: Crossing Boundaries and Changing Identities*, edited by G. Buijs. Oxford: Berg Publishers Ltd.

Chan, Kwok Bun, Jin Hui Ong, and Soon Beng Chew. 1995. Asian Transmigration: Themes, Issues and Debates. In *Crossing Borders: Transmigration in Asia*

Pacific, edited by J. H. Ong, K. B. Chan and S. B. Chew. Singapore: Simon and Schuster (Asia) Limited.

Chan, Sucheng. 1991a. *Asian Americans: An Interpretive History.* Boston: Twayne Publishers.

———. 1991b. The Exclusion of Chinese Women, 1870–1891. In *Entry Denied: Exclusion and the Chinese Community in America, 1882–1943,* edited by S. Chan. Philadelphia: Temple University Press.

Chang, Edward T.H. 2002. Korean transnational families. Riverside, CA, February.

Chang, Mau-kuei. 2000. On the Origins and Transformation of Taiwanese National Identity. *China Perspectives* 28:51–69.

Chang, Mau-kuei, and Hsing-yi Wu. 2000. *Identity and Sentiment in Nationality and Ethnicity: Respect and Recognition (text in Chinese).* 6 vols. Vol. 2, *Taiwan Research Foundation Series.* Taipei: Yueh Dan Publisher.

Chang, Shu Yuan. 1973. China or Taiwan: The Political Crisis of the Chinese Intellectual. *Amerasia Journal* 2:47–81.

Chang, Ying-hua, Cheng Tai-shi, and Yi Chih-wang. 1996. *Educational Tracking and Socioeconomic Status: Policy Implication on Technical and Vocational Education Reform (text in Chinese).* Taipei: The Executive Yuan Education Reform Committee.

Chao, Ruth. 2002. The Role of Children's Linguistic Brokering among Immigrant Chinese and Mexican Families. Paper read at Biennial meeting of the Society for Research in Child Development, at Minneapolis, Minnesota.

Chase-Dunn, Christopher, and Thomas D. Hall. 1997. *Rise and Demise: Comparing World-Systems.* Boulder, CO: Westview.

Chee, Maria W.L. 1995/96. Book Review on The First Suburban Chinatown: The Remaking of Monterey Park, California. By Timothy P. Fong. Philadelphia: Temple University, 1994. *Amerasia Journal* 21 (3):237–39.

Chee, Maria W.L., Gary A. Dymski, and Wei Li. 2004. Asia in Los Angeles: Ethnic Chinese Banking in the Age of Globalization. In *Chinese Enterprises, Transnationalism and Identity,* edited by E. T. Gomez and H. H. M. Hsiao. London: RoutledgeCurzon.

Chen, Fang-ming. 1988. *An Anthology on the 2–28 Incident (text in Chinese).* Irvine: Taiwan Publishing Company, Inc.

Chen, Hsiang Shui. 1992. *Chinatown No More: Taiwan Immigrants in Contemporary New York.* Ithaca: Cornell University Press.

Chen, Ta. 1940. *Emigrant Communities in South China: A Study of Overseas Migration and Its Influence on Standards of Living and Social Change.* New York: Institute of Pacific Relation.

Cheng, Lucie. 1984. Free, Indentured, Enslaved: Chinese Prostitutes in Nineteenth-Century America. In *Labor Immigration under Capitalism: Asian Workers in the United States Before World War II,* edited by L. Cheng and E. Bonacich. Berkeley: University of California Press.

Cheng, Lucie, and Edna Bonacich, eds. 1984. *Labor Immigration under Capitalism: Asian Workers in the United States Before World War II.* Berkeley: University of California Press.

Cheng, Lucie, and Philip Q. Yang. 1998. Global Interaction, Global Inequality, and Migration of the Highly Trained to the United States. *International Migration Review* 32:626–53.

———. 2000. The "Model Minority" Deconstructed. In *Contemporary Asian America: a Multidisciplinary Reader,* edited by M. Zhou and J. V. Gatewood. New York: New York University Press.

Chiang, Nora. 2001. Divorce in Taiwan. Taipei.

Chien, Wen-yin, and Cherng-tay Hsueh. 1996. Employment of Married Women in Taiwan: Its Pattern and Causes (text in Chinese). *Journal of Population Studies [Taiwan]* 17:113–34.

Chilcote, Ronald H. 1974. Dependency: A Critical Synthesis of the Literature. *Latin American Perspectives* 1 (1):4–29.

Chin, Ku-Sup, In-Jin Yoon, and David Smith. 1996. Immigrant Small Business and International Economic Linkages: A Case of Korean Wig Business in Los Angeles, 1968–1977. *International Migration Review* 30 (2):485–510.

Chin, Tung Pok, and Winifred Chin. 2000. *Paper Son: One Man's Story.* Philadelphia: Temple University Press.

Chiswick, Barry R. 1979. The Economic Progress of Immigrants: Some Apparently Universal Patterns. In *Contemporary Economic Problems 1979,* edited by P. D. W. Fellner. Washington, D. C.: American Enterprise Institute for Public Policy Research.

Chiu, Paul. 1992. Money and Financial Markets: The Domestic Perspective. In *Taiwan: From Developing to Mature Economy,* edited by G. Ranis. Boulder, CO: Westview.

Chong, Denise. 1995. *The Concubine's Children.* New York: Viking.

Chu, Louis. 1979. *Eat a Bowl of Tea.* Seattle: University of Washington Press.

Chun, Allen. 1996. Discourses of Identity in the Changing Spaces of Public Culture in Taiwan, Hong Kong and Singapore. *Theory, Culture & Society* 13 (1):31–75.

Chung, Chong-li Edith. 1994. An Investigation of the Psychological Well-Being of Unaccompanied Taiwanese Minors/Parachute Kids in the United States. Ph. D. dissertation, University of Southern California, Los Angeles.

Cohen, Myron L. 1976. *House United, House Divided: The Chinese Family in Taiwan.* New York: Columbia University Press.

Cohn, Bernard S. 1981. Anthropology and History in the 1980s. *Journal of Interdisciplinary History* 12 (2):227–52.

Coleman, James S. 1988. Social Capital in the Creation of Human Capital. *American Journal of Sociology* 94 (Supplement 1):S95-S120.

Comaroff, John, and Jean Comaroff. 1992. *Ethnography of the Historical Imagination.* Boulder, CO: Westview.

Coolidge, Mary. 1909. *Chinese Immigration.* New York: H. Holt and Company.

Copper, John F. 1996. *Taiwan: Nation-State or Province?* Boulder, CO: Westview.

Daniels, Roger. 1988. *Asian American: Chinese and Japanese in the United States since 1850.* Seattle: University of Washington Press.

Deo, Frederic C. 1987. *Beneath the Miracle: Labor Subordination in the New Asian Industrialism.* Berkeley: University of California Press.

Di Leonardo, Micaela. 1987. The Female World of Cards and Holidays: Women, Families, and the Work of Kinship. *Signs: Journal of Women in Culture and Society* 12 (3):440–53.

Dicken, Peter. 1992. *Global Shift: The Internationalization of Economic Activity.* New York: The Guilford Press.

Dill, Bonnie Thornton. 1988. Our Mothers' Grief: Racial Ethnic and the Maintenance of Families. *Journal of Family History* 12 (4):415–31.

———. 1994. *Across the Boundaries of Race and Class: An Exploration of Work and Family among Black Female Domestic Servants.* New York: Garland.

Dos Santos, Theotonio. 1970. The Structure of Dependence. *American Economic Review* 40 (2):231–36.

Douvan, Elizabeth, and Joseph Pleck. 1978. Separation as Support. In *Working Couples*, edited by R. Rapoport and R. N. Rapoport. London: Routledge and Kegan Paul.

Duvall, Evelyn M. 1964. *In-Laws: Pro & Con. An Original Study of Inter-Personal Relations.* New York: Association Press.

Edwards, Richard C., Michael Reich, and David M. Gordon, eds. 1975. *Labor Market Segmentation.* Lexington, MA: D.C. Heath and Company.

Evans, M. D. R. 1989. Immigrant Entrepreneurship: Effects of Ethnic Market Size and Isolated Labor Pool. *American Sociological Review* 54 (6):950–62.

Evans-Pritchard, E. E. 1940. *The Nuer: A Description of the Modes of Livelihood and Political Institutions of a Nilotic People.* Oxford: Oxford University Press.

Farris, Agnes. 1978. Commuting. In *Working Couples*, edited by R. Rapoport and R. N. Rapoport. London: Routledge and Keagan Paul.

Fawcett, J. T. 1989. Networks, Linkages, and Migration Systems. *International Migration Review* 23 (3):671–80.

Fernandez, John, and Mary Barr. 1993. *The Diversity Advantage: How American Business Can Out-perform Japanese and European Companies in the Global Market.* New York: Lexington Books.

Fields, Gary S. 1992. Living Standards, Labor Markets, and Human Resources in Taiwan. In *Taiwan: From Developing to Mature Economy*, edited by G. Ranis. Boulder, CO: Westview.

Findlay, Allan. 1990. A Migration Channels Approach to the Study of High Level Manpower Movements: A Theoretical Perspective. *International Migration Review* 28 (1):15–21.

Fong, Joe C. 1996. Transnational Newspapers: The Making of the Post-1965 Globalized/Localized San Gabriel Valley Chinese Community. *Amerasia Journal* 22 (3):65–77.

Fong, Timothy P. 1994. *The First Suburban Chinatown: The Remaking of Monterey Park, California.* Philadelphia: Temple University Press.

Fortune. 1998. February 2, 65–78.

Foucault, Michel. 1972. *The Archeology of Knowledge.* Translated by A. M. S. Smith. New York: Pantheon Books.

———. 1995. *Discipline and Punish: The Birth of the Prison.* Translated by A. Sheridan. New York: Vintage Books.

Fouron, Georges, and Nina Glick Schiller. 2001. All in the Family: Gender, Transnational Migration, and the Nation-State. *Identities* 74 (2):539–82.

Frank, Andre Gunder. 1991. The Underdevelopment of Development. *Scandinavian Journal of Development Alternatives* 10 (3):5–72.

Freedman, Maurice. 1958. *Lineage Organization in Southeastern China*. London: Athlone Press.

———. 1971. *Chinese Lineage and Society: Fukien and Kwangtung*. London: Athlone Press.

Gailey, Christine Ward. 1992. A Good Man is Hard to Find: Overseas Migration and the Decentered Family in the Tongan Islands. *Critique of Anthropology* 12 (1):47–74.

Gates, Hill. 1981. *Chinese Working-Class Lives: Getting by in Taiwan*. Ithaca: Cornell University Press.

———. 1981. Ethnicity and Social Class. In *The Anthropology of Taiwanese Society*, edited by E. M. Ahern and H. Gates. Stanford: Stanford University Press.

Gelb, Joyce, and Marian L. Palley, eds. 1994. *Women of Japan and Korea: Continuity and Change*. Philadelphia: Temple University Press.

Georges, Eugenia. 1992. Gender, Class, and Migration in the Dominican Republic: Women's Experience in a Transnational Community. In *Towards a Transnational Perspective on Migration: Race, Class, Ethnicity, and Nationalism Reconsidered*, edited by N. G. Schiller, L. Basch and C. Blanc-Szanton. New York: New York Academy of Sciences.

Gerstel, Naomi, and Harriet E. Gross. 1984. *Commuter Marriage: A Study of Work and Family*. New York: The Guilford Press.

———. 1987. Commuter Marriage: A Microcosm of Career and Family Conflict. In *Families and Work*, edited by N. Gerstel and H. Gross. Philadelphia: Temple University Press.

Giddens, Anthony. 1984. *The Constitution of Society*. Cambridge: Polity Press.

Gillespie, Dair L. 1971. Who Has the Power? The Marital Struggle. *Journal of Marriage and the Family* 33 (3):445–58.

Gilroy, Paul. 1991. It Ain't Where You're From, It's Where You're At. . . . The Dialectics of Diasporic Identification. *Third Text* 13:3–15.

Glenn, Evelyn N. 1983. Split Household, Small Producer and Dual Wager Earner: An Analysis of Chinese-American Family Strategies. *Journal of Marriage & the Family* 45 (1):35–46.

———. 1985. Racial Ethnic Women's Labor: The Intersection of Race, Gender and Class. *Review of Radical Political Economics* 17 (3):86–109.

———. 1986. *Issei, Nisei, Warbride: Three Generations of Japanese American Women in Domestic Service*. Philadelphia: Temple University Press.

———. 1992. From Servitude to Service Work: Historical Continuities in the Racial Division of Paid Reproductive Labor. *Signs: Journal of Women in Culture and Society* 18 (1):1–43.

Glenn, Evelyn N., and Stacey G. H. Yap. 1994. Chinese American Families. In *Minority Families in the United States: A Multicultural Perspective*, edited by R. L. Taylor. Englewood Cliff, NJ: Prentice Hall.

Glick Schiller, Nina, Linda Basch, and Cristina Blanc-Szanton. 1992. Introduction. Transnationalism: A New Analytic Framework for Understanding Migration.

In *Towards a Transnational Perspective on Migration: Race, Class, Ethnicity, and Nationalism Reconsidered,* edited by N. G. Schiller, L. Basch and C. Blanc-Szanton. New York: The New York Academy of Sciences.

Goldring, Luin. 1998. The Power of Status in Transnational Social Fields. In *Transnationalism from Below,* edited by M. P. Smith and E. Guarnizo. New Brunswick, NJ: Transaction Publishers.

———. 2001. The Gender and Geography of Citizenship in Mexico-U.S. Transnational Spaces. *Identities* 7 (4):501–37.

Gordon, David M., Richard Edwards, and Michael Reich. 1982. *Segmented Work, Divided Labor: The Historical Transformation of Labor in the United States.* Cambridge: Cambridge University Press.

Gordon, Milton. 1964. *Assimilation in American Life: The Role of Race, Religion, and National Origins.* New York: Oxford University Press.

Graham, Hillary. 1984. Survey Through Stories. In *Social Researching: Politics, Problems, Practice,* edited by C. Bell and H. Roberts. London: Routledge & Kegan Paul.

Gramsci, Antonio. 1971. *Selections from the Prison Notebooks.* Translated by Q. Hoare and G. N. Smith. New York: International Publishers.

Grasmuck, Sherri, and Patricia R. Pessar. 1991. *Between Two Islands. Dominican International Migration.* Berkeley: University of California Press.

Gross, Harriet E. 1980. Dual-Career Couples Who Live Apart: Two Types. *Journal of Marriage and the Family* 41 (2):567–76.

Guarnizo, Luis E. 1997. Transnationalism from Below: Social Transformation and the Mirage of Return Migration among Dominican Transmigrants. *Identities* 4 (2):281–322.

Gurak, Douglas T., and Fe Caces. 1992. Migration Network and the Shaping of Migration System. In *International Migration Systems: A Global Perspective,* edited by M. Kritz, L. L. Lim and H. Zlotnik. Oxford: Clarendon Press.

Hall, Thomas D. 2000. World-System Analysis: A Small Sample from a Large Universe. In *A World-Systems Reader: New Perspectives on Gender, Urbanism, Cultures, Indigenous People, and Ecology,* edited by T. D. Hall. Lanham, MD: Rowman & Littlefield Publishers, Inc.

Hannerz, Ulf. 1998. Transnational Research. In *Handbook of Methods in Cultural Anthropology,* edited by H. R. Bernard. Walnut Creek, CA: AltaMira Press.

Haraway, Donna. 1988. Situated Knowledges: The Science Question in Feminism and the Privilege of Partial Perspective. *Feminist Studies* 14 (3):575–99.

Hartmann, Heidi. 1981. The Family as the Locus of Gender, Class, and Political Struggle: The Example of Housework. *Signs: Journal of Women in Culture and Society* 6 (3):366–94.

Hartsock, Nancy C. M. 1983. The Feminist Standpoint: Developing the Ground for a Specifically Feminist Historical Materialism. In *Discovering Reality: Feminist Perspectives on Epistemology, Metaphysics, Methodology, and Philosophy of Science,* edited by S. Harding and M. B. Hintikka. Boston: D. Reidel Publishing Company.

Hendershot, Anne B. 1995. *Moving for Work: The Sociology of Relocating in the 1990s.* Lanham: University Press of America, Inc.

Hing, Bill Ong. 1993. *Making and Remaking of Asian America Through Immigration Policy, 1850–1990*. Stanford: Stanford University Press.

Ho, Elsie, Manying Ip, and Richard D. Bedford. 2001. Transnational Hong Kong Chinese Families in the 1990s. *New Zealand Journal of Geography* 301:24–30.

Ho, Elsie. 2002. Multi-local Residence, Transnational Networks: Chinese "Astronaut Families" in New Zealand. *Asian and Pacific Migration Journal* 11 (1):145–64.

Hobsbawm, Eric, and Terence Ranger. 1983. *The Invention of Tradition*. Cambridge: Cambridge University Press.

Hochschild, Arlie. 1989. The Economy of Gratitude. In *The Sociology of Emotion*, edited by D. Franks and E. D. McCarthy. Greenwich, CT: JAI.

Hochschild, Arlie, and Anne Machung. 1989. *The Second Shift: Working Parents and the Revolution at Home*. New York: Viking.

Hom, Marlon K. 1987. *Songs of Gold Mountain: Cantonese Rhymes from San Francisco Chinatown*. Berkeley: University of California Press.

Hondagneu-Sotelo, Pierette. 1994. *Gendered Transitions: Mexican Experiences of Immigration*. Berkeley: University of California Press.

———. 2001. *Doméstica: Immigrant Workers Cleaning and Caring in the Shadows of Affluence*. Berkeley: University of California Press.

———. 2003. Gender and Immigration: a Retrospective and Introduction. In *Gender and U.S. Immigration: Contemporary Trends*, edited by P. Hondagneu-Sotelo. Berkeley: University of California Press.

Hondagneu-Sotelo, Pierrette, and Ernestine Avila. 1997. "I'm Here, But I'm There": The Meaning of Latina Transnational Motherhood. *Gender & Society* 11 (5):548–71.

Horton, John. 1995. *The Politics of Diversity: Immigration, Resistance, and Change in Monterey Park, California*. Philadelphia: Temple University Press.

Hsia, Jayjia. 1988. *Asian Americans in Higher Education and at Work*. New Jersey: Lawrence Erlbaum Associates.

Hsiao, H. H. Michael, and Hua-pi Tseng. 1999. The Formation of Environmental Consciousness in Taiwan: Intellectuals, Media, and the Public Mind. *Asian Geographer* 18 (1–2):99–109.

Hsiao, H. H. Michael, and Christopher Smith. 1994. Adaptation Process and Return Migration of Taiwan Immigrants in the Country of Settlement: The Case of Los Angeles and New York (text in Chinese). Taipei.

Hsiao, H. H. Michael. 1999. Environmental Movements in Taiwan. In *Asia's Environmental Movements: Comparative Perspectives*, edited by Y. F. Lee and A. Y. So. Armonk, NY: M. E. Sharpe, Inc.

Hsiau, A-chin. 1998. Crafting a Nation: Contemporary Taiwanese Cultural Nationalism. Ph. D. dissertation, University of California, San Diego.

———. 1999. The Development of Taiwanese Cultural Nationalism Since the Early 1980s: A Study on "Taiwanese (National) Literature" (text in Chinese). *Taiwanese Sociological Review* 3:1–51.

Hsu, Madeline Y. Y. 1997. Gold Mountain Dreams and Paper Son Schemes: Chinese Immigration Under Exclusion. In *Chinese America History and*

Perspective, edited by Marion K. Hom, Him Mark Lai, Vitus Leung, Lilian Louie, and Lawrence Wu McClain. San Francisco: Chinese Historical Society.

———. 2000. *Dreaming of Gold, Dreaming of Home: Transnationalism and Migration Between the United States and South China, 1882–1943*. Stanford: Stanford University Press.

Hu, Tai-li. 1990. Taros and Yams: Ethnic Relations and Identities of "Honored Citizens" (Veteran-Mainlanders) in Taiwan (text in Chinese). *Bulletin of the Institute of Ethnology, Academia Sinica, Taiwan* 69:107–32.

Huber, Joan, and Glenna Spitze. 1983. *Sex Stratification: Children, Housework, and Jobs*. New York: Academic Press.

Hughes, Robert, Jr., and Jason D. Hans. 2001. Computers, the Internet, and Families: A Review of the Role New Technology Plays in Family Life. *Journal of Family Issues* 22 (6):776–90.

Hugo, Graeme J. 1981. Village-Community Ties, Village Norms, and Ethnic and Social Networks: A Review of Evidence from the Third World. In *Migration Decision Making*, edited by G. F. DeJong and R. W. Gardner. New York: Pergamon.

Hui, Y. F. 1993. Astronaut Family. *The Hong Kong Journal of Social Work* 27 (1):59–68.

Hune, Shirley. 2000. Doing Gender with a Feminist Gaze: Toward a Historical Reconstruction of Asian America. In *Contemporary Asian America: A Multidisciplinary Reader*, edited by M. Zhou and J. V. Gatewood. New York: New York University Press.

Ichioka, Yuji. 1977. Ameyuki-san: Japanese Prostitutes in Nineteenth-Century America. *Amerasia Journal* 4 (1):1–21.

Ignatiev, Noel. 1885. *How the Irish Become White*. New York: Routledge.

Iredale, Robyn. 1997. *Skills Transfer: International Migration and Accreditation Issues*. Wollongong, Australia: University of Wollongong.

Johnson, S. E. 1987. Weaving the Threads: Equalizing Professional and Personal Demands Faced by Commuting Career Couples. *Journal of NAAWDAC* 50 (2):3–10.

Kaplan, David. 1998. The Social Structure of Urban Ethnic Economics. *Urban Geography* 19 (6):489–501.

Kaufman, Debra R. 1989. *Rachel's Daughters: Newly Orthodox Jewish Women*. New Brunswick, NJ: Rutgers University.

Kawakami, Barbara F. 1985. *Picture Brides Slide Show: Lives of Hawaii's Early Immigrant Women From Japan, Okinawa, and Korea*. Manoa, HI.

Kearney, Michael. 1995. The Local and the Global: The Anthropology of Globalization and Transnationalism. *Annual Review of Anthropology* 24:547–65.

———. 2000. Transnational Oaxacan Indigenous Identity: The Case of Mixtecs and Zapotecs. *Identities* 7 (2):173–95.

Kellogg, Susan. 1993. Histories for Anthropology: Ten Years of Historical Research and Writing by Anthropologists, 1980–1900. In *Engaging the Past: The Uses of Histories Across the Social Sciences*, edited by E. H. Mokonnen. Durham: Duke University Press.

Kerr, George H. 1965. *Formosa Betrayed*. Boston: The Riverside Press.

Khoo, Tai-ling Terina. 1995. Stress-Coping of Recently Arrived Chinese High School Students (Hong Kong, Taiwan). Ph. D. dissertation, University of Southern California, Los Angeles.

Kibria, Nazli. 1990. Power, Patriarchy, and Gender Conflict in the Vietnamese Immigrant Community. *Gender & Society* 4 (1):9–24.

———. 1993. *Family Tightrope: The Changing Lives of Vietnamese Americans*. Princeton: Princeton University Press.

Kikumura, Akemi. 1981. *Through Harsh Winters: The Life of a Japanese Immigrant Woman*. Novato, CA: Chandler & Sharp Publishers, Inc.

Kim, Kwang Chung, and Moo Hurh Wong. 1986. The Burden of Double Roles: Korean Wives in the U.S.A. *Ethnic and Racial Studies* 11:151–67.

Kingston, Maxine Hong. 1977. *The Woman Warrior: Memoirs of a Girlhood among Ghosts*. New York: Vintage Books.

Kirschner, Betty F., and Laurel R. Wallum. 1978. Two-Location Families: Married Singles. *Alternative Lifestyles* 1 (4):513–25.

Komter, Aafke. 1990. Hidden Power in Marriage. *Gender & Society* 3 (2):187–216.

Kranichfeld, Marion. 1987. Rethinking Family Power. *Journal of Family Issues* 8 (1):42–56.

Kristoff, Nicholas D. 2002/03. Who Needs Love! In Japan, Many Couples Don't. In *Annual Edition: Anthropology, 02/03*, edited by E. Angeloni. Guilford, CT: McGraw-Hill/Dushkin.

Kulp, Daniel H., II. 1966. *Phenix [sic] Village, Kwantung, China*. Vol. 1, *Country Life in China: The Sociology of Familism*. Taipei: Cheng-Wen Publishing Company.

Kuo, Shu-yu. 1991. *Taiwan's Parachute Kids in the United States (text in Chinese)*. Taipei: Institute of European and American Studies, Academia Sinica.

Lam, Lawrence. 1994. Searching for a Safe Haven: The Migration and Settlement of Hong Kong Chinese Immigrants in Toronto. In *Reluctant Exiles?: Migration from Hong Kong and the New Overseas Chinese*, edited by R. Skeldon. Armonk, NY: M. E. Sharpe.

Lam, Theodora, Brenda S. A. Yeoh, and Lisa Law. 2002. Sustaining Families Transnationally: Chinese-Malaysians in Singapore. *Asian and Pacific Migration Journal* 11 (1):117–143.

Lamley, Harry J. 1981. Subethnic Rivalry in the Ching Period. In *The Anthropology of Taiwanese Society*, edited by E. M. Ahern and H. Gates. Stanford: Stanford University Press.

———. 1999. Taiwan Under Japanese Rule, 1895–1945: The Vicissitudes of Colonialism. In *Taiwan: A New History*, edited by M. A. Rubinstein. Armonk, NY: M. E. Sharpe.

Lamphere, Louise. 1993. The Domestic Sphere of Women and the Public World of Men: The Strength and Limitations of an Anthropological Dichotomy. In *Gender in Cross Cultural Perspective*, edited by C. B. Brettell and C. E. Sargent. Upper Saddle River, NJ: Prentice Hall, Inc.

Lauby, Jennifer, and Oded Stark. 1988. Individual Migration as a family Strategy: Young Women in the Philippines. *Population Studies* 42 (473–86).

Leacock, Eleanor. 1978. Status in Egalitarian Society: Implications for Social Evolution. *Current Anthropology* 19 (2):247–75.

Lee, Wen Ho, and Helen Zia. 2001. *My Country Versus Me*. New York: Hyperion.

Leong, Russell C. 1996. Transnationalism, Media, and Migration. *Amerasia Journal* 22 (3):iii-vi.

Lewellen, Ted C. 2002. *The Anthropology of Globalization: Cultural Anthropology Enters the 21st Century*. Westport, CONN: Bergin & Garvey.

Li, Wei. 1998. Los Angeles' Chinese Ethnoburb: From Ethnic Service Center to Global Economy Outpost. *Urban Geography* 19 (6):502–17.

Li, Wei, Maria Chee, Yu Zhou, and Gary Dymski. 2000. Development Trajectory of the Chinese American Banking Sector in Los Angeles. Paper read at Asian American Studies Association Annual Conference, at Phoenix, Arizona.

Li, Wei, Gary Dymski, Yu Zhou, Maria Chee, and Carolyn Aldana. 2002. Chinese American Banking and Community Development in Los Angeles County. *Annals of the Association of American Geographers* 92 (4):77–96.

Li, Wei, Yu Zhou, Gary Dymski, and Maria Chee. 2001. Banking on Social Capital in the Era of Globalization: Chinese Ethnobanks in Los Angeles. *Environment and Planning A* 33:1923–48.

Light, Ivan. 1979. Disadvantaged Minorities in Self-Employment. *International Journal of Comparative Sociology* 20 (1–2):21–35.

———. 1984. Immigrant and Ethnic Enterprise in North America. *Ethnic and Racial Studies* 7 (2):195–216.

Lin, Holin. 1998. The Crossroads of Ethnicity and Gender: Intergenerational Household Resource Allocation Strategies in Taiwan (text in Chinese). *Journal of Humanities and Social Sciences* 11 (4):475–528.

Lin, Sung-ling. 1999. Effects of Mother on Her Children's School Performance: The Comparisons of Cultural Capital, Economic Resources, and Supervisory Role (text in Chinese). *National Taiwan University Journal of Sociology* 27:73–105.

Ling, Huping. 1998. *Surviving on the Gold Mountain: A History of Chinese American Women and Their Lives*. Albany: State University of New York Press.

Liu, Alan P. L. 1987. *Phoenix and the Lame Lion: Modernization in Taiwan and Mainland China 1950–80*. Stanford: Hoover Institution Press.

Liu, Haiming. 1992. The Trans-Pacific Family. *Amerasia Journal* 18 (2):1–34.

Liu, John M., and Lucie Cheng. 1994. Pacific Rim Development and the Duality of Post-1965 Asian Immigration to the United States. In *The New Asian Immigration in Los Angeles and Global Restructuring*, edited by P. Ong, E. Bonacich and L. Cheng. Philadelphia: Temple University Press.

Liu, Paul C. H. 1992. Money and Financial Markets: The Domestic Perspective. In *Taiwan from Developing to Mature Economy*, edited by G. Ranis. Boulder, CO: Westview Press.

Loewen, James W. 1988. *The Mississippi Chinese: Between Black and White*. Prospect Heights, IL: Waveland Press, Inc.

Los Angeles Time. 1993. June 24.

Lu, Yu-hsia. 1982. Value Extension of Modern Women's Role (text in Chinese). *Thoughts and Words* 20 (2):135–50.

————. 1983. Women's Labor Force Participation and Family Power Structure in Taiwan (text in Chinese). *Bulletin of the Institute of Ethnology, Academia Sinica* 56:113–43.

————. 1996. Women's Role in Taiwan's Family Enterprises: A Preliminary Research (text in Chinese). In *Population, Employment and Welfare*. Taipei: Institute of Economics, Academia Sinica.

————. 1997. Facilitation or Inhibition: Family Interaction and Married Women's Employment (text in Chinese). In *Taiwanese Society in 1990s: Taiwan Social Change Survey Symposium Series II (Part 2), Monograph Series No. 1*, edited by L. Y. Chang, Y. H. Lu and F. C. Wang. Taipei: Institute of Sociology Preparatory Office, Academia Sinica.

Lu, Yu-hsia, and Chin-chun Yi. 1999. Employment and Family Status of Women in a Changing Society: Allocation of Household Chores (text in Chinese). Paper read at Chinese Family and Its Relationship Conference, at Taipei, Taiwan.

Lukes, Steven. 1976. *Power: A Radical View*. London: MacMillan Press Limited.

Lyman, Stanford M. 1968. Marriage and the Family among Chinese Immigrants to America, 1850–1960. *Phylon* 29: 321–30.

Mahler, Sarah J. 1999. Engendering Transnational Migration: A Case Study of Salvadorans. *American Behavioral Scientist* 42 (4):690–719.

————. 1999. Theoretical and Empirical Contributions Toward a Research Agenda for Transnationalism. In *Transnationalism from Below*, edited by M. P. Smith and L. E. Guarnizo. New Brunswick: Transaction Publishers.

————. 2001. Transnational Relationships: The Struggle to Communicate Across Borders. *Identities* 7 (4):583–619.

Man, Guida. 1993. Astronaut Phenomenon: Examining Consequences of the Diaspora of the Hong Kong Chinese. Paper read at Managing Changes in Southeast Asia: Local Identities, Global Connections, The 21st Meeting of the Canadian Council for Southeast Asian Studies, at The University of Alberta, Canada.

————. 1996. The Experience of Middle-Class Women in Recent Hong Kong Chinese Immigrant Families in Canada. In *Voices: Essays on Canadian Families*, edited by M. Lynn. Toronto: Nelson Canada.

————. 1996. The Experience of Women in Middle-Class Hong Kong Chinese Immigrant Families in Canada: An Investigation in Institutional and Organization Process. Ph. D. dissertation, Education, University of Toronto, Toronto.

Marcus, George E. 1986. Contemporary Problems of Ethnography in the Modern World System. In *Writing Culture: The Poetics and Politics of Ethnography*, edited by J. Clifford and G. E. Marcus. Berkeley: University of California Press.

Marcus, George E., and Michael M. J. Fischer. 1986. *Anthropology as Cultural Critique: An Experimental Moment in the Human Sciences*. Chicago: University of Chicago Press.

Margolis, Diane R. 1979. *The Managers: Corporate Life in America*. New York: William Morrow and Company, Inc.

Massey, Douglas S. 1990. The Social and Economic Origin of Immigration. *Annals of the American Academy of Political and Social Science* 510:60–72.

———. 1999. Why Does Immigration Occur? A Theoretical Synthesis. In *The Handbook of International Migration: The American Experience*, edited by C. Hirschman, P. Kasinitz and J. DeWind. New York: Russell Sage Foundation.

Massey, Douglas S., and Felipe Garcia Espana. 1987. The Social Process of International Migration. *Science* 237 (733–38).

Massey, Douglas S., Rafael Alarcon, Jorge Durand, and Humberto Gonzalez. 1987. *Return to Aztlan: The Social Process of International Migration from Western Mexico*. Berkeley: University of California Press.

Massey, Douglas S., Joaquin Arango, Graeme Hugo, Ali Kouaouci, Adela Pellegrino, and J. Edward Taylor. 1993. Theories of International Migration: A Review and Appraisal. *Population and Development Review* 19 (3):431–66.

McBeath, Gerald. 1998. *Wealth and Freedom: Taiwan's New Political Economy*. Aldershot, England: Ashgate Publishing Limited.

McClain, Charles J. 1994. *In Search of Equality: The Chinese Struggle against Discrimination in Nineteenth Century America*. Berkeley: University of California Press.

McDonald, Gerald W. 1980. Family Power: The Assessment of a Decade of Theory and Research, 1970–79. *Journal of Marriage and the Family* 42:841–54.

Meaney, Constance S. 1994. State Policy and the Development of Taiwan's Semiconductor Industry. In *The Role of the State in Taiwan's Development*, edited by J. D. Aberbach, D. Dollar and K. L. Sokoloff. Armonk, NY: M. E. Sharpe.

Mendel, Ernest. 1976. Introduction. In *Capital: A Critique of Political Economy*. Translated by B. Fowkes. London: Penguin Books.

Miles, Robert. 1989. *Racism*. London: Routledge.

Miller, Stuart C. 1969. *The Unwelcome Immigrant: The American Image of the Chinese, 1785–1882*. Berkeley: University of California Press.

Min, Pyong Gap. 1998. *Changes and Conflicts: Korean Immigrant Families in New York*. Boston: Allyn and Bacon.

Mintz, Sidney. 1985. *Sweetness and Power: The Place of Sugar in Modern History*. New York: Penguin Books.

Monterey Park 75th Anniversary Committee. 1991. *Monterey Park Past, Present and Future*. Monterey Park: Historical Society of Monterey Park and City of Monterey Park.

Narayan, Kirin. 1997. How Native is a "Native" Anthropologist? In *Situated Lives: Gender and Culture in Everyday Life*, edited by L. Lamphere, H. Ragoné and P. Zavella. New York: Routledge.

Nee, Victor G., and Brett de Barry Nee. 1986. *Longtime Californ': A Documentary Study of an American Chinatown*. Stanford: Stanford University Press.

Nelson, Cynthia. 1977. Public and Private Politics: Women in the Middle Eastern World. *American Ethnologist* 1 (3):551–63.

Newsweek. 2002. March 25, 41.

Ng, Franklin. 1998. *The Taiwanese Americans*. Wesport, CT: Greenwood Press.

Ng, Franklin, ed. 1995. *The Asian American Encyclopedia*. New York: Marshall Cavendish.

Ong, Paul, and John M. Liu. 1994. U.S. Immigration Policies and Asian Migration. In *The New Asian Immigration in Los Angeles and Global Restructuring*, edited by P. Ong, E. Bonacich and L. Cheng. Philadelphia: Temple University Press.

Ono, Kazuko. 1989. *Chinese Women in a Century of Revolution: 1850–1950.* Stanford: Stanford University Press.

Osajima, Keith. 1988. Asian Americans as the Model Minority: An Analysis of the Popular Press Image in the 1960s and 1980s. In *Reflections on Shattered Windows: Promises and Prospects for Asian American Studies,* edited by G. Y. Okihiro, S. Hune, A. A. Hansen and J. M. Liu. Pullman, WA: Washington State University Press.

———. 1993. Hidden Injuries of Race. In *Bearing Dreams, Shaping Visions: Asian American Perspectives,* edited by L. A. Revilla, G. M. Nomura, S. Wong and S. Hune. Pullman, WA: Washington State University Press.

Overseas Scholar. 1998. 8.

Pan, Lynn, ed. 1999. *The Encyclopedia of Chinese Overseas.* Cambridge, MA: Harvard University Press.

Papanek, Hanna. 1979. Family Status Production: The "Work" and "Non-Work" of Women. *Sign: Journal of Women in Culture and Society* 4 (4):75–81.

Park, Howard. 1992. New Perspectives on Industrial Growth in Taiwan. In *Taiwan: From Developing to Mature Economy,* edited by G. Ranis. Boulder, CO: Westview Press.

Parreñas, Rhacel S. 2000. New Household Forms, Old Family Values: The Formation and Reproduction of the Filipino Transnational Family in Los Angeles. In *Contemporary Asian America: A Multidisciplinary Reader,* edited by M. Zhou and J. V. Gatewood. New York: New York University Press.

———. 2001. Mothering from a Distance: Emotions, Gender, and Intergenerational Relations in Filipino Transnational Families. *Feminist Studies* 27 (2):361–90.

Pasternak, Burton. 1972. *Kinship and Community in Two Chinese Villages.* Stanford: Stanford University Press.

Peffer, George A. 1986. Forbidden Families: Emigration Experiences of Chinese Women under the Page Law, 1875–1882. *Journal of American Ethnic History* 6:28–46.

———. 1999. *If They Don't Bring Their Women Here: Chinese Female Immigration Before Exclusion.* Urbana: University of Illinois Press.

Pe-Pua, Rogelia, Colleen Mitchell, Robeyn Iredale, and Stephen Castles. 1996. *Astronaut Families and Parachute Children: The Cycle of Migration Between Hong Kong and Australia.* Canberra: Australian Government Publishing Services.

Pessar, Patricia R. 1982. The Role of Households in International Migration and the Case of U.S.-Bound Migration from the Dominican Republic. *International Migration Review* 16 (2):343–64.

———. 1995. On the Homefront and in the Workplace: Integrating Immigrant Women into Feminist Discourse. *Anthropological Quarterly* 68 (1):37–47.

———. 1999. Engendering Migration Studies. American Behavioral Scientist 42 (4):577–600.

Philips, Steven. 1999. Between Assimilation and Independence: Taiwanese Political Aspirations Under Nationalist Chinese Rule, 1945–1948. In *Taiwan: A New History,* edited by M. A. Rubinstein. Armonk, NY: M. E. Sharpe.

Piore, Michael J. 1975. Notes for a Theory of Labor Market Stratification. In *Labor Market Segmentation*, edited by R. C. Edwards, M. Reich and D. M. Gordon. Lexington, MA: D.C. Heath and Company.

Pleck, Joseph H. 1987. *Working Wives/Working Husbands*. Beverly Hills: SAGE Publications, Inc.

Portes, Alejandro, Luis E. Guarnizo, and Patricia Landolt. 1999. The Study of Transnationalism: Pitfalls and Promise of an Emergent Research Field. *Ethnic and Racial Studies* 21 (2):217–37.

Pyke, Karen. 1994. Women's Employment as a Gift or Burden?: Marital Power Across Marriage, Divorce, and Remarriage. *Gender & Society* 8 (1):73–91.

———. 1996. Class-Based Masculinities: The Interdependence of Gender, Class, and Interpersonal Power. *Gender & Society* 10 (5):527–49.

Radcliffe-Brown, A.R. 1987. Introduction. *In African Systems of Kinship and Marriage*, edited by A. R. Radcliffe-Brown and D. Forde. London: Kegan Paul International Limited.

Reimer, David M. 1983. An Unintended Reform: The 1965 Immigration Act and Third World Immigration to the United States. *Journal of American Ethnic History* 3 (1):9–28.

Reinharz, Shulamit. 1992. *Feminist Methods in Social Research*. Oxford: Oxford University Press.

Reiter, Rayna R. 1975. Men and Women in the South of France. In *Toward an Anthropology of Women*, edited by R. R. Reiter. New York: Monthly Review Press.

Rich, A. 1976. *Of Women Born: Motherhood as Experience and Institution*. New York: Norton.

Rodman, Hyman. 1967. Power in France, Greece, Yugoslavia, and the United States: A Cross-National Discussion. *Journal of Marriage and the Family* 29:320–24.

———. 1992. Marital Power and the Theory of Resources in Cultural Context. *Journal of Comparative Family Studies* 3:50–69.

Rosaldo, Michelle. 1974. Woman, Culture and Society: A Theoretical Review. In *Woman, Culture, and Society*, edited by M. Rosaldo and L. Lamphere. Stanford: Stanford University Press.

———. 1980. The Uses and Abuses of Anthropology. *Sign: Journal of Women in Culture and Society* 5 (3):389–414.

Rouse, Roger. 1991. Mexican Migration and the Social Space of Postmodernism. *Diaspora: A Journal of Transnational Studies* 1 (1):8–23.

Sacks, Karen Brodkin. 1994. How Did Jews Become White Folks. In *Race*, edited by S. Gregory and R. Sanjek. New Brunswick, NJ: Rutgers University Press.

Safilios-Rothschild, Constantina. 1970. The Study of Family Power Structure: A Review 1960–1969. *Journal of Marriage and the Family* 32 (4):539–53.

Sanders, Jimmy M., and Victor Nee. 1996. Immigrant Self-Employment: The Family as Social Capital and the Value of Human Capital. *American Sociological Review* 61:231–49.

Sandmeyer, Elmer C. 1991. *The Anti-Chinese Movement in California*. Urbana: University of Illinois Press.

Sassen, Saskia. 1988. *The Mobility of Labor and Capital: A Study in International Investment and Labor Flow*. Cambridge: Cambridge University Press.

Saxton, Alexander. 1995. *The Indispensable Enemy: Labor and the Anti-Chinese Movement in California.* Berkeley: University of California Press.

Schortman, Edward M., and Patricia A. Urban. 1992. Living on the Edge: Core/Periphery Relations in Ancient Southeast Mesoamerica. *Current Anthropology* 35(4):401–30.

Seagrave, Sterling. 1985. *The Soong Dynasty.* New York: Harper & Row.

U.S. Immigration and Naturalization Services. 1989. *Statistical Yearbook.* Washington, D.C.: Government Printing Office.

Siu, Paul C. F. 1952–53. The Sojourner. *The American Journal of Sociology* 58:33–44.

Skeldon, Ronald, ed. 1994. *Reluctant Exiles?: Migration from Hong Kong and the New Overseas Chinese.* Armonk, NY: M.E. Sharpe.

———, ed. 1995. *Emigration from Hong Kong: Tendencies and Impact.* Hong Kong: The Chinese University Press.

Skinner, George W. 1957. *Chinese Society in Thailand: An Analytical History.* Ithaca: Cornell University Press.

Sklair, Leslie. 1999. Competing Conceptions of Globalization. *Journal of World-Systems Research* 5 (2):143–62.

———. 2001. *The Transnational Capitalist Class.* Malden, MA: Blackwell Publishers, Inc.

Smith, Dorothy. 1987. Women's Perspective as a Radical Critique of Sociology. In *Feminism and Methodology,* edited by S. Harding. Bloomington: Indiana University Press.

Smith, Michael P., and Luis E. Guarnizo, eds. 1998. *Transnationalism from Below.* New Brunswick, NJ: Transaction Publishers.

Stack, Carol B., and Linda M. Burton. 1998. Kinscripts. In *Families in the U.S.: Kinship and Domestic Politics,* edited by K. V. Hansen and A. I. Garey. Philadelphia: Temple University Press.

Steil, Janice M. 1995. Supermoms and Second Shifts: Marital Inequality in the 1990s. In *Women: A Feminist Perspective,* edited by J. Freeman. Mountain View, CA: Mayfield Publishing Company.

Steiner, Christopher B. 1994. *African Art in Transit.* Cambridge: Cambridge University Press.

Stevenson, Mary. 1975. Women's Wage and Job Segregation. In *Labor Market Segmentation,* edited by R. C. Edward, M. Reich and David M. Gordon. Lexington, MA: D.C. Heath and Company.

Stier, Haya. 199. Immigrant Women Go to Work: Analysis of Immigrant Wives Labor Supply for Six Asian Groups. *Social Science Quarterly* 72:67–82.

Sun, Tsing-shan, and Wu Rong-chiao. 1993. Social Resources, Cultural Capital, and the Changing Process of Status Attainment (text in Chinese). Research Report. Taichung: Graduate Institute of Sociology, Tung Hai University.

Takagi, Dana. 1992. From Discrimination to Affirmative Action: Facts in the Asian American Admission Controversy. *Social Problems* 37 (4):578–92.

Takaki, Ronald. 1998. *Strangers from a Different Shore: A History of Asian Americans.* New York: Penguin Books.

Taiwan Daily. 2001. June 27.

Tanzer, Andrew. 1985. Little Taipei. *Forbes*, May 6, 67–81.

Thompson, E. P. 1977. Folklore, Anthropology, and Social History. *The Indian Historical Review* 3 (2):247–66.

Thornton, Arland, and Hui-sheng Lin. 1997. *Social Change and the Family in Taiwan*. Chicago: University of Chicago Press.

Thrift, N. 1985. Bear and Mouse of Bear and Tree? Anthony Gidden's Reconstitution of Social Theory. *Sociology* 19 (609–23).

Tian, Rukang. 1953. *The Chinese of Sarawak*. London: Department of Anthropology, London School of Economics and Political Science.

Tilly, Charles. 1984. *Big Structure, Long Processes, Huge Comparisons*. New York: Russell Sage Foundation.

Traeger, L. 1984. Family Strategies and the Migration of Women: Migrants to Dagupan City, Philippines. *International Migration Review* 18 (4):1264–77.

Tsai, Shu-ling. 1998. The Transition from School to Work in Taiwan. In *From School to Work: A Comparative Study of Educational Qualifications and Occupational Destinations*, edited by Y. Shavit and W. Muller. Oxford: Clarendon Press.

Tseng, Yen-fen. 1994. Chinese Ethnic Economy: San Gabriel Valley, Los Angeles County. *Journal of Urban Affairs* 16 (2):169–89.

———. 1995. Beyond "Little Taipei": The Development of Taiwanese Immigrant Businesses in Los Angeles. *International Migration Review* 29 (1):33–58.

Tuan, Mia. 1999. *Forever Foreigners or Honorary Whites?: The Asian Ethnic Experience Today*. New Brunswick, NJ: Rutgers University Press.

United Daily News. 2001. June 21.

Uno, Kathleen S. 1999. *Passage to Modernity: Motherhood, Childhood, and Social Reform in Early Twentieth Century Japan*. Honolulu: University of Hawaii Press.

Uzzell, Douglas. 1976. Ethnography of Migration: Breaking Out of the Bi-Polar Myth. *Rice University Studies* 62 (3):45–54.

Vogler, Carolyn. 2000. Money in the Household: Some Underlying Issues of Power. *The Sociological Review* 46: 687–713.

Waldinger, Roger, Howard Aldrich, and Robin Ward. 1990. Opportunities, Group Characteristics, and Strategies. In *Ethnic Entrepreneurs: Immigrant Business in Industrial Societies*, edited by R. Waldinger, H. Aldrich and R. Ward. Newbury Park, CA: SAGE Publications, Inc.

Waldinger, Roger, and Yen-fen Tseng. 1992. Divergent Diasporas: The Chinese Communities of New York and Los Angeles Compared. *Revue Europeene des Migrations Internationales* 8 (3):93–114.

Waller, Willard, and Reuben Hill. 1951. *The Family: A Dynamic Interpretation*. New York: Dryden Press.

Wallerstein, Immanuel. 1974. The Rise and Future Demise of the World Capitalist System: Concepts for Comparative Analysis. *Comparative Studies in Society and History* 16 (4):387–415.

———. 1976. *The Modern World-System: Capitalist Agriculture and the Origin of the European World-Economy in the Sixteenth Century*. New York.: Academic Press.

———. 1979. *The Capitalist World Economy*. Cambridge: Cambridge University Press.

————. 1989. *The Modern World-System III: The Second Era of Great Expansion of the Capitalist World-Economy, 1730–1840s*. New York: Academic Press.

————. 1997. Social Science and the Quest for a Just Society. *American Journal of Sociology* 102 (5):1241–57.

Wang, Fu-chang. 1993. Causes and Patterns of Ethnic Intermarriage among the Hokkien, Hakka, and Mainlanders in Postwar Taiwan: A Preliminary Examination (text in Chinese). *Bulletin of the Institute of Ethnology, Academia Sinica, Taiwan* 76:43–96.

————. 1993. The Consequences of Ethnic Intermarriages: The Impact of Intermarriages on Ethnic Assimilation in Taiwan (text in Chinese). *Journal of Humanities and Social Sciences, Academia Sinica* 5 (1):231–67.

Wang, L. Ling-chi. 1996. The Structure of Dual Domination: Toward a Paradigm for the Study of the Chinese Diaspora in the United States. *Amerasia Journal* 21 (1–2):149–69.

Wang, Peter Chen-main. 1999. A Bastion Created, a Regime Reformed, an Economy Reengineered, 1949–1970. In *Taiwan: A New History*, edited by M. A. Rubinstein. Armonk, NY: M.E. Sharpe.

Wang, Te-mu, Yu-chia Chen, and Wei-an Chang. 1986. The Changing Educational Structure and Equal Opportunity in Education (text in Chinese). In *Social and Cultural Change in Taiwan*, edited by H. Y. Chiu and Y. H. Chang. Taipei: Institute of Ethnology, Academia Sinica.

Watson, James L. 1975. *Emigration and the Chinese Lineage: The Mans in Hong Kong and London*. Berkeley: University of California Press.

Weber, Max. 1947. *The Theory of Social and Economic Organization*. New York: The Free Press.

Wilkinson, David. 1986. Central Civilization. *Comparative Civilizations Review* 17 (Fall):31–59.

Willis, Katie D., and Brenda S. A. Yeoh. 2000. Gender and Transnational Household Strategies: Singaporean Migration to China. *Regional Studies* 34 (3):253–64.

Willis, Katie, and Brenda Yeoh. 2000. Introduction. In *Gender and Migration*, edited by K. Willis and B. Yeoh. Cheltenham, UK: Edward Elgar Publishing Limited.

Wilmott, William E. 1980. The Chinese in Indochina. In *Southeast Asian Exodus: From Tradition to Resettlement, Understanding Refugees from Laos, Kampuchea and Vietnam in Canada*, edited by E. L. Tepper. Ottawa: The Canadian Asian Studies Association.

Wilson, Taqmar Diana. 1994. What Determines Where Transnational Labor Migrants Go? Modifications in Migration Theories. *Human Organizations* 53 (3):269–78.

Winfield, Fairlee E. 1985. *Commuter Marriage: Living Together, Apart*. New York: Columbia University Press.

Wolf, Margery. 1968. *The House of Lim: A Study of a Chinese Farm Family*. New York: Appleton-Century-Crofts.

————. 1972. *Women and the Family in Rural Taiwan*. Stanford: Stanford University Press.

Wong, Charles. 1989. Monterey Park: A Community in Transition. In *Frontiers of Asian American Studies,* edited by G. Nomura, R. Endo, S. H. Sumida and R. Leong. Pullman, WA: Washington University Press.

Woo, Deborah. 2000. *Glass Ceilings and Asian Americans: The New Face of Workface Barriers.* Walnut Creek, CA: AltaMira Press.

Wrigley, Julia. 1995. *Other People's Children.* New York: BasicBooks [sic].

Wu, Wan-yu. 1992. Women Under the Patriarchal System in Taiwan (text in Chinese). Master's thesis, Sociology, Tung Wu University, Taipei.

Xu, Xiaohe, and Shu-chuan Lai. 2002. Resources, Gender Ideologies, and Marital Power. *Journal of Family Issues* 23 (2):209–45.

Yanagisako, Sylvia J. 1987. Mixed Metaphors: Native and Anthropological Models of Gender and Kinship Domains. In *Gender and Kinship: Essays Toward a Unified Analysis,* edited by J. F. Collier and S. J. Yanagisako. Stanford: Stanford University Press.

———. 1995. Transforming Orientalism: Gender, Nationality, and Class in Asian American Studies. In *Naturalizing Power: Essay in Feminist Cultural Analysis,* edited by S. Yanagisako and C. Delaney. New York: Routledge.

Yeoh, Brenda S.A., and L. Khoo. 1998. Home, Work and Community: Skilled International Migration and Expatriate Women in Singapore. *International Migration Review* 36 (2):159–84.

Yi, Chin-chun, and Ying-hwa Chang. 1996. Change of Family Structure and Marital Power in Taiwan (text in Chinese). In *Families, Human Resources and Social Development,* edited by H. H. N. Chen, Yia-ling and M. O. Hsieh. Taipei: The Department and Graduate Institute of Sociology, National Chengchi University.

Yi, Chin-chun, and Yuay-ling Tsai. 1986. Analysis of Marital Power in Taipei Metropolitan Area: An Example of Familial Decision-Making (text in Chinese). In *Social Phenomena in Taiwan: An Analysis,* edited by C. C. Yi and C. C. Chu. Taipei: Academia Sinica.

Yi, Chin-chun, and Wen-shan Yang. 1995. The Perceived Conflict and Decision-Making Patterns Among Husbands And Wives in Taiwan (text in Chinese). In *Family Formation and Dissolution: Perspectives from East and West,* edited by C. C. Yi. Taipei: Academia Sinica.

Young, K. 1985. The Creation of a Relative Surplus Population: A Case Study from Mexico. In *Women and Development: The Sexual Division of Labor in Rural Societies,* edited by L. Beneria. New York: Praeger.

Yu, Connie Young. 1989. The World of Our Grandmothers. In *Making Waves: An Anthology of Writings by and about Asian American Women,* edited by Asian Women United of California. Boston: Beacon Press.

Yung, Judy. 1999. *Unbound Voices: A Documentary History of Chinese Women in San Francisco.* Berkeley: University of California Press.

Zhong, Yen-yiu. 1999. *Political Immigrants' Mutual Aid Associations (1946–1995): Out of Province Hometown Associations (text in Chinese).* Taipei: Tao Hsiang Publisher.

Zhou, Min. 1998. "Parachute Kids" in Southern California: The Educational Experience of Chinese Children in Transnational Families. *Educational Policy* 12 (6):682–704.

Zhou, Min, and James V. Gatewood. 2000. Introduction. In *Contemporary Asian America: A Multidisciplinary Reader,* edited by M. Zhou and J. V. Gatewood. New York: New York University Press.

Zhou, Yu. 1998. How Do Places Matter? Comparative Study of Chinese Immigrant Communities in Los Angeles and New York. *Urban Geography* 19 (6):531–63.

Zolberg, Aristide R. 1989. The Next Waves: Migration Theory for a Changing World. *International Migration Review* 223 (3):403–30.

Index

For Product Safety Concerns and Information please contact
our EU representative GPSR@taylorandfrancis.com Taylor & Francis
Verlag GmbH, Kaufingerstraße 24, 80331 München, Germany

T - #0104 - 270225 - C0 - 229/152/15 - PB - 9780415654326 - Gloss Lamination